Supporting Vulnerable Babies and Young Children

by the same author

Helping Babies and Children Aged 0–6 to Heal After Family Violence
A Practical Guide to Infant- and Child-Led Work
Dr. Wendy Bunston
Foreword by Dr. Julie Stone
ISBN 978 1 84905 644 1
eISBN 978 1 78450 138 9

of related interest

The Child's World, Third Edition
The Essential Guide to Assessing Vulnerable
Children, Young People and Their Families
Edited by Jan Howarth and Dendy Platt
ISBN 978 1 78592 116 2
eISBN 978 1 78450 382 6

Creative Ideas for Assessing Vulnerable Children and Families
Katie Wrench
ISBN 978 1 84905 703 5
eISBN 978 1 78450 225 6

Tackling Child Neglect
Research, Policy and Evidence-Based Practice
Edited by Ruth Gardner
Foreword by David Howe
ISBN 978 1 84905 662 5
eISBN 978 1 78450 165 5

Risk in Child Protection
Assessment Challenges and Framework for Practice
Martin C. Calder with Julie Archer
ISBN 978 1 84905 479 9
eISBN 978 0 85700 858 9

Supporting Vulnerable Babies and **Young Children**

Interventions for Working with Trauma, Mental Health, Illness and Other Complex Challenges

Edited by
Wendy Bunston and **Sarah J. Jones**

Foreword by **Graham Music**

Jessica Kingsley *Publishers*
London and Philadelphia

First published in 2020
by Jessica Kingsley Publishers
73 Collier Street
London N1 9BE, UK
and
400 Market Street, Suite 400
Philadelphia, PA 19106, USA

www.jkp.com

Library of Congress Cataloging in Publication Data
A CIP catalog record for this book is available from the Library of Congress

British Library Cataloguing in Publication Data
A CIP catalogue record for this book is available from the British Library

ISBN 978 1 78592 370 8
eISBN 978 1 78450 714 5

Printed and bound in Great Britain

Contents

Part 3: Culture and the Infant

Part 4: Political and Legal Systems

Part 5: Mental Health, Community Nursing and Medical Systems

Foreword

BY GRAHAM MUSIC

This wonderfully rich book provides a truly international perspective on the importance of infancy as a vital developmental period, highlighting the challenges we face in ensuring that knowledge from clinical work and research is catapulted up the agenda of policy makers and service development.

While such issues been well described in many books, academic papers and policy documents (Gerhardt, 2014) it is worth reiterating why the kind of work championed by this book is so vitally important.

The human infant is extraordinarily adaptive, psychologically, physiologically, emotionally, culturally and neurobiologially. Prenatally the foetus is already adapting to its environment (Music, 2013), and the human brain is extraordinarily adept at responding to whatever environment it finds itself in. Indeed we are beginning to learn how intergenerational epigenetic effects, the 'sins of the fathers', are transmitted intergenerationally and leave their mark (Bouvette-Turcot, Meaney and O'Donnell, 2018).

In our early years our neurochemical systems are becoming programmed, our brain architecture being wired, our autonomic nervous system is developing specific patterns, our inner worlds are being framed, even our genes are coming to be expressed in specific ways via epigenetic processes, all so we learn to survive and if possible, thrive, in the family, culture, social group and emotional environment that fate has landed us in.

Babies within days even cry differently, if they born into a French or German family, for example. Yet how much more profoundly important are the early adaptations to, for example, serious trauma, or neglect, or loving parenting, each giving rise to profoundly different behavioural and emotional responses which become later templates for 'being-with-others-in-the-world'.

This book brings alive so many of these fundamental processes. We read about powerful interventions, rooted in psychoanalytic, attachment and other depth psychology approaches, but each delivered with a sensitivity to the importance of engaging real, distressed parents and infants at a level they can relate to. The infant is always placed centre stage, as a real person with feelings, thoughts, and a huge range of potentials. Yet the chapters all keep very much in mind the context around the child, the families, cultural issues, political agendas, providing a masterly synthesis of macro and micro issues.

Several key issues recur throughout the chapters that are dear to my heart and I hope bear reiterating. As already hinted at, an understanding of cultural issues and diversity runs through many chapters, and such cross-cultural awareness challenges any idea that there is one way to raise a child, to live a life, avoiding the dangers of an overly normative approach to infancy and parenting which can become another form of cultural imperialism.

Trauma is central to many chapters and trauma shows its face and takes its toil in a variety of ways and at many levels. We are increasingly aware of the devastating effects of violence, abuse and neglect on the developing brain (Teicher *et al.*, 2016). In addition, we absolutely know how the state of mind of the parent affects the developing mental and emotional state of the infant. Beebe's work on disorganised attachment (Beebe *et al.*, 2012) should leave us in no doubt how babies adapt to overwhelming experiences. At just 4 months babies whose mothers display frightening behaviours learn to adapt, such as by starting to whimper in the face of threat, but then shifting the whimper to placatory smiles so as not to alienate mothers who cannot bear negative affect. Such reactions and states then become engrained personality traits (Perry *et al.*, 1995) that are hard to shift without timely skilled help. Indeed, since Fraiberg's pioneering early week, we have known how infants adopt profound defences in the face of trauma and abuse (Fraiberg, 1982).

Such understanding from micro-analysis has shown for example, how maltreatment in a parent affects their very capacity to make sense of and be attuned to their infant's states of mind (Thompson-Booth *et al.*, 2018), something that child psychotherapy, as well as research which looks at the inner world and symbolic communications of children have long asserted (Hodges *et al.*, 2003). This is of course another argument for early interventions with parents and their infants.

Many chapters in the book are influenced by both the traditions of infant observation (Miller, 1989), and of parent-infant psychotherapy (Hopkins, 1992; Baradon *et al.*, 2016). The thinking is imbued with the psychoanalytic capacity to bear and face the unthinkable nature of much that the authors have helped their clients bear, heling their clients to face issues as diverse as natural disasters such as Tsunamis, children suffering horrendous cancers, the fallout from the refugee crisis and asylum seeking, intergenerational ethnic discrimination, family violence, alcohol and other addictions, and so much more. We read accounts in which these issues are faced head-on, and yet in which hope and resilience shine though.

One theme which I feel needs underlining and shouting loudly about is one which often leaves people cold, uninterested and too quiet, and hence is not taken seriously enough. This is the issue of serious child neglect, which is too often itself neglected (Music, 2018b). Emotional neglect is different to the kinds of physical neglect that social workers often act on and is hard to recognise and prove. However its consequences are often more devastating than overt trauma, on brains, psyches, relationship capacities (Nelson, Zeanah and Fox, 2019). The classic examples were seen in some of the infamous depriving orphanages (Rutter *et al.*, 2007), but in fact this is far more widespread yet goes unrecognised as such neglected children rarely elicit worry and concern, having shut-down their evolved inherited expectation of and demand for interpersonal contact (Music, 2018a). The babies who do not cry and seem 'just fine' can become children unnoticed at backs of classrooms and adults who live lives deadened and unfeeling. They often have far worse prognoses, but their plight goes silently unnoticed.

The thinking in this book is about extremely serious matters. As the science backs up what therapists have long known, we can no longer deny how adverse experiences are not about soft 'touchy-feely' matters, but have profound effects on later psychological and physical health outcomes, including deadly diseases and early death (Hughes *et al.*, 2017). We know how trauma and other early adverse experiences affects the brain (McCrory, Gerin and Viding, 2017), the nervous system (Porges, 2011), and a range of biomarkers from telomeres to DNA expression (Ridout, Khan and Ridout, 2018) We ignore this at our peril.

This book is full of deep thinking and good practice about such cases, describing a wide range of work with infants in a variety of contexts, infants experiencing an array of distressing experiences which are a challenge both to those in contact with them, and of course to the extraordinarily sensitive and adaptive infants themselves. The following chapters will offer something invaluable to anyone working with infants, from experienced practitioners to the novice to the policy-maker to the researcher, and many more. The reader is invited to partake of a feast, a veritable *smorgasbord* of practical wisdom, insight, research findings, interventions, all with the infant and their inner world and emotional needs at its centre. The work described might be a challenge at times to digest, but with our hand held by these skilled practitioners and writers, we soon realise that, in the words of Bion (1962), digesting and metabolizing such experiences, understanding them not just intellectually but emotionally, will be health-enhancing not only for the reader, but of course also for the infants and families we work with, and indeed for the subsequent generations of those we offer help to.

References

Baradon, T., Biseo, M., Broughton, C., James, J. and Joyce, A., 2016. *The practice of psychoanalytic parent-infant psychotherapy: Claiming the baby.* Oxford: Routledge.

Beebe, B., Lachmann, F.M., Markese, S., Buck, K.A., Bahrick, L.E., Chen, H., Cohen, P., Andrews, H., Feldstein, S. and Jaffe, J., 2012. On the Origins of Disorganized Attachment and Internal Working Models: Paper II. An Empirical Microanalysis of 4-Month Mother–Infant Interaction. *Psychoanalytic Dialogues*, 22(3), pp.352–374.

Bion, W.R., 1962. *Learning from experience.* London: Heinemann.

Bouvette-Turcot, A.-A., Meaney, M.J. and O'Donnell, K.J., 2018. Epigenetics and Early Life Adversity: Current Evidence and Considerations for Epigenetic Studies in the Context of Child Maltreatment. In: *The Biology of Early Life Stress.* Springer, pp.89–119.

Fraiberg, S., 1982. Pathological defenses in infancy. *Psychoanalytic Quarterly*, 51, pp.612–635.

Gerhardt, S., 2014. *Why Love Matters: How Affection Shapes a Baby's Brain.* Oxford: Routledge.

Hodges, J., Steele, M., Hillman, S. and Henderson, K., 2003. Mental representations and defences in severely maltreated children: A story stem battery and rating system for clinical assessment and research applications. In: R.N. Emde, D.. Wolf and D. Oppenheim, eds., *Revealing the Inner Worlds of Young Children. The MacArthur Story Stem Battery and Parent-Child Narratives.* Oxford: Oxford University Press, pp.240–267.

Hopkins, J., 1992. Infant-parent psychotherapy. *Journal of Child Psychotherapy*, 18(1), pp.5–17.

Hughes, K., Bellis, M.A., Hardcastle, K.A., Sethi, D., Butchart, A., Mikton, C., Jones, L. and Dunne, M.P., 2017. The effect of multiple adverse childhood experiences on health: a systematic review and meta-analysis. *The Lancet Public Health*, 2(8), pp.e356–e366.

McCrory, E.J., Gerin, M.I. and Viding, E., 2017. Annual Research Review: Childhood maltreatment, latent vulnerability and the shift to preventative psychiatry–the contribution of functional brain imaging. *Journal of child psychology and psychiatry*, 58(4), pp.338–357.

Miller, L., 1989. *Closely observed infants*. London: Duckworth.

Music, G., 2013. Stress pre-birth: How the Fetus is Affected by a Mother's State of Mind. *International Journal of Birth & Parent Education*, 1(1), pp.12–15.

Music, G., 2018a. Avoiding avoidance, neglecting neglect and deactivating attachment strategies. In: L. Cundy, ed., *Attachment and the Defence Against Intimacy: Understanding and Working with Avoidant Attachment, Self-hatred, and Shame*. Oxford: Routledge.

Music, G., 2018b. Neglecting neglect, another form of turning a blind eye. In: C. Bonovitz and A. Harlem, eds., *Developmental Perspectives in Child Psychoanalysis and Psychotherapy*. Oxford: Routledge.

Nelson, C.A., Zeanah, C.H. and Fox, N.A., 2019. *How Early Experience Shapes Human Development: The Case of Psychosocial Deprivation*. Neural Plasticity.

Perry, B.D., Pollard, R.A., Blakley, T.L., Baker, W.L. and Vigilante, D., 1995. Childhood trauma, the neurobiology of adaptation, and Use-dependent" development of the brain: How states" become traits". *Infant Mental Health Journal*, 16(4), pp.271–291.

Porges, S.W., 2011. *The polyvagal theory: Neurophysiological foundations of emotions, attachment, communication, and self-regulation*. New York: Norton.

Ridout, K.K., Khan, M. and Ridout, S.J., 2018. Adverse Childhood Experiences Run Deep: Toxic Early Life Stress, Telomeres, and Mitochondrial DNA Copy Number, the Biological Markers of Cumulative Stress. *BioEssays*, 40(9), p.epub.

Rutter, M., Beckett, C., CASTLE, J., Colvert, E., Kreppner, J., Mehta, M., Stevens, S. and Sonuga-Barke, E., 2007. Effects of profound early institutional deprivation: an overview of findings from a UK longitudinal study of Romanian adoptees. *European Journal of Developmental Psychology*, 4(3), pp.332–350.

Teicher, M.H., Samson, J.A., Anderson, C.M. and Ohashi, K., 2016. The effects of childhood maltreatment on brain structure, function and connectivity. *Nature Reviews Neuroscience*, 17(10), pp.652–666.

Thompson-Booth, C., Viding, E., Puetz, V.B., Rutherford, H.J.V., Mayes, L.C. and McCrory, E.J., 2018. Ghosts in the nursery: An experimental investigation of a parent's own maltreatment experience, attention to infant faces, and dyadic reciprocity. *Emotion*, p.epub.

Graham Music (PHD) is Consultant Child and Adolescent Psychotherapist at the Tavistock and Portman Clinics and an adult psychotherapist in private practice. His publications include *Nurturing Children: From Trauma to Hope using neurobiology, psychoanalysis and attachment (2019), Nurturing Natures: Attachment and children's emotional, sociocultural and brain development* (2016, 2010), *Affect and Emotion* (2001), and *The Good Life: Wellbeing and the new science of altruism, selfishness and immorality* (2014). He has a particular interest in exploring the interface between developmental findings and clinical work. Formerly Associate Clinical Director of the Tavistock's child and family department, he has managed a range of services working with the aftermath of child maltreatment and neglect, and organised many community based psychotherapy services. He currently works clinically with forensic cases at The Portman Clinic. He teaches, lectures and supervises in Britain and abroad.

Acknowledgements

Thank you to my very dear friends (Karen Glennen, Bez Robertson, Jane Miller, Liz Orr and Jenny Conrick) who have held me in ways they may have never realised through what has been a very tough two years. To my very dear co-editor Sarah J. Jones in our journey to create this book – thank you.

Wendy

Sincere acknowledgements to my parents, whose intellectual energies inspired my own. To my generous husband for his kindness and support; whose criticisms have made me a better writer. To my co-editor and dear friend, WB.

Sarah

PART 1

Honouring Beginnings

Introduction

As editors, our aim was to create a book which offers a broad spectrum of work with infants and young children. In particular, we wanted to explore the lives of infants and their families who may receive little attention in the literature and who require considerably more attention than has usually been afforded them. The idea for this book emerged from our work as social workers, family therapists and infant mental health practitioners. As senior consultants we supervise and train others in infant and child-led practices. Alongside this we also both work therapeutically with infants, young children and their families.

Our brief to the authors invited to participate in this book was to:

Make prominent the voice, experience and perspective of infants and young children who have endured considerable and complex vulnerabilities. This is through providing a range of expertise which brings together a collection of disparate, contemporary and often underexamined areas of working with the world's youngest citizens.

Our quest was that each chapter should examine what can be cumulative disadvantages experienced by infants and very young children, their parents and caregivers. We further asked the authors in this book to consider that:

The children written about here may not fit one category, or one culture, or experience only one kind of violence or one kind of adversity. The goal is to show readers how to work with complexity, and to demonstrate what is considered 'good practice'. The book is intended for a wide audience of professionals who work in the early years and who have the potential to bring healing and therapeutic engagement to the lives of these infants, young children and families. It also intends to increase the confidence and ability of workers to see infants and children, to think about them and effectively work with them.

Our authors have met the challenge admirably! We believe this book offers a vast array of differing arenas of practice with the unifying principle being the authors' commitment to honouring the experience of the infants and young children, and their relationship with their caregiving world.

Chapter 1: Introducing the Infant: And How to Support Vulnerable Babies and Young Children

This book begins with **Wendy Bunston** and **Sarah J. Jones** introducing the world of the infant, and the very young child. This chapter lays the foundation for how to approach infant- and child-led practice. It offers a frame to work within for those new to, as well as those experienced in, working with the very young. Their work firmly places the infant and young child at the centre of interventions, actively respecting their right to be involved in work which directly impacts them. The salient aspects of the infants' and families' historical, relational, cultural and subjective experiences inform our ability to create a nuanced therapeutic relationship.

Chapter 2: Reflective Supervision's Essential Place in Thoughtful Practice

Three supervisors, all working in the arena of infant mental health and infant- and child-led practice, **Julie Stone, Sarah J. Jones and Wendy Bunston**, provide a comprehensive description of what reflective supervision is, how it differs from other types of supervision offered in either the workplace or privately, and why these differences are integral to good practice. All three authors share examples taken from their own practice as supervisors or supervisees. These examples illustrate why reflective supervision is essential in facilitating our abilities as workers or therapists to competently, respectfully and effectively support vulnerable babies, young children and their families.

Chapter 3: Restoring Ruptured Bonds: The Young Child and Complex Trauma in Families

Fiona True describes an innovative model of working through the multiple dynamics which operate within a family system after there has been a traumatic rupture. This approach allows the therapist to not only 'discover and explore the child's experience of their family, it also provides the opportunity to share that experience with their parent(s)'. This family systems approach holds both the parent's perspective and the child's in equal measure. A diversity of modalities is used to tease out the communication constraints within the family system to respectfully untangle the complexities of the trauma and safely relay this between the family subsystems of relationships. Using a case example with 4-year-old twins, 'Catherine' and 'Clarissa', Fiona powerfully illustrates a way of therapeutically amplifying the voice of the very young child whilst simultaneously offering the therapist a way of processing this emotionally challenging material.

Chapter 4: Developing an Intervention for Infants and Young Children in Foster Care: 'Watch Me Play!'

Play and discovery are imperative to healthy early development. In order to engage in beneficial play and creative discovery, an infant or very young child requires a relational space which supports, protects and engages with such play. **Jenifer Wakelyn** describes her involvement in the London-based intervention program 'First Step' with infants and children in foster care. She provides case illustrations of how workers can support meaningful play in and 'out of their family home' care setting whilst enhancing the relational experiences of the very young child and their foster carers. Fundamental to this approach is encouraging the emergence of 'reflective tenderness' that the young infant or child would ordinarily receive from their caregiving world. Jenifer explains how 'First Step' takes this a step further by using what is directly observed within this play space to further advocate for the infant's or child's psychological needs within professional planning discussions and decisions.

Chapter 5: Keeping the Child in Mind When Thinking About Violence in Families

Canadian author **Angelique Jenney** sets the scene of how past practices under reported the severe consequences for children's mental health when violence was not theorised and recognised. This chapter outlines an early intervention community-based programme in Calgary, focused on promoting the safety and wellbeing of very young vulnerable children under the age of 4 years. The programme works with the mother–child dyad, particularly those affected by family violence and currently involved with child protection services. Through the example of a troubled, disenfranchised mother and her baby, the author provides a realistic understanding of when fearful responses are evoked in both the clients and the staff participating in a programme that operates within the context of child protection services. Through this detailed and humane account, attention is given to an honest appraisal that sometimes children are not safe with their parents. However, attachment repair and parental growth are possible through infant/child-focused work which maintains open communication with the family and child protection, whilst offering an infant-led therapeutic programme.

Chapter 6: 'Murder in Their Family': Making Space for the Experience of the Infant Impacted by Familial Murder

It has taken a long time for society to realise that infants are not inured to the shattering impacts of familial murder. From the events leading to the murder and through the consequences of such circumstances, a complex stain of meaning seeps out into the lives of immediate and extended family members, and the service systems dealing with the aftermath. The infant or young child may in fact be present when a murder occurs; however, records are not commonly kept regarding the number of infants and very young children impacted by the loss of a family member or what the experience has been like for such children. **Kathy Eyre**, **Nicole Milburn** and **Wendy Bunston** share their knowledge and expertise in working with infants and young children impacted by the murder of a family member, and guide the reader through what they believe are important practice principles and, crucially, the need to hold as paramount space for the infant or young child's experience.

Chapter 7: Homelessness in Infancy: Finding 'Home' for Babies in Crisis Accommodation after Family Violence

The infant is the least researched, written or thought about person in the area of homelessness. Yet it is often the mother's high motivation to protect her infant from violence which leads to her decision to leave their home and seek crisis accommodation. **Wendy Bunston** is fearless when it comes to both articulating and then addressing the multiple ways the sector unwittingly adds to rather than redresses the trauma experienced by the infant with the mother. Using an infant-led approach, this chapter offers a way whereby the homelessness sector could support 'building a home for the infant' through helping to support and grow the infant–mother relationship. This calls for a reorientation which focuses on building relational shelter as much as securing housing and attending to the infant whose crisis may be rendered invisible by adult-orientated practices. Wendy's chapter concludes with a realistic and compassionate imagining of what a baby would feel like if the relational home was restored via a more attuned system of care.

Chapter 8: Self-Determining Support for Indigenous Children in Australia: The Bubup Wilam Case Study

Indigenous children in Australia are still experiencing the aftermath of the disadvantage and dispossession created by longstanding, historical transgenerational trauma and ongoing institutional racism within Australia. **Angie Zerella**, **Lisa Thorpe**, **Luella Monson-Wilbraham** and **Kerry Arabena** beautifully introduce us to the work of Bubup Wilam, an Aboriginal Child and Family Centre which each year supports the education, health and wellbeing of about 100 Aboriginal children aged 6 months to 6 years, and their families. The centre emphasises a strengths-based approach to learning and wellbeing that promotes high expectations and supports the self-determination and aspirations of the children and families they work with. Case examples powerfully bring to life the hope, spirit and pride of these children and the richness of the experiences within and created by the environment within Bubup Wilam.

Chapter 9: Infants and Young Children in the Aftermath of the Great East Japan Earthquake, Tsunami and Fukushima Daiichi Nuclear Power Plant Accident

In exquisite detail **Hisako Watanabe** captures profound and powerful therapeutic moments in the work she and her colleagues have undertaken with infants, children and families since the triple disaster of the earthquake, tsunami and nuclear explosion in Japan in 2011. In a context where vast numbers of people lost their lives, where large tracts of the Japanese landscape were stripped bare and replaced with mangled debris, strewn across what were once thriving cities and towns, Hisako speaks about how her work with other team mates reverted back to that which was most basic: the need to rebuild relationships and restore trust in themselves and one another. Hisako most eloquently demonstrates 'the power of children in reviving vitality affect and hope in the community' after large-scale disasters.

Chapter 10: Play With Us: Bringing Hope and Healing to Kwazulu-Natal's Children

This chapter takes us to the province of KwaZulu Natal (KZN) in South Africa. **Rachel Rozentals-Thresher**, **Robyn Hemmens** and **Julie Stone** describe work undertaken by Dlalanathi, a small community development team. This work is with caregivers and grandparents and is concerned with how Dlalanathi has responded to the devastation of the HIV and AIDS pandemic. It is staggering to learn that as a result of this pandemic, one in five children mourned the loss of one or both parents before they turned 5 years of age. Dlalanathi began as a bereavement service which helped and supported caregivers to begin to have difficult conversations with children who felt bereft and confused by what they imagined to be their parents' abandonment of them. The authors bring to life how love and acknowledgement form the basis of strong positive parenting, yet for those adults whose own early life was difficult and demanding it can be challenging to provide this to the young. The chapter outlines how Dlalanathi's relationship-centred approach is core, and that long and enduring relationships are often required. Via the universal language and need for play, the 'Play for Communication Program' was developed.

Chapter 11: The 'International Infant': Examining the Experiences and Clinical needs of Separated and Reunited Transnational Infant–Parent Dyads

At first glance an infant described as an 'international infant' seems out of place. **Natasha Whitfield** explores the term by examining the experiences and clinical needs of separated and reunited transnational infant–parent families. In her pithy essay, drawn from her PhD research, she describes the custom of extended family caretaking practices for young infants, which perhaps was once more local but is increasingly now global. Whilst Natasha describes the work from a Canadian perspective, there is no doubt there are those in other countries who share similar experiences. Creative ways to perhaps bring these families together in mind and spirit, if not in body, may be one of the most helpful interventions.

Chapter 12: 'Invisible Children': How Attachment Theory and Evidenced-Based Procedures Can Bring to Light the Hidden Experience of Children at Risk from Their Parents

Ben Grey and **Jeremy Gunson** offer insight into the way organisational defences can, often unconsciously, influence professionals, thereby obstructing the ability to truly reach traumatised children. They examine and make overt the adaptive behavioural strategies of the abused child. Due to their need to be acquiescent and acquire a false sense within their attachment contexts, these children's subtle displays of distress can be rendered invisible and tragically misinterpreted. In a rich chapter exploring one troubled infant and her parent, we can see an agency responding to phenomena in a way that ultimately does not serve the infant. The authors' reflections and suggestions are situated in the context of high-profile child abuse enquiries, which they argue fail to explore the reasons why some children, despite multi-agency involvement, can be overlooked.

Chapter 13: Infants and Young Children Living Within High-Conflict Parental Disputes: 'Keep Me Safe and Organise My Emotional World'

Jennifer McIntosh is well known in Australia for her academic contribution, clinical acumen and working just with the judiciary. Jennifer's work has also been commissioned by the Australian Government Attorney-General's Department. Her expertise involves examining how to maintain the focus on the child's developmental needs in high-conflict court-related parent disputes. Interviewed by editor **Sarah J. Jones**, Jennifer offers her refreshingly clear views on supporting infants in the highly charged arena of litigation. Her experience in advising disputatious parents is described in her own humane and infant-centred voice. She comments on the particular plight of sperm donors, who subsequently might want a role in the life of an infant, and what the infant may gain if the parties can collaborate.

Chapter 14: Playing Behind the Barbed-Wire Fence: Asylum-seeking Infants and Their Parents

Christine Hill brings into sharp focus an account of the inhumane and extreme neglect of infant and parent asylum-seekers that a wealthy democratic country enforces. She affirms the purpose of this book when she notes that in the literature on immigration detention, infants are rarely mentioned. They are forefront and central in Christine's mind, despite the absence of care and attention in the detention centre that she persistently visits. In this moving account, Christine provides a stark contrast between the bleak experience of visiting the detention centre and her attempts to welcome infants and parents by bringing colourful flowers from home, as well as fruit and materials to offer to those incarcerated. She tells us that 'our focus was the babies' play – often our only shared language'. This chapter provides a harrowing and courageous account, distressingly relevant for our time.

Chapter 15: Infants With Cancer: The Oncology Unit as Their Second Home

It is hard to imagine the impact on parents who finally meet their newborn baby and celebrate the relief to have that child in their arms, only to be subsequently informed that their young infant has cancer. **Maria McCarthy** and **Helen Shoemark** are specialists in the area of paediatric psychosocial oncology. They write about the kind of psychosocial care every infant in every hospital ward needs to receive. The detailed way they capture the life of one child on an oncology ward and the ward's system of care is their central story. A mother's perspective brings alive the way a resilient mother on a cancer ward can still protect her young. With these two authors she exemplifies the way a mother advocates for her child to be centre stage.

Chapter 16: High-Risk Infant Mental Health Outreach: Creating a Professional Community of Caregivers Using a Collaborative Mental Health and Nursing Approach

This chapter, written by **Paul Robertson**, **Amity McSwan** and **Louise Dockery**, offers a way that two traditional child and family clinical services can marry their efforts to meet and respond to the mental health needs of infants in vulnerable families. They describe an innovative collaboration between child and adolescent mental health clinicians and their colleagues in maternal and child nursing (home visiting) and how to engage with troubled infants on their own terms and in their own homes. Via the example of troubled 30-month-old 'John', we are offered an ultimately optimistic collaboration that other services might consider worthwhile replicating.

Chapter 17: The ART of Finding Authentic Discourses for Parents About and With Their Donor-Conceived Children

Concluding our book is a chapter about the cutting-edge work undertaken by **Sarah J. Jones** as she writes about the area of Assisted Reproductive Treatments (ART) and the needs of infants born via donor conception. By applying a legislative and child rights framework, she argues that professionals and parents need to grapple with the importance of conception histories for the infant's identity. When an infant's needs for identity get lost in unacknowledged feelings in participating in the ART process, Jones describes how this may impinge on the way parents develop meaningful stories. This in turn can adversely affect the parent–infant relationship and thus the mental health of the baby. This is because an infant may be denied some or all of the details of their conception story by parents. Parents participating in the ART process can feel judged by others, ashamed of themselves or fearful for their relationship with their infant if they are made aware of the full story and implications of being conceived through ART. This can then have profound ramifications for how the child over time develops a sense of themselves and their relationships.

* * *

It has been a true privilege to share with each author the journey of compiling this book. We have learnt much about their work and have enormous respect for the contribution they are making to not just the lives of vulnerable infants, young children and their families, but to our collective knowledge. We hope you find their work as inspiring as we do.

Wendy Bunston and Sarah J. Jones

CHAPTER 1

Introducing the Infant

And How to Support Vulnerable Babies and Young Children

WENDY BUNSTON AND SARAH J. JONES

Allow us to introduce you to the unique world of the infant. This is a world much larger than society in general tends to acknowledge or feel comfortable exploring. There is a myriad of reasons for this, some of which will be covered in this book. We commence with our regard for the infant as a person, a young citizen who has their own self and their own history, along with rights and an urgent need to feel safe and valued. This regard for the infant is even more important when she/he is born into life circumstances of great vicissitude, which renders them even more vulnerable and often invisible. We believe it is of crucial importance to develop ways to fully hold an expansive and sensitive consideration of what influences who this little person is, within their own unique family and culture.

Once upon a time infancy and the early years were disregarded as a rather nebulous stage in life's journey. Our work, building on those of so many before us, affirms that the formative years lay foundations for what follows. The newborn, within the cradle of their formative relationships, begins storing early physiological (bodily) memories which accumulate, remain implicit and help shape neural pathways within the infant's brain. The repetition of experiences, particularly those which are relational, contribute to the infant's emerging subjectivity. In their second year of life the infant develops greater motor coordination and self-mastery. In general, movement, mobility and language serve to further enhance their discovery of the world within which they live, and during the second to third year of life their developing cognitive abilities become more sophisticated and memories more explicit. Memories will remain available to the toddler, and as they grow, even more memories become stored and available for retrieval.

In working to support vulnerable infants and young children, we are concerned with understanding their earliest experiences. We are interested to discover them in both dyadic and triadic relationships, within the family matrix of parents, caregivers and grandparents and with siblings. All these relationships will create the attachment system for the young infant. They will store the interpersonal experiences, and create memories, implicit and explicit. We are keen to know the children we work with and learn from them. We know that very young children communicate something of their experiences, traumatic or otherwise, through their way of being with us. We wish to support them, to make ourselves available to meet them, welcome them and be curious to their tiny cues and sometimes loud cries. The infant and young child is an emotional being; so are we. As adults we can sometimes obscure our emotional selves with our rational selves. Sometimes we can over-rely on what we are told, more than what we really feel and what we see. Often, subtle communications can easily be missed if our attention strays or stays only with what we are told by caregivers. We need to be attentive to what the infant or young child expresses through their body, notice their interactions with their primary caregivers and discern their capacity for play. Being with our clients involves observing the ways a young child is spoken about and held, and how they behave. We often have an unspoken sense about this small baby or child, and this may be as critical to our understanding as what is spoken.

Working with vulnerable infants and young children is 'relational'. By this we mean that all features of an interpersonal connection are relational experiences. Our emerging relationship with the infant and with their parents/attachment figures, the way we feel when we sit ourselves on the floor to engage with the toddler, and the way we feel when we talk about these babies in supervision are subjective and relevant to our way of working. The evolving relational world of the infant and young child is shaped by the culture in their caregiving world, including influences and biases about race, gender, class, religion and a multitude of other factors.

The life of the infant

The infant has an important history pre-conception – a particular journey in utero – and then in the pathways they traverse as they enter the world and rapidly develop into the growing, relationally connected person they are, and continually become.

Pre-conception

As people who work with infants and their caregiving systems, by coming to know the infant's genesis story we may illuminate important familial history, with intergenerational threads of meaning emerging as the narrative unfolds. Some parental histories are marred by violence or other traumatic incidents or catastrophic events that make the telling of any stories intolerable or incoherent (Jones & Bunston 2012). These stories, whether spoken or unspoken, are important to try to understand as context for appreciating the caregiving world of the vulnerable infant and young child and how we might support them.

Conception

The conception itself may have been one of many for a mother, or a first. It may have been distressing, magical, or too difficult to simply reduce to words. What is important for all of us working in this area is to take the time, make no assumptions and allow for a therapeutic connection where this history may be explored. For example, in our work with parents experiencing family violence we very gently explore the conception story, creating space to speak about consent, non-consent, feeling pressured into sex and rape (Bunston *et al.* 2016). Some parents may have wanted the pregnancy terminated, but their ambivalence or the control exercised by others around them prevented this (Bunston & Sketchley 2012). Such circumstances very often leave an indelible emotional and psychological residue that remains unresolved. This knowledge informs us to be aware of the often-traumatic relational undercurrents which contribute to how the infants develop their sense of self and sense of others.

The infant in utero

What occurs in utero has received increased attention from the scientific community as the embryonic stages of the development of the brain, spine, major organs and central nervous system are becoming better understood. The potent impact of not only physical health but also psychological health of women during pregnancy is still a new frontier of undiscovered knowledge. What happens on the outside of the body, within the body and within the mind of the woman carrying the baby (and those significant others) directly impacts the infant in utero. Just as it is now commonly accepted within the health professions that smoking, excessive alcohol and substance misuse directly impact the foetus, so too do high levels of cortisol and other potent neural chemicals induced by distress and trauma experienced during pregnancy.

The infant's birth

Birth itself is an enormously significant life event for the baby and parent/s. Both authors have had the privilege of working with many professionals, particularly midwives and maternal child health nurses (home-visiting nurses) who have been present during vast numbers of births and who can recall, with exquisite elegance and deep sensitivity, amazing, terrifying and traumatic births. We ourselves have explored with parents their stories, fears and hopes as their babies were born; or with parent/s using assisted reproductive technologies or donor mothers, complicated and fraught journeys that led to and may then enshroud the birth experience.

Whether difficult, painful, uneventful, life threatening, all birth stories begin a narrative and add meaning to who this newborn member of a family is or might become. Circumstances and events that occur during and immediately after birth may conspire to impinge on the world of this new infant. For example, the extremely premature baby, the very unwell or the terminally ill infant may have, as their earliest experiences, intrusive and painful medical interventions. Their distress may go unrecognised as the parent/s themselves struggle to cope, let alone see who this new, growing little person is beyond the medical crisis; or perhaps to protect themselves from even imagining that their little baby may be suffering (Jones 2007).

The early years

Work with infants and young children during the early years has of course received a lot of attention from parents and practitioners, as this is where most believe it all begins. In the arena of child and family practice, the older the infant the more that has been researched and written. Perhaps this relates to our reliance on the spoken word; and as children grow older and attend day care, kindergarten or school, others outside a family are more likely to pick up on a child's difficulties.

The newborn or young infant seems more fragile and less like us until they learn to stand and start to speak. The younger the infant, the more we may need to rely on speculation and tolerate uncertainty. We need to find other ways to come to know the infant and allow them to know us. For some very new to infant work, a baby can be a little frightening, and we may believe we can't really come to know them, assuming we can only really rely on a parent's description.

Parents and professionals may quell their inherent anxiety in not always understanding babies' or even older children's communications by sweeping these away with generalised assumptions. Unfortunately, it is not uncommon to believe that preverbal babies do not really feel, see, hear or experience what others around them experience. Nor is it uncommon to discount what the verbal child expresses. This can lead, and has led, to grave errors in professional decision making. Child abuse enquiries in the UK have commonly found that, tragically, professionals have over relied on parent reports and made assumptions about cultural norms (see Chapter 12). For example, The Victoria Climbié Inquiry (2003), regarding 8-year-old West African child Victoria who died after suffering severe abuse at the hands of her caregivers, found that there were multiple service systems failures that contributed to this tragedy. A decade later, another case of abuse and neglect in the UK involved Baby P. Again, similar systems failures were reported (Jones 2014). There are lessons here to apply to our work with children all over the world. One of these lessons is captured by the analysis of Margaret Rustin (2005), who offered profound insights into understanding little 8-year-old Victoria Climbié's state of mind, and that of those around her. Rustin concluded that much is missed when children and professionals emotionally defend themselves against the horror of believing that a parent would deliberately harm, torture or even want to kill their own child. Unless this is understood, we will continue to miss what is most important to see.

Crucial to the infant and young child are their significant attachment figures, for they are the centre of their universe. Should the growing child feel safe and secure enough in this relationship matrix, they will begin to reach out, to discover and learn, to seek self-mastery, and become more creative and imaginative in their play and in other relationships. Should a secure relationship not be available from the very beginning, or suddenly and traumatically withdrawn, their relationship world shrinks. Often, both their physical and emotional growth becomes restricted as well. If there is a total absence or loss of a previously available and reliable caregiver to buffer, support, enjoy and protect a young child, this will have far-reaching consequences. For each young child, we know there will be different accounts given in family stories about those who suffer devastating loss, even if there are factors in common as to what caused the loss. When there are natural disasters or man-made disasters – accidental or deliberate – each caregiving system will create its own stories. Our role is to respectfully and empathically hold in mind the subjective experience of each infant or young child and their family or caregivers, privileging the experience of our youngest citizens, and creating new stories with the infant as part of this experience. In this book we are seeking to explore, with our colleagues, knowledge about the theories and research that informs them as professionals working within infant and family fields. We bring their practice experience to the constantly challenging place of infant work in our changing world.

Introducing the infant and young child into our work

Infant mental health and early childhood development practice is well established. There are training courses and associations for Infant Mental Health across the world. The most useful and applicable theoretical constructs that inform this field are drawn from the work of attachment theory (Bowlby 1988; Salter-Ainsworth 1991), the philosophy of 'good enough parenting' (Winnicott 1953) and, more recently, the introduction of the constructs of 'subjectivity and intersubjectivity' (Trevarthen & Aitken 2001) and the neurological explorations of how experience shapes early brain development (Schore 2016; Siegel 2012). In distilling the essence of how we have come to engage with the mind and subjectivity of the infant, we endeavour to do less in order to explore more. That is, we do not rush forth with solutions. Although sometimes the circumstances warrant urgent intervention to prevent immediate harm to the infant/child, we ordinarily need to slow down in order to work and think; not rushing the infant but allowing space for the infant to come to know us, at their pace. We accept overtures when they are given to us by the infant or young child and spend time simply being with them in their space. This can be summarised as six practice principles:

1. welcome

2. curiosity

3. observation

4. exploration

5. mentalisation/reflective functioning

6. relationship-oriented practice.

Welcome

To engage well with the infants, children and families we see, we offer our warmth, compassion and interest. Our work starts with the first meeting, with our welcome. With each new encounter we welcome families with an open mind and an open heart. Our welcome must not be clouded by our busy-ness or filled up with attention to tasks and goals. Rather, we provide a sense of unrushed time to be with a new family, and the meeting often includes having space to be on the floor with the infant or young child, providing some, though not too many, toys to explore. We need to start well if a family is to join us in further work together.

Curiosity

Curiosity is a state of mind, which means that we are interested in the other and their experience. It is open-ended. We are required to be interested in, and curious about, all kinds of family experience, which often include disharmony. This may be unhappy couple relationships, violence, alcohol abuse, thoughts about suicide, eating disorders, disagreements and worries about the children and their behaviour. We need to be open to thinking about these things, which can feel tricky, because our curiosity in the family's experience will move beyond normal conversational etiquette. It can be difficult to find a place for curiosity when we are listening to aspects of peoples' lives that are intimate and evoke strong feelings in them and in us. To be curious does not mean we have the answers or solutions to people's dilemmas; it means we are courageous enough to ask and to talk together. When we are openly curious, we can help people find ways to put their experience into words and help them become more curious as to their own feelings and thoughts.

Observation

Just as active listening is a skill, so is reflective attention and observation. Observation is more than hurried watching; it is active and demanding. To observe well, we must still our mind. It is a skill that comes with patience and practice. When we are with babies and their parents, the parent is often both troubled and distracted; urgently needing to talk. Sometimes they are in such distress that their baby or toddler can disappear amidst all the talking, even when a distressed child is casting toys around the room. The thrown objects are often a plea or communication asking to be noticed.

When we start working with young children, we may not see or perceive their tiny signals. We may not notice their tightly scrunched-up fingers, the blood rush to their face. We may misunderstand that the quiet, 'good' baby has quietly withdrawn from the world. Over time, with practice and, for some, the experience of formal Infant Observation training (see Chapters 3 and 4), we become more able to notice the details and tiny clues which are the infant's ways of communicating.

By honing our observation skills, we become more attuned with all those we work with. Whilst in the beginning we might 'see' only the child the parent tells us about, over time we might build our own picture and see more nuance and complexity. The aim of our work is to make a child more alive and more known to their parents. We share our observations with the parents and listen to theirs to open new understandings.

Exploration

Exploring is having the courage to search and go into unknown territory. By engaging them, taking them along with us, we can explore with the parents/caregivers and the child. To venture into a new or foreign direction, we must first establish ourselves as trustworthy guides who can lead the way safely. A client who does not let us in, who restricts exploration, might be frightened of where we might take them. When an infant or toddler cannot or will not engage or play with us, we might need to explore in our own minds how we can make sense of these refusals. We explore with the family in the room, and we explore through silently reflecting within ourselves. Supervisors and trusted colleagues can help us explore our experience of being with the clients in the room. Our training and theoretical frameworks are useful guides for discovery – the maps that inform explorations and alert us to possible dangers.

Reflective functioning/mentalisation

To mentalise, we need to have the capacity to think and reflect on our experience and to accept that another person's experience will be different. Mentalisation, also referred to as 'reflective functioning', offers us a way of thinking about, and making sense of, how our experiences, observations, physical responses and feelings influence us and our interactions with others. There are two aspects of this: first, we come to an understanding of what happens in our own mind. Second, we explore what might be happening between us and the people we work with.

Our own capacity to mentalise supports us in the work we do. It strengthens our capacities to think about what it feels like to be with our clients and offers insight into how they might feel. This helps us also understand what happens between ourselves and our clients, both adults and young ones. The parent's state of mind (mental state) and their capacity for reflection about emotional states – their own and others' – influences and shapes the parent–infant relationship and the way an infant comes to know their own mind.

Relationship-oriented practice

In working with children and families, we don't come with fancy equipment, or a step-by-step instruction manual. Our work is the relationships we make with the children and families we see. The welcome is the invitation and extended hand, relating from the first moments. We offer our self, our curiosity, and openness to exploration in the service of this unique family. On the one hand it is understood that we need to use our own minds and emotions to guide us through our work. On the other hand, using our emotional guide can also mean we feel things we don't wish to feel. Using ourselves in the work means we bring our humour, our joy and our compassion. We also bring our minds and our purpose to creating 'therapeutic relationships' with all family members, including the infant.

Innovative practices that support vulnerable infants, young children and their families

Fundamental to this way of working is the belief that:

> Infants and children are not objects that we do things to, nor are they passive participants in the therapeutic process whom we work on. Rather, they are willing, able and available unique subjects who are communicating volumes to their external world about how their internal world is faring. (Bunston 2008, p.335)

When working with families with young children, commonly used terms such as 'child-centred', 'child-sensitive' or 'child-friendly' are often used. These typically refer to the workers and therapists and parents 'keeping in mind' the needs of infants or younger children. Whilst these approaches are very important, we aim to extend this further.

Should the adults, particularly the parent(s), struggle to make good decisions on behalf of the young infant or child, such as may occur within highly vulnerable families, then increasing focus is often placed on enhancing and growing the 'capacity of the parent(s)'. Meanwhile, it is common practice that the parent/caregiver is the main recipient of most interventions, overlooking the infant or younger child. It may be an assumption that the work that occurs with the parent will automatically transfer to the child. Gunlicks and Weissman (2008) found the transfer of learnings from research into practice when treating the adult's postnatal maternal and parental depression had limited success in impacting parent-child relationships. However, Forman *et al.* (2007) argue that 'treatment for depression in the postpartum period should target the mother–infant relationship in addition to the mothers' depressive symptoms'.

Infants and small children, as the newest members of families, can often be the quickest to respond. They may provide crucial entry points for undertaking complex therapeutic work with 'at risk' families. An infant-/child-led approach considers the infant, from utero through to the age of five, as an active participant in the change process, and from the outset to be as important as any other. This approach concerns itself with 'how to bring the subjectivity of infant and child alive, and the need to recognise and employ the potential hope, and healing the new-born brings, as well as the motivation for change' (Bunston 2017, p.7). Simultaneously, whilst we have an infant focus, from the moment we welcome a new family we engage in an exploration as to how to support all its members. We are aware that if we lose this engagement with the parent(s), we lose the infant too.

Infant-ready, responsive therapeutic practice

Working with infants is messy and unpredictable work, and ever more so with highly vulnerable and chaotic families. This work requires therapeutic stamina but also systemic thinking. All who are significant in the caregiving world of the infant, need to be thought about. A women's refuge worker or a hospital social worker may become a temporary attachment figure of enormous importance. One of the most significant tasks for the developing infant is developing their socio-emotional and neurophysiological regulation (Stern 2003). Their emerging subjective and emotional selves and how they manage their internal world occur within the context of their caregiving relationships (Beebe 2006; Stern 2003). Their capacity to develop healthy strategies to manage their emotional regulation is dependent on a caregiving response that is timely, emotionally safe and appropriate. Where the mother or father is themselves traumatised, both by past and present traumas (for example, ongoing family violence), infant responsive therapeutic practices can offer immediate, flexible and healing therapeutic opportunities, for both mother and baby (Jordan 2007; Thomson-Salo 2007).

It is imperative to provide a rapid and flexible therapeutic response (Bunston *et al.* 2016; Bunston & Glennen 2015). The longer and more often an infant is left alone in a dysregulated, dissociative or hyper-aroused state, the more enduring the damaging biochemical consequences for the developing brain (Cirulli, Berry & Alleva 2003; Schechter & Willheim 2009). The sooner the infant is emotionally attended to, and within the context of their caregiving system, the greater the capacity for relational and regulatory repair. This requires 'infant-ready responses' that are not solely dependent on healing the parent first, whilst the infant waits; but on responses that involve using the relationship between the infant and their mother/father together, and now, to act as the starting point for repair and healing.

Infant mental health-trained relational therapists and early childhood workers need to be flexible and available to respond as traumatic events occur, in a space which feels safe for the family (perhaps their home or the primary worker's office) and within the context of their ongoing working relationship with their primary worker. The primary worker is often, but not always, working with the mother and her young children. They provide the primary, substantive and ongoing working relationship.

We must be alert to our biases of working with men and assumptions that only they, and not the mother, are capable of intimate partner violence. When specialist infant–parent therapists become involved, involving other practitioners, such as a previous primary worker, in therapeutic sessions builds on their prior working relationship with families. Further, it enhances the worker's skills and understandings as to how to implement an infant-led approach. When managed well, this also augments the capacity to continue the therapeutic thread of the sessions in their day-to-day work. This often occurs outside of the more structured therapeutic sessions. Sometimes, to provide a family with a stronger caregiving system, more effort needs to go into bringing together all the key professionals, such as child care educators, maternal and health nurses, paediatricians, family support workers, etc. This approach prevents or reduces compartmentalising the therapeutic systems that are engaged with vulnerable families. Just as Winnicott (1953) argued that mothers needed to be 'good enough', we also need to be 'good enough' when we are engaged in working with young families. An infant-ready response means that practitioners work with the infant at the centre, work with each other and work with all family members. Most of all it means not losing sight of the baby.

Conclusion

Infant- and child-led work brings with it an immediacy and imperative that generates hope, growth and discovery. We can sometimes gain access to the most difficult-to-engage families through their baby, as parents might seek help when they are less certain and often more anxious about the health needs of these little ones than they are for themselves. Introducing parents to the emotional and psycho-physiological world of their infant/young child, and their baby/ young child's urgent need for relational health can be revelatory. We say: 'Bring on the revolution!'

References

Beebe, B. (2006) 'Co-constructing mother–infant distress in face-to-face interactions: Contributions of microanalysis.' *Infant Observation 9*, 2, 151–164.

Bowlby, J. (1988) *A Secure Base: Clinical Applications of Attachment Theory.* London: Routledge.

Bunston, W. (2008) 'Baby lead the way: Mental health groupwork for infants, children and mothers affected by family violence.' *Journal of Family Studies*, Volume 14, Issue 2–3.

Bunston, W. (2017) *Helping Babies and Children (0–6) to Heal After Family Violence: A Practical Guide to Infant- and Child-Led Practice.* London: Jessica Kingsley Publishers.

Bunston, W. & Sketchley, R. (2012) *Refuge for Babies in Crisis.* Melbourne, Australia: RCH-IMHP. Retrieved 16/01/19 from www.dvrcv.org.au/sites/thelookout.sites.go1.com.au/files/Refuge%20for%20Babies%20Manual%20FinalWEB.pdf.

Bunston, W. & Glennen, K. (2015) 'Holding the baby costs nothing.' *DVRCV Advocate*, Spring/Summer, 46–49.

Bunston, W., Eyre, K., Carlsson, A. & Pringle, K. (2016) 'Evaluating relational repair work with infants and mothers impacted by family violence.' *Australian & New Zealand Journal of Criminology 49*, 1, 113–133.

Cirulli, F., Berry, A. & Alleva, E. (2003) 'Early disruption of the mother–infant relationship: Effects on brain plasticity and implications for psychopathology.' *Neuroscience & Biobehavioral Reviews 27*, 1–2, 73–82.

Forman, D., O'Hara, M., Stuart, S., Gorman, L., Larsen, K. & Coy, K. (2007) 'Effective treatment for postnatal depression is not sufficient to improve the developing mother–child relationship.' *Development and Psychopathology 19*, 2, 585–602.

Gunlicks, L. & Weissman, M. (2008) 'Change in child psychopathology with improvement in parental depression: A systematic review.' *Journal of the American Academy of Child and Adolescent Psychiatry 47*, 4, 379–389.

Jones, R. (2014) *The Story of Baby P: Setting the Record Straight.* Bristol: Bristol University Press.

Jones, S. (2007) 'The baby as subject: The hospitalised infant and the family therapist.' *Australian and New Zealand Journal of Family Therapy 28*, 3, 146–154.

Jones, S. & Bunston, W. (2012) 'The "original couple": Enabling mothers and infants to think about what destroys as well as engenders love, when there has been intimate partner violence.' *Couple and Family Psychoanalysis 2*, 2, 215–232.

Jordan, B. (2007) 'Infancy and Domestic Violence.' In F. Thomson-Salo & C. Paul (Eds) *The Baby as Subject.* Melbourne: Stonnington Press.

Rustin, M. (2005) 'Conceptual analysis of critical moments in Victoria Climbié's life.' *Child and Family Social Work 10*, 11–19.

Salter-Ainsworth, M.D. (1991) 'Attachments and Other Affectional Bonds Across the Life Cycle.' In C.M. Parkes, J. Stevenson-Hinde & P. Marris (Eds) *Attachment Across the Life Cycle*. London: Routledge.

Schechter, D.S. & Willheim, E. (2009) 'The Effects of Violent Experiences on Infants and Young Children.' In C.H.Z. Jr (Ed.) *Handbook of Infant Mental Health*. New York: The Guilford Press.

Schore, A.N. (2016) *Affect Regulation and the Origin of the Self: The Neurobiology of Emotional Development*. New York: Routledge.

Siegel, D.J. (2012) *Developing Mind: How Relationships and the Brain Interact to Shape Who We Are* (2nd ed.). New York: Guilford Press.

Stern, D.N. (2003) *The Interpersonal World of the Infant: A View From Psychoanalysis and Developmental Psychology*. London: Karnac Books.

Thomson-Salo, F. (2007) 'Relating to the Infant as Subject in the Context of Family Violence.' In F. Thomson-Salo & C. Paul (Eds) *The Baby as Subject*. Melbourne: Stonnington Press.

Trevarthen, C. & Aitken, K. (2001) 'Infant intersubjectivity: Research, theory, and clinical applications.' *Journal of Child Psychology and Psychiatry 42*, 1, 3–48.

Winnicott, D.W. (1953) 'Transitional objects and transitional phenomena.' *International Journal of Psycho-Analysis 34*, 89–97.

Suggestions for further reading

The Interpersonal World of the Infant: A View From Psychoanalysis and Developmental Psychology. Stern, D.N. (2003). London: Karnac Books.

Forms of Intersubjectivity. Beebe, B., Knoblauch, S.H., Rustin, J. & Sorter, S (2005). New York: Other Press.

Attachment Theory and Psychoanalysis. Fonagy, P. (2001). London: Karnac Books.

Handbook of Infant Mental Health (4th ed.). Zeanah Jr, C.H. (2019). New York: The Guilford Press.

Winnicott on the Child. Winnicott, D.W. (2002). USA: Perseus Publishing.

CHAPTER 2

Reflective Supervision's Essential Place in Thoughtful Practice

JULIE STONE, SARAH J. JONES AND WENDY BUNSTON

The authors of this chapter believe it is crucial for all who work with or for distressed young children and their families, regardless of seniority or role, to engage in reflective practice. This chapter outlines the key reasons why reflective supervision is vital for sustained, thoughtful work, explains some of the essential ingredients for 'good enough' reflective supervision, and explores some of the pitfalls or obstacles that can, and do, get in the way of supervision being creative and helpful. Supervision as discussed in this chapter includes both individual and group supervision, whether supported by a service or agency or self-funded.

The authors have extensive experience of reflective supervision as both supervisor and supervisee. Each of us has found reflective supervision to be one of the most potent aspects in our professional development. Now, as experienced supervisors, the relationships we had with our supervisors – both the unhelpful and the helpful – have shaped, influenced and enriched the way we supervise others. By way of illustration, at the end of the chapter, we will each describe vignettes from supervision. Julie and Wendy write from the point of view of the supervisor, and Sarah from the point of view of being supervised.

Reflective supervision's contribution to thoughtful practice

The purpose of reflective supervision is to help build our capacity, competence and confidence in working effectively with or for distressed children and families. In essence, reflective supervision is about making a commitment to a regular space in our diaries and our minds, to meet with another or group of others, to reflect upon and to think about the multitude of thoughts, feelings and emotions that swirl around and within us in response to our work. When we make a commitment to doing this, our thoughts, feelings and emotions provide rich data we can mine to help us make sense of that which does not make sense, or to tolerate 'not knowing'. Supervision enables us to be more creative and to thoughtfully hold the child and family at the centre of our work.

Recognising and negotiating challenges

Working with distressed infants and their families is difficult and demanding. Our recognition and identification with the infant or other family members' distress, dependence or vulnerability, consciously or unconsciously, arouses painful feelings within us all. Anxiety, chaos, distress, fantasies of rescue, hurt, indignation, outrage, preoccupation, shame and stirred memories are some of the many feelings that are part of this work. When confronted by a child's or parent's disclosure of family violence, for example, we might need our supervisor to help us with our outrage. Good reflective supervision should be able to help participants think about the feelings that might be getting in the way of their thinking or clouding their view of the infant's and family's experience. When unacknowledged or unattended to, our feelings hijack our ability to think, which then impairs our ability to work effectively.

Supervision offers a place and an opportunity to untangle and think about what belongs to the work and what belongs to us. Sometimes our own experience and memories are evoked. Once recognised and acknowledged, they can be better tolerated, contained and kept separate from the work. Our work is enhanced when we can clarify what is frustrating or worrying us, and when we can think about something we might not wish to feel or to know. Reflective supervision can also highlight areas of our understanding or knowledge that need to be strengthened.

Pioneering Infant Mental Health clinician Janet Dean, the founding Director of the Boulder Colorado Community Infant Mental Health Program, argues that reflective supervision is 'the guarantee and insurance policy' to help us sustain thoughtful and effective work (Janet Dean made this statement to Julie Stone in a personal communication in 1999). The relationships formed in reflective supervision foster the opportunity to think together about our experience in our work. Reflective supervision helps us hone our practice. Supervision helps us hold on to, reclaim and develop our thinking mind. It helps us to safely navigate the vicissitudes of our work, to be with the family's distress and to be open and curious in the face of our uncertainties.

Reflective supervision is essentially different from other forms of supervision, which might, for example, be about governance or an organisational requirement to measure performance (Key Performance Indicators (KPIs). Such management supervision might be to focus on monitoring an individual's workload, or to ensure that practice is within agency guidelines or meeting professional standards. In contrast, the focus in reflective supervision is on the participants' experience and what is evoked in them in their work with the children and families. Reflective supervision helps us explore the ways that our responses and experience can help us better understand something important about the children and families and their experience.

Getting started

When you are curious and have some confidence that reliable and regular reflective supervision will help you in your practice, but this is not supported by your workplace, approach your manager or team leader to discuss how such supervision may be accessed. You might need other colleagues to support you with this conversation. Campaign robustly if you can. If unsuccessful, then consider sourcing supervision for yourself, or pooling resources to pay for an external supervisor. If neither of these options is possible, set up a structured peer group process to reflect together to help deepen your explorations – via case studies, exploring practice dilemmas or reading professional literature.

Establishing a contract

Before supervision begins, there are many questions to be asked and answered: Why? Where? When? How often? For how long? What do I expect? What's expected of me? Who pays? How do we evaluate whether or not it is working? How will difficulties be addressed? Asking and answering these and other questions, discussing them and coming to an agreed 'supervision contract' is an important place to begin. Some practitioners find it helpful to formalise the supervision contract by writing out the agreed terms, which are then signed by all participants. When the supervision is being supported and paid for by an agency, some, but not all, agency managers request a formal contract from the supervisor. This can help establish an explicit professional relationship with the agency and reinforce their support and commitment to the process.

When the relationship between a supervisor and an individual or group develops well, trust is established. Then reflective supervision becomes a creative space where discovery becomes possible. As within all good relationships, trust builds over time, experience by experience. Trust is facilitated when the expectations and 'terms' of the supervision are clear, explicit, understood and agreed to by the supervisor and participant(s).

Before beginning supervision, it can be helpful to agree on a time frame for review. This allows for the progress and helpfulness, or otherwise, to be explored, and the relationship reflected upon and talked about. Without a clear invitation to do so, we understand that many participants might not feel able to talk about their concerns with us. Practitioners embarking on their first experiences in reflective supervision may feel wary and apprehensive. It can take them some time before they feel comfortable in their relationship with the supervisor, other group members, the reflective supervision space and the task.

An experienced supervisor will expect and respect these feelings and allow time for participants to find their way to discover what supervision has to offer. They will encourage participants to explore new ways of thinking about their work. If the supervisory relationship becomes too comfortable or cosy, this too can inhibit robust discussion and discovery.

Reflective supervision as a scaffold for practice

Parents and their infants, often unknowingly perhaps, look to us to scaffold and contain them, individually and together, in their struggling relationship. To work effectively, practitioners themselves need to have a steady, firm frame or scaffold to help hold and contain them, as sometimes they themselves might feel 'shaky'. The families we work with are often aroused, distressed, emotionally disorganised, victims of social injustices and/or may live in poverty. The service systems we work in, for, or with are often demanding, overwhelmed and inadequate. It is little wonder we quake at times. The families we work with look to us, needing us to withstand the onslaught of their feelings, not to crumble in their wake.

The metaphor of the frame or scaffold reminds us that we all need a structure around us to help hold us steady. We must consciously build or construct a suitable frame to hold and help us hold our thinking mind, in our minute-to-minute and day-to-day encounters and experiences in our work. Our training and experience, the teams we work in, our senior colleagues, and our organisation's administrative processes and procedures are all part of the frame. Our theoretical models could also be regarded as scaffolds for holding our thoughts. Our understanding and clarity concerning our role and the task provide other essential elements in our scaffold. Reflective supervision can – and the authors propose it should – be a central organising structure in the holding frame.

In difficult and challenging cases, supervision helps us think about all those involved, including paying attention to a non-verbal infant. It helps us gather a coherent understanding of the complexity of the family and the various services or agencies they may be involved with. Supervision can help us be alert to dangers and help us clarify what is needed from us in our role.

The good enough supervisor

The good enough supervisor is one who encourages, challenges and helps us grow in our confidence, competence and capacity to work effectively. In part we measure this by whether or not, over time, we feel free to share our thoughts and feelings about our work, especially when it seems it is not going well. The 'good enough' supervisor encourages and facilitates participants to become courageous and creative in their work. They may encourage us to be less serious and more playful, to have a go, to take thoughtful risks, to try something new. They remind us that none of us 'gets it right' all the time and invite us to experience that in a good enough relationship, every rupture is an invitation for repair.

Some, but not all, supervisors will help us integrate new knowledge, theory and research evidence. Some participants bring one family to supervision session after session; others bring the challenge or worry that is uppermost in their mind. A good enough supervisor will not prescribe the required content; their commitment will be to think together to help enrich our understanding and our work.

Pitfalls and obstacles

The need to talk or debrief with a colleague after a particularly difficult or painful encounter may have a place in our day-to-day work. However, the need or urge to do this too frequently can also be a defence against thinking, a way of pushing the feelings away. Such 'debriefing' can bring relief, yet it is useful to consider if at the same time we might rob ourselves of the understanding that comes from grappling thoughtfully with our troubled and troubling feelings.

Participants may feel ambivalent about their supervisor. It is important that this is noted and assessed over time. It is usually unhelpful to flee from supervision at the first sign of discomfort. When uncertain, it can be difficult to voice this; however, having the courage to talk about what is not going well can be a rich and instructive experience. How the experienced supervisor listens to, responds and guides exploration and reflections on the participant's concerns, and how the participant feels after such reflections, will be important markers for the ongoing supervision partnership.

If a supervisor defensively responds to any challenge or perceived criticism, there is a problem. If a supervisor finds that repeatedly the people they are supervising 'flee', it behoves them to reflect and closely examine what might be going on and what part they play in the exodus. Supervisors also need to make the space and time to reflect and think about their work, to help them remain clear about their role and responsibilities, and to ensure that what they offer is in the service of the participants and their work.

Vignettes from supervision

Challenges in supervision: Julie Stone

Over the last 20 years in my professional life as an infant, child and family psychiatrist, it has been my privilege to engage in reflective supervision with colleagues from many differing disciplines, with differing theoretical orientations and working in a wide range of roles. These colleagues have worked in public and private health, mental health, child protection, government and non-government family services, including family violence services, community development and family advocacy, most recently with advocates supporting families seeking asylum in Australia.

The common thread across all the supervision I have offered is my explicit commitment to strive to give children and their experience a central place in our explorations. Despite not always getting it right for those being supervised, my intention is to be open to the experience of those seeking supervision, to listen and to make my mind, understanding and experience available to them in the service of their understanding and their work. Two recent experiences in my supervision practice are offered to illustrate differing challenges. For one colleague, without something changing in our relationship, creative discovery would not have been possible. For another, our shared exploration facilitated a painful and valuable understanding.

Not held, not safe, not contained

The first colleague, a director and clinician for a programme supporting mothers and their babies, contacted me to request a 'time to talk' about our supervision. In her email she wrote she had 'put on her brave pants' to make the request. For some months, after our supervision sessions I had been left with a vague feeling of having failed this colleague. I sensed that my disquiet and my colleague's need for bravery were related and part of what we needed to talk about.

When she rang, I said her comment about being brave alerted me to her perhaps feeling some trepidation. She agreed. She explained she had become reluctant to 'turn up' for supervision. Far from experiencing me as open, available and interested in her, she experienced me as someone 'with a big personality', who thought and spoke very quickly, and who left her feeling unsure of herself. She had noticed an eagerness to please and appease, fearing that otherwise I would 'spit her out'.

Clearly what she experienced in supervision was far from what she wanted, and very far from what I wanted to offer her. Thinking and talking quickly are things I always consciously try to hold in mind, and to temper. I had failed her in not pacing myself well enough for her, and in not thinking more deeply about my own disquiet at the end of our supervision hour. She said she was left feeling bombarded by a potentially destructive force. There is no opportunity for creative discovery within that experience.

My colleague's bravery allowed us to begin to explore some of the possible antecedents and meanings of the gaps between our agreed intention for supervision and her experience, perhaps opening the way for future creative discovery. I valued the opportunity to discuss together her experience and was left pondering and taking responsibility for my contribution to the gaps. We agreed to work together in our joint effort to create a comfortable space for her to think about her work. We agreed that if after an agreed period she still felt it was not working, then we would think together about who as supervisor might be a better fit for her.

Sometimes knots and misunderstandings in the relationship need to be teased apart and attended to. Some are sorted, deepening and enriching the relationship, while others cannot be. When this is the case, then the best outcome is a mutual acknowledgement of the mis-match, and a shared discussion about potential alternative supervisors promising creative possibility for the practitioner.

Black, white, right, wrong, mistrust and conflict

The second colleague, working in a statutory organisation, began a supervision session by saying she had just left a 'horrid meeting', which left her feeling distressed, angry and completely useless. She was flushed and tearful. Over the hour we were able to sort through some of the fragments of the exchange between her in her role as child protection worker' and an angry, vocal, older woman, already caring for a number of grandchildren, who was determined to 'take on' another child. My colleague had hoped to engage and help this woman to see and understand this other child and his experience.

The boy had lived in the care of an unrelated foster mother since he was 6 weeks old. Following a recent discovery about his hitherto unknown racial heritage, he was being moved to live 'with family'. Sadly, somewhere in her effort to open a space for thinking together with the grandmother, it seems my colleague came to represent, and to be blamed and held to account for, aeons of racial and cultural difference, misunderstanding and oppression. She became caught in a toxic exchange as she felt the need to defend and explain her position.

In the polemic that raged between these women, both arguing for what they believed was right for this little boy, my colleague felt dismissed as yet another bossy white woman who could not and would never understand. An opportunity to come together to think about the boy and his experience was lost. I remarked that the odds were stacked against their meeting.

Through our reflections, she began to make sense of her unease. She saw that, unwittingly and unwillingly, she was part of a statutory service's sanctioned 'removal' of this boy from his psychological and loved mother. She felt caught in a repetition of the heinous acts that led to the devastating experiences of 'the stolen generation'. When able to acknowledge and feel her sense of powerlessness, shame and sadness, my colleague was able to think about what she could do for this boy.

She resolved to write a letter to his mother-to-be, acknowledging and accepting her own part in their failed attempt at meeting. She also determined to document her understanding for this little boy, who might someday wish to read his official agency file. Creative discovery is no guarantee of a happy ending. Supervision does, however, help us bare (and bear) our sorrows and enables us to continue thinking about the children we meet in our work.

Seeing the infant clearly in supervision: Wendy Bunston

A large part of my work involves running monthly reflective group supervision for counselling teams, maternal child health nurses, refuge workers and workers in the homelessness sector. Keeping the infant and their experience in mind and at the centre of the work holds true for this kind of supervision, as illustrated in the following supervision vignette reflecting on an 18-month-old toddler, Selma.

Aarushi, a child support worker, presented a case for discussion in her family support programme team's regular group supervision. She had been working with Selma, now 18 months old, and her mother Ratu and father Samuel, since Selma's birth. The family had a complex history and had been referred by child protection services. Aarushi had found herself becoming increasingly anxious when doing home visits with Selma and her mother. Even before stepping into the home, she found herself having heart palpitations. As soon as Aarushi arrived, Ratu would sweep her into the kitchen, leaving Selma alone to entertain herself in the lounge room next door. As Aarushi spoke about this, she became flushed and her words were hurried. When asked to describe what was happening for Selma during these visits, Aarushi became even more flustered.

As Aarushi's supervisor, I spoke slowly and softly and asked her to slow down, to shut her eyes and to describe where Selma was and what she was doing during these visits. Then I asked her to imagine what Selma might make of her mother and Aarushi's interactions. Aarushi remarked that Ratu's intensity might be overwhelming for Selma, as it was for her. She expressed shock when she realised that she might have unwittingly added to, rather than reduced, the anxiety and feelings of isolation Selma could have been feeling.

Together, the group played with ideas about what might happen if Aarushi took herself to where Selma was and sat down beside her. Aarushi started to imagine what this might look like, what she might do to gently engage Selma and how this might shift the dynamics in the space. Aarushi became excited about how she might be different in the space and hopeful that she could bring something new to Selma.

In the next supervision session, Aarushi described how she sat on the floor with Selma. She started to read to her, and Ratu came to join them. After the story ended, Aarushi continued to play with Selma, and Ratu spoke about how her grandmother would sometimes sit her on her knee and tell her stories. She remembered how this led to them both drifting off to sleep, with her cuddled up in her grandmother's arms.

These reflections in supervision created a space for Aarushi to mentally stand outside of herself and imagine and consider herself, Selma and Ratu, and their interactions differently. For the first time Aarushi felt that she gained some insight into how Selma might experience her mother and how Ratu experienced herself. This revelation was incredibly powerful for her work with this family and other families.

Aarushi marked this moment in supervision as the moment she realised just how her ability to think about what the space felt like for others brought something new and important to thinking about her own experience. Rather than feeling lost and overwhelmed, Aarushi slowly found that she began to welcome whatever feelings came her way. She began to reflect on them and what they might be telling her about the infants and families.

This experience in reflective supervision changed Aarushi's practice. Selma and her mother's interactions with Aarushi helped Aarushi develop her confidence that by engaging Selma directly, she was helping both Selma and her mother. She nurtured Selma's capacity to experience being seen and feeling felt, both necessary experiences in the development of a thinking and creative mind. Aarushi was able to play a part in helping mother and baby build a stronger emotional foundation for their relationship.

The experience also helped Aarushi gain insight into Ratu's own experience. When parents are still trapped in their own early wounds of neglect, trauma and abuse – sometimes at the hands of their own parents, the very people who were there to care for them – it is hard for them to see themselves or their infants differently. What happened in the past and how they were cared for can be re-enacted in their methods of caring for their infants/children, transferring the ghosts of the past from one generation to the next (Fraiberg, Adelson & Shapiro 1975; Lieberman *et al.* 2005).

In our infant/parent work, supervision offers the space to still the mind and to make these ghosts apparent. Deliberately reflecting on the relational patterns, and the associated feelings floating underneath what we see, may reveal the real struggle being played out. Aarushi's work over time with Selma and Ratu revealed longstanding threads of relational neglect handed down from one generation to the next. The sight of Aarushi seeing and engaging with Selma as real and worthy enabled Ratu to rediscover something good from her past whereby she could claim something real and worthy in herself.

The inter-subjective space, where minds grow and develop in and through the meeting with other minds, can only happen within a relational context. It is important for the infant to be physically present in the working space and mentally present in our considerations, something which could not happen when Aarushi disappeared into the kitchen with Ratu.

We all exist, respond and make meaning through context and relationships. Relationships are at the heart of Infant Mental Health work. 'Being with' is at the heart of relationships. And the supervisory relationship must sit at the heart of our work as Infant Mental Health practitioners and workers concerned with enhancing the quality of life of the infant and their families.

The supervisee's perspective: Sarah J. Jones
Feeling overwhelmed

Many years ago, I was working with a couple, whose emotional distress overwhelmed them both and myself. When considering my experiences as a supervisee, my work with this couple came to mind. Following a session where they had erupted into humiliating anger, I felt great guilt at my lack, my absence and inability to be present for them in this torrid session. Their children were not present, and had they been, I would have responded differently.

Despite my considerable training, clinical experience and supervision of working with couples, I felt defeated and hopeless. Later that afternoon at my regular weekly supervision session, my supervisor noted I seemed shaken. My feelings of inadequacy felt persecutory. By the end of the supervision session, I felt restored. What had she done? First of all, she asked me to recount the experience in detail. I had discussed my therapeutic work with this couple many times in supervision with her, and the dynamics of the couple were well known to her. During this supervision, we were able to gain a deeper understanding of how this couple related to one another.

Second, she pointed out they might have felt supported well enough by me and our work to bring their rage and their messy, inchoate feelings to it. They had kept coming, she reminded me, and so maybe I could see this as some form of progress, not only failure? Third, she helped me explore how my own feelings of humiliation experienced with this couple were a way of understanding something more of their emotional life. My guilt, she posed, might be a projection of their own unbearable affect. The couple continued to come and we continued to explore and work together productively. It was my ongoing supervision which held and supported me, allowing me to endure and go on working with their distress and, in time, many others like them.

Over the 15 years I have spent with this supervisor, I have felt greatly enriched by all she has given me and taught me. Through her steady, challenging guidance I have internalised a good enough supervisor, enabling me to know that I am a good enough clinician and supervisor in the work that I do. She helped me understand that, just as the couple trusted me enough to expose their rage and humiliation, I trusted her enough to take my humiliation and sense of inadequacy to her. I learnt that my fear of being judged was not actually her judgement but my own.

Process notes: a powerful supervision tool for reflecting on our work with infants

Many years ago, social workers in training were expected to write up 'process notes' (Trowell & Miles 2004). Process notes, written following a clinical encounter, strive to be a verbatim account, in full narrative form, of the session. Optimally, everything that happens is captured by the practitioner: all the verbal and non-verbal exchanges of client(s), of infants and children when present, and of the practitioner. When writing process notes, the tone, affect, mood, timing and way the clients arrive, where family members sit, children's play, end of the session, and departure are all deemed noteworthy. Such intense reflection on one's work teaches the writer a great deal and is a wonderful way to develop a more nuanced and effective clinical practice.

Whilst, sadly, process notes are no longer an essential part of social work training, they remain essential and standard practice in child psychotherapy training. Process notes are also an integral component of Infant Observation (Bick 1964; Rustin 2009). Infant Observation is a specialised 1-year training course involving the practitioner visiting a family with a newborn infant once a week for a year, with weekly supervision to participants' observations of the infant in the context of their family and other caregivers. The experience of group members, as detailed in their process notes, structures the weekly reflective supervision session for participants.

Initially, many observers struggle to capture the infinite myriad of details that present themselves. In my own group of three infant observers, over the year we noticed that our notes became richer and more detailed. The hours we took to write up our notes increased and so did the depth of our observations. A cornerstone of this training experience is how we grapple with the 'process' of our observations and then make sense of them in our thinking. The task of writing the process notes, committing our memories to paper in a coherent form, is labour-intensive and takes time. However, without the presentation of diligent and detailed notes, the supervision seminars could never reach the richness of detail which makes Infant Observation such a powerfully informative experience.

Writing process notes every week, to discuss with my current supervisor of nearly 10 years, is still a challenge and an inimitable task. With her acute eye and ear to process, she is regularly able to notice that which I could not. Once, when I was discussing a particular client, my supervisor noted that following this client's disclosure of something very intimate, I would often 'step away from', rather than 'step towards' her. With the written details in front of us, examining the minutiae of a session, I could see she was right. I became aware of this when, in the next encounter with my client, I caught myself about to repeat the step to move away.

Discussions with my supervisor, reflecting on what happened and what I have written, sharpen my capacity to learn more about the way my mind works, alongside the emotional life of my clients. As supervisees, when we are with a trusted supervisor/guide, when we stop and think, and then write, we go more slowly with them, enabling us to go more deeply along the path of the experience 'in the room'. As we hone our reflections, more is caught in our gaze and more stays in mind. Our practice deepens with our capacity to observe and to understand the infants, young children and families we work with.

Conclusion

Making and taking the time to think about and to reflect on our work is vital in supporting vulnerable infants, young children and their families, whatever our role. The good enough supervisor encourages and facilitates participants to become comfortable and creative in their work, to take therapeutic risks, become more playful, accept their mistakes and to consider what these teach us about themselves and the work they do. Importantly, reflective supervision provides us with a safe base, grows confidence and provides us with the direct experience that in a good enough relationship, every rupture offers an opportunity for repair.

Reflective supervision is NOT:

- *administrative*, where caseloads and organisational or management matters are discussed

- *directive or didactic*, where the practitioner is told what he or she must do or should think
- *disciplinary*, where the practitioner is told what he or she is not doing well enough.

Reflective supervision IS:

- founded in a *relationship* between a supervisor and one or a group of others, with a clear and agreed purpose for their meetings
- a *regular* event
- held in a *protected*, quiet and private space
- for an *agreed time*
- run by a supervisor who is committed to facilitating and supporting *thoughtful* practice
- attended by practitioners who enter the supervision relationship *willingly*, if cautiously at the beginning
- acknowledging that we all learn most from the difficult areas of our practice, and ensures that with encouragement, practitioners are *enabled* to bring the challenging and troubling aspects of their work to supervision
- where the practitioner being supervised leaves the supervision with a sense that their thinking has been *challenged, encouraged and supported*.

Acknowledgements

Julie Stone would like to acknowledge and thank her colleagues who kindly agreed to material from their supervision becoming the vignettes in her contribution.

Sarah J. Jones would like to acknowledge the late Ms Riva Miller (Royal Free Hospital, London), Ms Anne Clancy, Ms Frances Hattam and Dr Julie Stone. All of them have been inspiring as supervisors, and without them my work would be less courageous.

Wendy Bunston would like to acknowledge Frances Thomson-Salo and Ruth Wraith for their commitment to infants and children. And my many supervisees who have taught me so much.

References

Bick, E. (1964) 'Notes on infant observation in psycho-analytic training.' *The International Journal of Psycho-Analysis 45*, 558–566.

Fraiberg, S., Adelson, E. & Shapiro, V. (1975) 'Ghosts in the nursery.' *Journal of the American Academy of Child Psychiatry 14*, 3, 387–421.

Lieberman, A.F., Padrón, E., Van Horn, P. & Harris, W.W. (2005) 'Angels in the nursery: The intergenerational transmission of benevolent parental influences.' *Infant Mental Health Journal 26*, 6, 504–520.

Rustin, M. (2009) 'Esther Bick's legacy of infant observation at the Tavistock – some reflections 60 years on.' *Infant Observation 12*, 1, 29–41.

Trowell, J. & Miles, G. (2004) 'The contribution of observation training to professional development in social work.' *Journal of Social Work Practice 18*, 1, 49–60.

Suggestions for further reading

'Creating a "nest" of emotional safety: Reflective supervision in a child–parent psychotherapy case.' Many, M.M., Kronenberg, M.E. & Dickson, A. B. (2016). *Infant Mental Health Journal 37*, 6, 717–727.

'The significance of reflective supervision for infant mental health work.' O'Rourke, P. (2011). *Infant Mental Health Journal 32*, 2, 165–173.

PART 2

Relationship Traumas

CHAPTER 3

Restoring Ruptured Bonds

The Young Child and Complex Trauma in Families

FIONA TRUE

Catherine and Clarissa, 4-year-old African American identical twins, tentatively entered my office, both girls wide-eyed with curiosity. Their father, James, 23 years old, and their stepmother for the past three years, Natalie, also 23, accompanied them. Together the twins sat on the floor in front of the large sheets of paper I had laid out and visibly relaxed as they began to draw what I had termed "the story of their lives from when they were tiny babies until today." By contrast, their parents—charged with the same task—sat uncomfortably holding paper pads. James, their father, did eventually put paper to pencil, but Natalie seemed frozen in place.

These small girls were with me in my office because James and Natalie had observed sexualized behavior directed from Catherine toward Clarissa and had approached our program for help. In the first meeting with just the parents, James had described this behavior as "though they were going through the motions of having sex." When Clarissa was asked by James and Natalie about her experience, Clarissa had been clear that she did not like it when her sister acted in this way and wanted it to stop. Natalie had seen redness in the vaginal area after Clarissa complained of pain on urinating, and there was a concern that objects were being inserted. This was not healthy sex play between sisters (Johnson 2013). An additional concern for the parents was the safety of their own little son, 1½-year-old Jon.

In this first family meeting, each child drew and talked about their earlier childhood experiences with their mother, Marisol. Clarissa drew a remarkably complex timeline of figures and talked about the various mothers she had had. She told me of her birth mother, and her maternal grandmother who had raised her from 12 months of age and who had recently died. Clarissa then pointed to Natalie: "This is my mother now." The girls had been living with James and

Natalie for the past five months. Catherine had more difficulty with the task of drawing her family. Her picture was chaotic in comparison with her sister's complex illustration, featuring crude faces and many scribbles through her pictures. She asked questions, primarily about her grandmother, and was frequently interrupted by Clarissa.

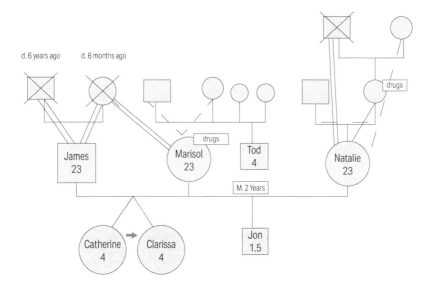

The conversation between the girls revealed a theme previously described in the first parent session by James; that of their constant enquiry about the whereabouts of their biological mother. As Clarissa drew, she talked about her mommy "whose tummy I was in," before telling a convoluted story about how Mommy Marisol was in the hospital today "for eating Junk." She told us that "Sam," a nursery school friend, had told her about mommy and the junk food, and she asked her father if this was so. In response, James looked confused and said he did not know anything about this.

A therapeutic method for restoring and strengthening relational bonds

Catherine and Clarissa were being seen at the Center for Children and Relational Trauma at the Ackerman Institute for the Family in New York. For the past 25 years, this center has engaged in clinical research addressing the therapeutic needs of families and children where relational bonds have been ruptured (Sheinberg & Fraenkel 2001).

The work of the center has endeavored to honor and repair familial bonds while simultaneously privileging safety. An essential component of our work with families with young children is to try to ensure that attuned, safe, and protective choices are made on their behalf, and that opportunities to repair and strengthen parent/child attachment bonds are created (Bowlby 1972, 1973).

The center is located within a family-therapy postgraduate training institute that engages in clinical practice research to develop systemic approaches to working with families and children with a variety of presenting problems. We work in pairs, with one partner behind a one-way mirror and the primary therapist in the room with the family members. In the work with this family, my partner was Marcia Sheinberg, Licensed Clinical Social Worker (LCSW). The work of the center has been documented in a book, *The Relational Trauma of Incest* (Sheinberg & Fraenkel 2001), and two published papers (Sheinberg & True 2008; Sheinberg, True & Fraenkel 1994).

We define *relational trauma* as occurring when a child's sense of emotional and/or physical safety has been violated by the behavior of their significant attachment figures—usually family members or caregivers (Sheinberg & True 2008). Such traumas include, but are not limited to, incest, the witnessing of domestic violence, physical abuse, bitter divorce and custody battles, parental death, neglect, and/or abandonment. Our approach is systemic, using a *multimodal, recursive process* (Sheinberg & True 2008) to link different components of individual, dyadic, and family sessions: an approach designed to provide safe, private, and developmentally appropriate opportunities for individual family members to explore the idiosyncratic experience of each family member and unearth relational constraints. This recursive process simultaneously provides privacy and promotes connection. This approach to therapy has been replicated in many social service agencies that would not otherwise identify as "family therapy" focused.

Elements of the child's experience that emerge in an individual session, and that are also evidence of an emotional constraint, are returned to the family through a *decision dialogue* in which the child actively participates (Sheinberg, True & Fraenkel 1994). The decision dialogue is a conversation with a child/or parent to enable linking individual and family sessions, offering privacy but promoting connection. Where a child expresses reluctance for certain content to be fed back to their family, we respect that confidence unless a mandated reporting of risk is required. This process and the mandated exception are thoroughly explained to the entire family prior to individual work with a child. When a child refuses to give permission for the content to be talked about with a caregiver, we actively turn that "wall" into a "corner" by exploring the relational constraints undermining an open conversation, asking process questions such as: "What would the worry be if you were to talk to Mommy/Daddy?" Invariably, we discover the child fears emotional or physical consequences of some kind, the specifics of which can then be addressed and potentially changed by the parents. We also know that distressed children often have no words, and that trauma creates a vacuum in expression, and a fear in finding words, for then the awfulness might be true.

The integration and linking of different therapy modalities (i.e. individual, family or dyadic sessions) not only allows the therapist to discover and explore the child's experience of their family; it also provides the opportunity to share that experience with their parent(s). We aim to work in such a way that does not usurp parental primacy but simultaneously recognizes family members' needs for privacy to explore their thoughts and feelings in an individual session.

This recursive process provides a unique opportunity to add *complexity* and, with it, more opportunities for effective therapeutic change. It has been our experience that children may be angry or are reluctant to express feelings of love or affection for a caregiver who may have harmed them in some way. This may relate to a child's fear of being seen as disloyal and putting at risk any existing, safe parental bond. We respect and understand that it is very important for a child to be given an opportunity to express their complex, often confusing, and conflicting feelings about their parents/caregivers and to have those feelings validated. For example, Clarissa said: "I love my mommy. I am angry that she is not here with me."

The decision dialogue *avoids confidentiality binds* as family members have agreed that the child's privacy will be respected, with the exception of a need for a mandated report. All family members understand that it is the therapist's aim to promote the family members' connection to each other and that the family is seen as the primary resource for healing.

For many children, their sense of *personal agency*—the ability to achieve ordinary things, such as having a friend, or feeling they are important—has been disrupted by the relational trauma (Ford & Thompson 1985). This experience may have compromised their ability to express themselves in play, in words, and to openly ask for what they need. By giving the child a clear role in deciding to share in the transfer of information or feelings back to a family session, the child is determining outcomes for herself, promoting her own sense of personal agency. It is our experience that very young children benefit from being taken seriously and shown respect by us.

Additionally, being with a therapist who is interested in a young client and engages with her in the session lends weight to the decision dialogue process. It can encourage the child to find words, try out ways of understanding her distress and thus *process her feelings*, through rehearsing how feelings are expressed in words, pictures, puppet play, and stories. We help children find ways to express what might be their fears about confiding in their parent(s). By finding out how they feel through this combination of talking and playing and processing those feelings with the therapist, the child frequently becomes more able to identify the causes of reluctance to share her feelings with her caregiver(s). The process also offers caregivers opportunities to enter their young children's experience by hearing directly from them (or in some cases initially from the therapist), and is used to promote empathy and understanding.

Our approach draws on play techniques to understand a young child's inner life and relational needs, utilizing drawing, storytelling, puppetry, and other metaphorical means of expression (Gil 1991). Catherine and Clarissa, at 4, were able to use language to describe their experience. They also benefited from the use of play to help capture feelings they were unable to fully express through language.

▨ Catherine and Clarissa: Therapeutic developments ▨

It is this recursive relational frame which informed our work with Catherine, Clarissa, and their parents. We had learned from James and Natalie that since they observed this sexualized behavior, the twins were no longer allowed to bathe together and had been separated at night. The father and stepmother were being vigilant in hopes of preventing the behavior from occurring again. This allowed us the freedom to proceed without worrying about ongoing inappropriate, unsafe behavior. However, these changes also fueled a concern in us that the twins might be confused about their sudden use of separate bedrooms and loss of shared bath times. It is possible that this parental decision meant they were missing out on important aspects of their relationship with each other.

The twins had recently started to live in James and Natalie's apartment in a new neighborhood. It was following this move and the loss of their grandmother that the sexualized behavior by Catherine had begun. The parents told us they had not noticed this occurring before this move.

Developmental history

Catherine and her sister were conceived during a high-school relationship between James and Marisol when both were 18. James broke off the relationship shortly before being told of the pregnancy. Whilst James expressed that he cared deeply for Marisol, he had become increasingly concerned that her recreational drug use had developed into a more serious substance abuse problem involving crack cocaine. Additionally, he told us that he felt that remaining in the relationship with Marisol might significantly affect his career plans to become an attorney.

Our only knowledge of the twins' mother's history came from James. We learnt from him that when Marisol was a young child her father had left the family. She had a fraught relationship with her mother and had experienced a very unsettled life, moving frequently and often living in shelters. When Marisol told James she was pregnant, he committed to honoring her choice to have the child, which turned out to be twin girls. However, he was also clear that he did not want to remain in the relationship.

Marisol stayed drug-free for the duration of her pregnancy. James was present for the twins' birth. However, in their first year, Marisol's drug habit became increasingly problematic, and on two occasions James visited the apartment to find the infants alone. Marisol had left them in their crib in order to meet her drug dealer.

James described coming from a very close and supportive family. The year before the twins' birth, his own father died. Marjorie, his mother, had been very involved in the girls' childcare from their birth. When Marjorie heard that Marisol was putting the girls at such risk, she invited Marisol with her granddaughters to live with her in her Harlem home. She wanted to offer support to Marisol to try to ensure the children's safety. Unfortunately, over the next two years, Marisol's drug use escalated, and she resorted to prostitution to support her drug habit. The situation deteriorated rapidly, and after several occasions during which the twins "disappeared" for several days with their mother, returning unwashed, hungry, and distressed, Marjorie felt the risks posed for her granddaughters were too high. She worried that they were being exposed to their mother's prostitution and applied to the family court for guardianship. Marisol's disappearances with the girls became increasingly prolonged and unpredictable. When Clarissa and Catherine were 3 years old, their grandmother applied for full custody. James was by then living with Natalie, his new wife, who was pregnant with their first child. James supported his mother's legal efforts. He remained committed to the girls' welfare and stayed very emotionally and physically connected.

The girls' paternal grandmother, Marjorie, had suffered from chronic asthma her entire life. On the date of the court hearing, after many months of delays and where the judge was due to formally afford full custody to Marjorie, their mother Marisol unexpectedly appeared. She attended the hearing in order to contest a previously signed waiver of her parental rights. The judge granted a stay in the process, as Marisol argued that she was trying to improve her life and was enrolled at a residential treatment center for substance abuse and hoped to be able to care for the girls in the future

This event devastated Marjorie, as she had felt on the brink of giving her much-loved granddaughters security and safety. The stress brought on by this ruling led to an asthma attack that was so severe it induced a heart attack. She was taken to the hospital and died two days later. The family story of the event is that "Grandma died of a broken heart." Marisol was unable to complete the rehabilitation program and left the treatment center within days of Marjorie's death; her whereabouts were unknown.

James described Catherine and Clarissa's response to their grandmother's death as showing intense sadness, being unable to speak and generally withdrawn. They became inseparable, getting upset if the other was not within sight; they had difficulty sleeping and both lost weight. When his mother died, James moved into her house to care for the twins, leaving Natalie and baby Jon in his and Natalie's apartment. He applied to the court to grant him full custody and to block their mother's right to access.

After being ordered to take a paternity test so that the judge could rule, James discovered that the daughters he regarded as his own were in fact not his biological children. Devastated by this news, he appealed to the court to afford him custody, noting that to the twins he was "the only father they have known" and that he regarded them as his children. The judge could offer only a foster-care placement, with a view to James and Natalie being able to apply for adoption over time. The twins, now 4 years old, moved from their grandmother's house to the apartment shared by James, Natalie, and Jon, their 13-month-old foster-brother.

As stated above, not long after the three children all started living together, James and Natalie observed Catherine's sexualized behavior toward Clarissa. As well as contacting our center, they also contacted the foster-care agency the court had appointed to supervise the girl's care. That agency had already conducted a forensic child abuse evaluation of both twins to determine past or ongoing sexual abuse. The report was inconclusive but speculated that due to Marisol's history of prostitution, the twins had likely been exposed to sexual behavior or victimized by someone in that context. James was not considered a risk to the girls.

Before meeting with the whole family (this included Jon), I had met with James and Natalie. This is a standard practice of our approach and provides an opportunity to hear the adult's version of the history of all members of the family and the presenting problem in full. We do this so that we don't overwhelm or upset young children; additionally, it is an opportunity to form a working alliance with the parents that is focused on the needs of the children. In the initial session, James appealed for help, describing how out of his depth he was: "I am only 23, and never had to deal with anything like this." He also described feeling worried that this sexualized behavior, especially that of Catherine, could somehow put both Catherine and Clarissa at risk in the future of being sexually exploited. Natalie was upset and angry. Describing finding Catherine lying on Clarissa, she said: "I caught her, it was disgusting." Understandably, Natalie was also expressing a worry that Catherine could harm her young son, Jon, in some way.

Natalie was exasperated and angry that the twins, who had recently been discovered to not be James's biological children, were causing such disruption in their lives. Natalie and James both described the additional problem of both girls, but especially Clarissa, constantly wanting to know where their mother was, and their frustration at not knowing how to help them with their upset, especially because they did not know of Marisol's whereabouts and had no way of being able to provide the girls with an answer.

We hypothesized that Catherine might be attempting to soothe herself, albeit in a misguided attempt at connection, as a way to cope with the significant losses she had experienced, her disrupted attachments, and the unpredictability of her biological mother. The use of sexual stimulation as a secondary soothing mechanism might be mimicking behavior she could have observed when her mother was engaged in prostitution, or she may have been abused (and stimulated) at some earlier time (Gil & Johnson 1993; Schwartz & Galperin 2002). Whatever the underlying cause of Catherine's behavior, it was potentially putting her at risk of being exploited, and Clarissa was being subjected to unwanted, intrusive sexual behavior. We worried that the sibling bond had been damaged by Catherine's sexualized behavior. The immediate therapeutic goals were to interrupt Catherine's sexualized behavior, try to understand its genesis, and strengthen and repair the bonds between the twins that may have been ruptured.

Our frame holds that *the repair and strengthening of safe relational bonds* is essential when the child has experienced relational ruptures. The usual time frame of a therapy in our program is 9 months of work and we actively work toward building increased capacity in the caregivers to tolerate a range of feelings expressed by the child. The therapeutic goal for the child(ren) is to be able to express themselves without fear of repercussions, so that the parent–child bond remains an emotional resource as the child navigates through her life. For Catherine and Clarissa, it was our goal to ensure that they were attached in a safe, connected relationship and that any broken trust was repaired.

Catherine and Clarissa were little girls with different therapeutic needs. Catherine was imposing her sexualized behavior upon Clarissa; Clarissa was being subjected to unwanted behavior. We needed to understand each child's particular experience and decided after meeting with the whole family to see them individually. I had explained to the family the use of a *decision dialogue*, saying that it would be an opportunity to talk and play and get to know them. If there were concerns that we thought were important for James and Natalie to know, we would ask the girls' permission to tell James and Natalie, either themselves or with my help. We reiterated that if either girl did not want to tell James and Natalie certain things, we would honor that, unless they were being hurt in some way. The decision dialogue thus afforded Catherine and Clarissa privacy while also promoting connection back to their parents. If a child refuses to transfer material back to a parent, we always explore why: "What would the worry be if you were to do so?" It is often in this back and forth that we uncover the *relational constraints*, which can then be explored and addressed without necessarily bringing the original content back.

Clarissa

Meeting alone with Clarissa, I asked which of the people in the drawing she had done in our first family meeting she would like to talk about. She chose her mother, Marisol. Clarissa described longing for her mother to come live with her, for "the whole family to live together in a very big house." When I asked whether she had ever told her daddy and Natalie about this wish, she answered that she couldn't do that because they "would not like me to say that and they would put me on punishment." This conversation revealed an awareness of James and Natalie's disapproval of Marisol. She explained that punishment would take the form of time out, where the girls were sent to their rooms for 15 minutes. I then explored whom else she might talk to about this wish, and she replied "no one." When asked about Catherine, she was clear that she didn't want to talk with her "because now she is an ugly sister." Pursuing this theme, I asked if it had been okay for her to talk with her grandma about her mother, and she was clear that it would have been, saying: "Grandma loves Mommy Marisol."

Clarissa then repeated the story about her mother being in the hospital "for eating junk" (perhaps a child's understanding of the term "junkie"), that Sam at nursery school had told her this, and that she was sad and worried about her mother. She said: "I want Daddy to take me to hospital, but he won't like me to do that." Using a *decision dialogue* with Clarissa, I asked if she would be willing to say these things to her daddy and Natalie with me there. She adamantly refused, saying: "You can talk to them about something else." However, she did give me permission to ask about "Sam" and to try to get information about the story he had told her.

The session revealed the considerable constraints, fear and confusion in speaking about ruptures in connection, loyalty binds, and anxieties that Clarissa felt. She was unable to express her feelings and concerns for her mother's wellbeing for fear this would be experienced as disloyalty and she would be punished. The description of Catherine as an "ugly sister" also suggested that the bond with her sister was damaged in some way, and perhaps reflected some level of anger and shame which was too hard to find words for—likely because of the sexualized behavior. We thought that her grandmother's death had deprived her of an open and accepting outlet for her concerns about her mother's wellbeing. Clarissa had lost her mother, and then her grandmother suddenly and dramatically.

Catherine

In my first session with Catherine alone, immediately following the first family session, she chose to talk about her grandmother. As in the first family session, Catherine's narrative was more jumbled, yet there was also coherence; for example, when she told me about her grandmother, she said: "She died, got sick, and was in a hospital." She told of how sad she felt, how she cried when no one was looking, and that she missed her grandma. She also revealed a considerable constraint in speaking and a misguided belief/fantasy that if she told anyone how sad she was, they might also "die of a broken heart." As a

4-year-old, she had taken the family "story" of her grandmother's death and made a literal, and profoundly emotionally inhibiting interpretation. She went on to describe not being able to talk to anyone else in the family because it would make her too sad and "I don't want anyone else to die."

Catherine was open to a recursive process, bringing her feelings and this constraining belief back to a meeting with her father alone, pointedly asking that Natalie not be there. I offered to write her thoughts down, so as to capture her voice rather than mine, and so that these could then be shared with her father. These were: "Daddy, I miss my Grandma because I love her very much. And I like her. And I miss her. Daddy, could you help me? I don't want you to get sadder and sadder and die. Thank you. And he would say 'yes'."

James joined this session. After my reading of Catherine's words, he responded gently, saying that he missed grandma too, but adding that it helped him to talk about it; that talking did not make him "sadder and sadder," it made him feel "better and better." He invited Catherine to tell him her feelings, and I suggested they take a few minutes alone each day to do this. He told me that he thought that his mother "babied" Catherine, as Marjorie believed that she needed more attention than Clarissa. These sessions helped me understand that as the girls were now living with the only man they knew as their father, their stepmother and baby foster-brother, Jon, Catherine had lost the special position of "the baby." I suggested that James and Catherine make time to talk every day and that Catherine "play baby" (Wachtel 2004), cuddling on James's lap and being rocked.

These sessions gave me insight into the complexities of these little girls' interior lives. What had emerged was the overarching theme of fear, loss, and sadness, leading to the lack of stories, and thus such a constraint/restraint for both Catherine and Clarissa in talking about what they felt, wanted, and needed. The general lack of trust in talking openly needed to be both understood and addressed if we were to successfully address Catherine's sexualized behavior and make room for the children's concerns about their mother.

Natalie and James

In the third (couple) meeting, I asked who in their extended family would be proud of each of them, given the decision they took to fight for the girls and take them in. James was quick to answer with a long list of family members, but Natalie was unable to answer, shaking her head and looking down. I mentioned that I had noticed she been unable to able to draw a picture of her own family, and I asked about her history. Natalie described a neglectful, drug-addicted mother who was also unreliable and often absent. She too was raised by her maternal grandparents, who never told her "the truth." She told me that she spent most of her childhood anxious and concerned. She went on to describe how when Catherine and Clarissa asked about Marisol's whereabouts, she would dismiss them, sending them to James for answers. Her logic was that it would be worse for her to "lie," since that was what had happened to her and she did not want to hurt them in the way that she had been hurt. She articulated a belief that "talking only makes things worse, it's better to forget." This may have inadvertently compounded Clarissa's fears.

In an effort to challenge Natalie's belief and create a greater comfort with reflecting and talking, I asked Natalie if she could imagine anything good coming from James's daughters being able to express their thoughts and feelings more openly. She replied: "Perhaps they would learn to trust, they wouldn't have to keep the hurt inside." In response to this opening in her rigid belief system, I suggested they create a ritual where each week they take 15 minutes, gather, and light three candles: one for the people they have lost, one for the people who have disappointed them, and one for the hopes for the family in the future (Imber Black & Roberts 1992). Anyone in the family could speak, but nobody was forced or required to. I hoped, by using this structured yet playful ritual, to create a more emotionally tolerable opportunity for the expression of feelings. Additionally, it offered the twins overt permission to express their feelings.

Later in the same session I enquired about the little boy Sam who told Catherine the story about their mother and junk food. It emerged that he was Marisol's 4-year-old brother, essentially the girls' uncle. He was enrolled in their new nursery class. James and Natalie had not known this until they heard the story in the first session with the twins. James agreed to reach out to Sam's mother to try to find out Marisol's whereabouts. He hoped this knowledge would enable himself and Natalie to answer the twins' constant enquiry about her. I described how the fear of "being put on punishment" was inhibiting the girls and reflected that whilst sound parenting was helpful, it may not be emotionally the best intervention given the children's recent losses. They both agreed to no longer send them to their rooms, using instead a chair in their living area and for only five minutes.

The next week, I met with Clarissa alone for the second time and I returned to her wish for her mother to live with her. She proudly announced that she did not need to talk about that anymore as she had told "Mommy Natalie" about the wish after our last session. I was curious about how she had changed her mind. Clarissa described telling her in the car, when she knew she couldn't be put in time out. She said that Natalie had "talked and talked and it was very happy, a very big happy." Natalie had told her that she and James would try to find out how her mother was and where she was living. The relief that she was not "put on punishment" was palpable. The *decision dialogue* in the first meeting had offered her an opportunity to rehearse her feelings, process her fears, and find a novel way forward to avoid the feared consequence of punishment.

The parents supported and maintained the sanctioned time ritual each week. Natalie reported to us that she had greater tolerance for the girls' questioning their mother's whereabouts, saying: "I don't like to answer them, but I am finding a way." On one occasion she told the girls that it was okay to love and miss Marisol and that she had also loved and missed her mother when she was growing up.

With the constraints in speaking lifting, I felt better able to address the sexualized behavior directly with the twins and specifically with Catherine. In the sixth family meeting the parents gave permission to both girls to speak about what they experienced, explicitly saying that whatever they said, they would not be punished. The session was organized in this way so that I could immediately meet with Catherine and Clarissa together. In response to my stating that "Mummy and Daddy have told you it's okay to talk about the touching that has happened and that you won't be punished," Clarissa quickly said: "I never touch you, I don't want you to touch me," and Catherine reluctantly admitted: "I touch myself and sometimes I touch her."

Meeting alone with Catherine that same day and using puppet play, I asked her to describe where in her body she got the feeling that would prompt her to seek out her sister for the sexualized behavior. She said: "I get the feeling in my head to make a mistake," and described a "tickle feeling," pointing to her groin. Using her language, I asked that the next time she got "the feeling in her head," she find Natalie or Daddy and tell them instead of going to Clarissa. I told her that they would be asked to give her a big hug. We role-played this scenario with puppets and then called James and Natalie into the room. I had not told the parents of this plan but was confident, at this point in the work, that the therapeutic relationship was robust enough and that they would be receptive. Using the puppets, Catherine played out the scene of her "getting the feeling in her head" and approaching Natalie and James in turn. The atmosphere was playful and there was laughter as they each hugged the puppet. I next asked Catherine to be herself and pretend she had the "feeling" and ask for help. Both parents responded warmly with large hugs. Later that day, alone with the parents, I asked that they also seek out Catherine for hugs and moments of affection so that the association was not just to her sexualized experience. In an individual session six weeks later, Clarissa reported no unwanted sexualized behavior from Catherine. Natalie and John reported that Catherine had approached them for hugs but with decreasing frequency.

Our early hypothesis that Catherine was engaged in a misguided attempt at secondary soothing to manage her disrupted attachments and losses had proved accurate. By helping the parents and children in this family to tolerate the expression of a range of feelings, and with Catherine now equipped to seek out appropriate affection, the sexualized behavior had stopped. There followed some weeks of therapeutic work to repair the bond between the siblings and for Clarissa to express her upset at Catherine. James and I both tried to reach out to Marisol to help her to participate in the therapy sessions. Unfortunately for everyone, we were not successful.

In this *recursive, multimodal approach* and using a *decision dialogue*, the twins' experiences of their multiple losses emerged and were understood by their parents. James and Natalie in turn embraced the changes needed to provide a safe, accepting, and open connection so that the *relational bonds could be repaired and strengthened*, and the problematic behavior understood and addressed. Catherine and Clarissa were again able to enjoy their close bond as twins, to relate safely to their little stepbrother, and, importantly, to be loved and cared for by James and Natalie.

Over many years we have conducted multiple community trainings in agencies that were not using a family therapy frame. Family members were being assigned to several different clinicians, hindering the possibility of bringing about relational change and repair. With young children, opportunities were being missed to strengthen attachment bonds because clinicians did not have the opportunity of working with all the family members.

Through changing our intake process and allowing a worker to treat the whole family, this approach offers a template where workers are able to see different combinations of family members and use the *decision dialogue* to explore, expand, and return to important elements of experience which need to be addressed. Most importantly, this approach brings front and center an understanding of the young child's experience, respects their privacy, and uses the *recursive process* to help the parents respond to that child's specific needs. Confidentiality binds are avoided by the use of the transparent description of the process, enabling workers to move seamlessly back and forth between different family members as well as ensuring the child's right to be heard, kept safe and responded to respectfully.

References

Bowlby, J. (1972) *Attachment and Loss: Attachment, Vol. I*. London: Penguin Books.

Bowlby, J. (1973) *Attachment and Loss: Separation, Vol. II*. New York: Basic Books.

Ford, E. & Thompson, R.A. (1985) 'Perceptions of personal agency and infant attachment: Toward a life-span perspective on competence development.' *International Journal of Behavioral Development 8*, 4, 377–406.

Gil, E. (1991) *The Healing Power of Play: Working with Abused Children*. New York: Guilford.

Gil, E. & Johnson, T.C. (1993) 'Sexualized children: Assessment and treatment of sexualized children and children who molest.' Rockville, MD: Launch Press

Imber-Black, E., & Roberts, J. (1992). *Rituals for our times: Celebrating, healing and changing our lives and our relationships*. New York: HarperCollins.

Johnson, T. C. (2013). *Understanding children's sexual behaviors: What's natural and healthy*. San Diego, CA: Institute on Violence, Abuse and Trauma.

Schwartz, M.F. & Galperin, L. (2002) 'Hyposexuality and hypersexuality secondary to childhood trauma and dissociation.' *Journal of Trauma and Dissociation 3*, 4, 107–120.

Sheinberg, M. & Fraenkel, P. (2001) *The Relational Trauma of Incest*. New York: Guilford Press.

Sheinberg, M. & True, F. (2008) 'Treating family relational trauma: A recursive process using a decision dialogue.' *Family Process 47*, 2, 173–195.

Sheinberg, M., True, F. & Fraenkel, P. (1994) 'Treating the sexually abused child: A recursive, multimodal program.' *Family Process 33*, 263–276.

Wachtel, E. (2004) *Treating Troubled Children and Their Families*. New York: Guilford Press.

CHAPTER 4

Developing an Intervention for Infants and Young Children in Foster Care

'Watch Me Play!'

JENIFER WAKELYN

Introduction

When 5-year-old Sam asked me to 'shut the door and watch me play', we could not think of a better name for the therapeutic intervention we had been developing in a mental health service in outer London. The service, called First Step, provides 'psychological health screening and assessment' for children and young people in the care of the local child protection authority and brief interventions where indicated. In the intervention approach we have now come to call 'Watch Me Play!' (WMP) the focus is on observing, with undivided attention, play that is child-led. This involves using warmth and an authentic interest in helping facilitate children's play, and actively encouraging foster carers, social workers and clinicians to notice, take in and remember the child's communications – both the enjoyable and the less enjoyable aspects of their play.

'"*Watch Me Play!*" *is the voice of the child through their play*' was the astute comment of a social worker who participated in a recent evaluation of the programme. Mutual delight, and even mutual distress, may be openly experienced as child and carer become more attuned. Greater feelings of safety in developing exploration may begin, and playfulness may afford relief from the sequelae of trauma.

My role in First Step is as the lead child psychotherapist. When our service identifies the need for further assessment or for long-term treatment, children are referred to the relevant local services. Our service identifies early signs of mental health or attachment difficulties in our young child clients, allowing for appropriate mental health support to be put in place and risk factors to be flagged early in the child's life in (out of the family home) care. Our multi-disciplinary mental health team staff work closely alongside local child protection and children in care social workers, foster carers and the paediatricians and nurses who conduct mandated health assessments for children in care.

Over a third of children who enter the care of the state in the UK are aged from birth to 4 years. The 'psychological health screening' model allows for an assessment of the needs of the youngest children entering care, who are rarely referred to mental health services. Many young children in care have experienced the cumulative traumas of abuse and neglect in their birth families, compromised development in the formative period of infancy, and disrupted primary caregiving relationships (Anda *et al.* 2006; Klee, Kronstadt & Zlotnick 1997; Wade *et al.* 2010). Infants and young children in care are also more likely to have been exposed to drugs and alcohol in utero and to environmental disadvantage (Birk Irner 2012; Needell & Booth 1998; Schore 2001; Ward, Munro & Dearden 2006). Children who are maltreated by their parents experience the trauma of fearing the adult upon whom they rely (Fraiberg 1982; Main & Solomon 1986). Children who have been abused by their primary attachment figures are also likely to lack the attuned, responsive care that is needed for healthy brain development, and as a result they may struggle to relate, communicate and learn (Brandon *et al.* 2014; McCrory, De Brito & Viding 2011; Schore 2001).

Some children in foster care may present with emotional, relationship or behavioural difficulties, and may be withdrawn and unresponsive; some children may be hyper-active, vigilant and wary or subject to sudden mood changes or extreme tantrums. In other cases, social workers and foster carers are concerned about the impact of early trauma for a child's later development. Social workers may also be concerned when adoption plans require children to leave foster carers to whom they have become deeply attached.

When a child enters our service, initial screening is carried out by asking the child's foster carer to complete the Under-Two Questionnaire devised by First Step (First Step 2016) or, for children aged over 2, the Strengths and Difficulties Questionnaire (Goodman 1997; Goodman,

Renfrew & Mullick 2000). Should any concerns arise as a result of these questionnaires, or because of the foster carer's or social worker's worries, an assessment and brief intervention process begins.

Our work begins with a consultation with the social worker and foster carer. We compile a detailed history of the child's experiences and history of significant relationships before and after entering care, identify the likely risk and protective factors for psychological well-being, gather observations of the child and contribute to care planning discussions. Where indicated, we also offer a brief intervention. As a service we recognise our need as mental health practitioners to provide our staff with access to regular reflective supervision to enable our own capacity to sit back, quieten ourselves and watch, as well as think about what the child, the foster carers and the system may be playing out (see Chapter 12).

In this chapter I will outline the brief intervention model developed by First Step which has been developed specifically with the needs of infants and young children in temporary foster care in mind. I will explain the imperative of discovery and the excitement of play, so necessary for the healthy development of the child and their relationships. I will illustrate the approach with clinical examples that have been de-identified for confidentiality and will end the chapter with some considerations for practice.

'Watch Me Play!' – and why this is so important!

The developmental value of play and the need for individual attention that are fundamental in early years education and child development research are often undervalued in emergency family care contexts. Trainings for foster carers in the UK mainly focus on physical care and behaviour management; busy foster homes can create routines where children's physical needs are met, but the fundamental needs for individual attention and intimacy may be overlooked (Hardy *et al.* 2013; Meakings & Selwyn 2016).

When children have been injured, or when the adults in their lives are intimidating, the necessary focus on physical safety may result in a blunting of alertness to psychological dimensions of experience. Fragmented parenting, when children are looked after by a succession of different adults, or where different aspects of parenting are divided among many adults, can also result in an erosion of the reflective tenderness that the young infant ordinarily elicits from caregiving adults (Robertson & Robertson 1989). The dynamics of child protection work can also impact on adults' sensitivity to children's emotional experiences and communications (Emanuel 2006; Ferguson 2017; Halton 1994).

Patient observing and engagement in children's play allows us to know more about a child's inner world of turmoil and need. From this, we are better informed to advocate for the psychological needs of infants and young children and to bring their emotional experiences to the forefront of adult attention in a way that can bring something alive in care planning discussions and legal proceedings. 'Watch Me Play!' is not a 'brand' or an attempt to market a supposedly new way of intervening; instead, it highlights generic elements common to evidence-based approaches and clinical practice with distressed and troubled young children that are validated by decades of child development research (Elliot & Reis 2003; Gerhardt 2004; Trevarthen 2001).

Child-led play, with the full attention of the primary caregiver for regular short periods of time, is central to interventions for young children with psychological vulnerability or developmental delay. Speech & Language therapy, the Solihull Approach, Incredible Years and Fostering Changes, Watch, Wait and Wonder, Floor-time, and Special Time as well as psychoanalytic child psychotherapy and parent–infant psychotherapy (Alvarez & Phillips 1998; Bratton *et al.* 2006; Cohen *et al.* 2002; Pallet *et al.* 2000) all share a common focus on promoting child-directed play. Approaches in which the caregiver provides their undivided attention and puts the child's play into words have been found to enhance confidence, trust, self-efficacy, imagination, self-esteem, concentration, regulation and co-ordination in the child, as well as mutual understanding and communication between child and caregiver, and sensitivity and attunement in the caregiver (Ayling & Stringer 2013; Dozier *et al.* 2009; Panksepp 2007; Sunderland 2007). In Africa, studies of children recovering from malnourishment report reduced mortality and increased speed of recovery in children who received intensive feeding and psychosocial support, in the form of promoting play and attention on the child, compared to children who received intensive feeding only (World Health Organization 2006). A focus on psychological well-being was found to be critical in generating life-giving emotional connectedness between children and their caregivers. Slade (1994) highlights the role of play as the means to consolidation and integration, and comments that in 'putting experiences and feelings into play rather than into words, the child is creating structure' (p.91).

One distinctive aspect of the WMP approach with young children in care is advocacy for their psychological needs by contributing direct observations to care planning discussions with professionals. A second distinctive aspect relates to the roots of psychoanalytic child psychotherapy in Infant Observation. The naturalistic Infant Observation model first developed at the Tavistock in the UK as part of the training of child psychotherapists is now widely used in mental health and social care trainings across the world (Bick 1964; Rustin *et al.* 1997; Trowell & Rustin 1991; Urwin & Sternberg 2012). Therapeutic observation has been developed as a clinical intervention from formal Infant Observation training (Houzel 2010; Rhode 2007; Rustin 2014; Wakelyn 2011, 2012). This way of working involves a weekly, one-hour visit to the family of the observed infant. The observer aims to provide a friendly and receptive presence without initiating interactions. After the visit, the observer writes detailed notes on the child's activities and interactions, and also of his or her own emotional responses as to what was observed. The notes are discussed and explored in a small group seminar, where links are made to child development research and psychoanalytic theory.

The WMP approach draws on this model of attention to the experience of being with the child. A particularly strong emotional response in the observer is thought to provide some indication of what might be going on for the child, and a way of homing in on significant moments in the child's play. The process of reflecting together with the foster carer on the child's play can help to bring something alive in a regulated way about the experiences of young children, encompassing delight and achievement as well as post-traumatic disturbances. Over time, the communications of young children who have experienced trauma can be taken in, made sense of and processed without becoming too overwhelming. The following case examples illustrate how WMP has helped to facilitate fundamental shifts in the way children experience themselves and their relationships within foster care placements.

■ Children who seem unable to play: Where to begin? ■▬▬▬

Case example 1

Alex (2 years) and his sister, Julia (3 years), entered care with serious physical injuries which required hospitalisation. They experienced feeding and sleeping difficulties following physical abuse and force-feeding by their parents. Alex and Julia had been placed with short-term foster carer Lynette on discharge from hospital until foster carers with more experience with toddlers could be found; Lynette's previous experience of fostering was with teenagers. After three weeks in foster care, their social worker was worried about the children's feeding difficulties, hyper-activity and dysregulation. By the time potential longer-term foster carers had been identified, both children had formed such a close bond with Lynette that a move away from her could be re-traumatising. It was agreed the children would stay with Lynette with help from professionals as well as support from her adult daughter. My role included direct work in the foster home and contributing to care planning discussions with professionals about the children's current and future placement needs.

Lynette vividly described the children's arrival in the foster home as 'like a tornado hitting us'. In my first visit, the two children hurtled around the room making ear-piercing shrieks. Despite their difference in age, the two siblings looked almost identical, and were similar in size, perhaps a sign of failure to thrive in one or both. Each had curly brown hair, large dark eyes and huge smiles. At night they slept in the same bed and clung to each other. The impact of both their physical and emotional neglect and abuse, and their attachment trauma, felt overwhelming; it was hard to know where to begin.

As part of my work, I learned about the children's early history and the trauma of physical abuse that led them to spend four weeks in hospital while their fractures began to heal. I also observed them in their foster home, absorbing and feeling what it was like to be with these children. When they entered Lynette's care they had no experience of routines, but they quickly adapted to Lynette's nurturing care and consistent meal and bed times. At first terrified of water and being washed, with Lynette's patient reassurance they began to enjoy bath times. This seemed encouraging. However, their restless, hyper-aroused physicality, flitting from one toy to another, and high-pitched shrieking were beginning to wear Lynette and her daughter out.

In my third visit to the foster home, as I sat on the floor watching, I noticed that first Alex and then Julia came fleetingly to sit down near me, before taking off again. Lynette commented that this was the first time she had seen them slow down during the day. I said to Lynette that I thought that maybe what drew the children to me in this way was the fact that I was sitting on the floor where they could see I was not going to suddenly go away, and that I was giving them my full attention. This seemed a good starting point to try introducing short play sessions for each child, where Lynette or her daughter simply sat on the floor, observed the child's play and described in simple sentences what the child was doing.

Lynette was sceptical but ready to try anything, and she and her daughter made time in their busy routines to provide each child with their undivided attention for five or ten minutes, two or three times a day. We worked together to create a quiet and comfortable environment with a few cushions and a small number of toys, turning the television off and putting away battery-operated toys (Lerner & Barr 2015). I sat with Lynette and her daughter and encouraged them to allow each child to take the lead in their play, as long as what they were doing was safe, and to quietly describe what they could see happening in the play. My visits fortnightly alternated with pre-arranged phone calls to Lynette when I could support her to put into words and think through Alex and Julia's play and about the experience of being with them. I would ask: 'Has anything changed or have things stayed the same?'

For some weeks, I noticed that Lynette found herself describing a repetitive piece of play: the toy cars were crashed together, over and over again. Then the cars were repeatedly pushed under a sofa and Alex would ask Lynette to find them for him. Lynette described the deadening, controlling atmosphere of this repetitive, driven play. Ten minutes of this was as much as she could manage. Drawing on what was known of Alex's early history, I reflected with Lynette and his social worker how the quality of his play might express something about terrifying experiences of unpredictable adults and the drastic changes in his young life. This interpretation led to a subtle shift in how Lynette experienced Alex and how he experienced her.

Lynette was rewarded for her persistence after some weeks by seeing improvements in Alex's feeding and a more relaxed bearing with less of the running around and shrieking that had felt so exhausting. Alex was rewarded too. He was helped by having another's thinking mind available to him, and his world began to become more predictable and his play less stuck.

The moment when Lynette was able to tell me that Alex had started to find his cars for himself marked an important development. Lynette told me how much the feeling of being with Alex had changed. She was able to enjoy Alex's newly found sense of his own agency and his new confidence to retrieve the toys for himself. With Lynette sitting on the floor alongside him, Alex was able to begin to explore other toys, talk in a lively voice to the toy animals, or to join in with singing a nursery rhyme. The feeding difficulties resolved, and it became possible for Alex to relax a little of his vigilant watching. The siblings started to sleep in separate beds and Alex was able to start nursery for a few hours a day.

Alex and Julia's parents and extended family were assessed to see if they might be able to resume the care of the two children. This proved unsuccessful. The process lasted over a year and concluded with legal proceedings that determined orders for the children to be adopted. During this period, a specialist health visitor – a trained nurse who visits homes to advise parents with young children – supported the focus on play with Alex and Julia, while I convened meetings for the professional network and met the nursery staff when first Alex, and later Julia, were gradually introduced to nursery. Visits from the nursery keyworker to the foster home were followed by short sessions at the nursery while Lynette stayed in the background. After three weeks' preparation, each child was ready to manage a half-day at nursery. Alex formed a particular attachment to one of the nursery staff. Julia began to demonstrate a love of singing and listening to songs in her small group at nursery.

When appropriate adoptive parents were matched with Alex and Julia, I supported their transition into their new, permanent home. Despite earlier practices in England which tended to promote the idea of a 'clean break' for children from their previous carers, having observed the strength of their attachment with Lynette, I was able to advocate for a slower transition to the adoptive home and for continuing visits from Lynette to the children in the first months after their move (Browning 2015; Lanyado 2003). This advice is consistent with practice guidance on moving children from foster care to adoption being developed by researchers at the University of East Anglia (Neil, Beek & Schofield 2018). This practice programme identifies three stages of a child's move to adoption: before, during and after the move. This is a shift from the traditional focus on the introductions as the critical element of the move. The first stage of the adults getting to know each other creates a context for the child's move, and visits by foster carers after the move, where possible, reassure the child that they are remembered and may also be helpful for the adoptive parents.

The children's adoptive parents were keen to discover what had helped Alex and Julia while in foster care and were interested to try to observe their play – an approach which had so benefited the children and Lynette. Both the children and the adoptive parents were provided with a sense of ongoing connection through play, and provided with a most important thread of continuity in helping the children and their new parents find each one another

(Winnicott 1986). First Step's model also provides for continuity through episodic telephone support. These adoptive parents received two years of telephone consulting from me, and I, to my great pleasure, heard about Alex and Julia's progress and how they were thriving in a stable and loving family environment.

Setting aside time to reflect – with Lynette and also in my own reflective supervision sessions – on something that felt driven and controlled in the children's play, and linking this with their early experiences of physical abuse and mis-attunement, was important to this work. Eventually, over time, my sitting close to the foster carer with a selection of simple toys in a quiet environment created conditions in which the children's anxieties and high arousal could begin to be contained, and, over time, more exploratory play could flourish. The capacity to think about communications through play allowed something within the relationship between caregiver and child to shift over time. Play that was attended to, and thought about, provided a starting point and a transitional space that helped the children express distress, rage, their own violence and hatred. It helped the carers to get to know each child, and the children to begin to get to know that their rage and distressing experiences, with the help of another, could be contained and metabolised in a way that felt gradual and safe (Winnicott 1951).

'Do I matter to her?' Helping a baby born prematurely and addicted to heroin
Case example 2

The following brief intervention brought home to me how hard it must have been for a first-time foster carer to feel that she could be important for, and close to, the traumatised infant in her care. Aisha was exposed to heroin in the womb, and spent her first weeks of life in a special care baby unit. Due to the case plan developed at birth, Aisha's foster carer, Tamara, was obliged to take Aisha, from 3 weeks of age, on a two-hour journey for contact with her parents five times a week.

Aisha was 5 months old when concerns were expressed about her shrill, persistent crying and sudden mood changes. When Tamara described her worries to me, it was hard for me to hear over the sound of a large television nearby. I noticed that Aisha was surrounded by battery-operated toys, each making random, piercing sounds and flashing lights as she pressed their buttons. Aisha repeatedly glanced briefly in Tamara's direction after a particularly loud noise and then dropped her gaze when Tamara was looking elsewhere. As this went on, Aisha's face became paler and her arms and legs seemed to stiffen. It seemed to me that Tamara may have lost, or perhaps had never had, the confidence to believe that her presence and attention were important for Aisha.

My work involved helping Tamara and the social worker supporting her to think about what might help Aisha to regulate her high levels of arousal. Turning the television off for some of the time and putting away the mechanical toys created a quieter environment in which Tamara could hold Aisha in her arms, talk quietly or sing to her. It gave Aisha the experience of being attended to and of having her feelings taken in as Tamara came to recognise her rapid, fleeting facial expressions (American Academy of Pediatrics 2012). This helped Tamara to respond to Aisha's cues, and to see when Aisha was ready for play and when she needed to rest. It also helped Aisha to send clearer signals and cues to the caregiver whose attention was now on her.

Encouraging Tamara to provide Aisha with her undivided attention for regular periods of ten or twenty minutes increased Tamara's confidence in attuning to a foster baby who had seemed worryingly withdrawn. Repeatedly experiencing familiar responses in a trusted space provided by play created a 'rhythm of safety' (Tustin 1986; Winnicott 1951). Increasingly pleasurable interactions began to be described as Aisha began to seek Tamara's attention, her long gazes giving way to slow smiles as Tamara talked to her and waited for her response. Tamara reported to her social worker that she felt she was getting to know Aisha in a different way. She began to recognise the likely stressors for Aisha, felt more able to anticipate her changes of mood, and more confident about soothing her when she was upset; the long periods of inconsolable crying lessened.

■■■ 'The house feels lighter' ■■■■■■■■■■■■■■■■■■■■■■■■■
Case example 3

Rani (2½ years) and her foster carer, Shaquille, both appeared depressed when I met them. The referral from Rani's social worker followed concerns that the care being provided in the foster home was basically 'functional'. After a visit to the foster home, I offered a series of play-based sessions in the clinic playroom. Rani was a sturdy, thick-set toddler with a sombre expression who glanced at the doll's house in the playroom without moving towards it or looking or turning towards her carer or myself. I sat on the floor with a small selection of toys that I placed near to Rani. Slowly she picked up one animal after another and looked at it. In a loud voice, Shaquille began to tell Rani the names of the animals and asked her to repeat them. Rani turned away and stared into space. Shaquille told me that this was Rani acting like a sulky teenager.

I encouraged Shaquille to sit on the floor and suggested we just watch what Rani chose to do and talk afterwards about what we had each seen. When Shaquille sat down near her, Rani put some cushions on the floor, took a blanket and played at going to bed. Shaquille now talked to her in a quieter voice, describing what she was doing. In the next two sessions, Rani repeated this game with increasing delight, and began to play peekaboo with Shaquille, hiding behind the blanket.

In the third session, Rani lifted her arms to be held by Shaquille. I felt a deep relief as I saw her relax into Shaquille's lap, her rigid muscle tone softened. Rani's sombre expression lifted more often into a smile and she vocalised more freely; Shaquille told me: 'The house feels lighter.'

Many factors may lead to foster carers becoming distant from the children they are looking after. Burn-out is a professional risk, under the impact of repeated, often unprocessed losses, and repeated experiences of rejection by children whose interactive styles appear indifferent or dismissive. Foster carers may not feel that their efforts are supported in a climate that militates against validating the parenting that they provide. I did not have the scope to explore the underlying causes of the alienation that seemed to have come about between Shaquille and Rani, or the opportunity to follow up this intervention, but it seemed that the transitional space created through play and the subsequent experience of mutual delight that it afforded had allowed something to become freed up and created more warmth between carer and child (Winnicott 1951).

Becoming a child
Case example 4

Foster carers may not be supported enough in their trainings and supervision to know that in looking after toddlers, who come to them following abuse and neglect, free play is important in providing opportunities for children to express themselves. For Samuel, a shy 4-year-old who spoke in a whisper and avoided any physical comfort from his thoughtful foster carers, a shift was seen after two WMP sessions and telephone support for his foster carer, Lee. In an intervention that I had the opportunity to supervise, my colleague, clinical social worker Martina Weilandt, noticed that as soon as Samuel started to play, Lee asked many questions and made suggestions about what he could do next. It seemed that Lee very much wanted to find a way of giving something to

Samuel, and in doing so, at times, unwittingly, became intrusive. When Lee was able to take a step back and started to see how Samuel was then able to play more freely, a new side of Samuel began to emerge. Now he could show the toy animals fighting, shout when he was winning at Snap, and ask to be held on Lee's lap when he got upset. Lee felt that Samuel had come alive, and had become a 3-year-old child instead of a 'mini-adult'. He began to enjoy looking after Samuel much more, even when the placement became more challenging as Samuel became less compliant.

In this brief intervention, the focus on play and attention helped child and carer to find each other.

Practice considerations

Our experience in using the WMP approach is with qualified child mental health practitioners receiving regular supervision. The containment and support of clinical supervision from an experienced supervisor, separate from management supervision, is essential to support ways of working that bring clinicians closer to the harrowing experiences of traumatised children and the, at times, upsetting events and uncertainties that mark many lives in care. Our team also has the support of a psychodynamic consultant who provides monthly group sessions that, like supervision, have a role in preventing secondary trauma, and in preventing or addressing signs of professional burn-out.

Doing 'Watch Me Play!'

When we suggest a WMP approach to foster carers and social workers, the aim is often to help carer and child to get to know each other better. The intervention involves a particular type of attention that is appropriate to provide for periods of up to twenty minutes, not something that a carer would be expected to do all the time. Carers who worry that a child is excessively clingy sometimes find that once the WMP routine has become established and the child is confident of having their carer's undivided attention at regular times during the week, the clingy behaviour lessens and the child becomes more able to play on their own.

Role-play activities in trainings with foster carers can be useful and fun ways to convey the key aspects of WMP. Modelling the approach and joining in to watch alongside the foster carer can help to reinforce the message that a quiet environment is needed, with televisions and screens off and battery-operated toys put to one side. Foster carers, just like parents, may struggle to provide their undivided attention, or to allow the child to take the lead and choose what to do in their play. For some carers, it can take time and encouragement to give up being in charge and instead to allow ideas to come from the child, while for other carers it can come as a relief to feel that they do not always have to direct the child's play.

The tasks of the WMP clinician are to model the approach with carer and child, showing interest both in the child's play and the carer's observations. It is helpful to encourage the carer to share observations and reflect together on how it feels to be with the child. Offering sensitive understanding to the child and to the foster carer helps them to find words and stories for feelings that may never have been named. Feeding back from time to time to the child and carer, and to the professional network, requires a relationship of respect and acceptance. Tact, sensitivity, imaginative empathy and playfulness are important qualities for this work.

We find that around six sessions provides a good basis for many carers and children, but the nature of our service means that we are flexible about frequency: sometimes a one-off session is all that is possible, while more complex cases may warrant a longer intervention. WMP is also used as a way in before a more intensive treatment, such as a video-interactive approach, or child or parent–child psychotherapy, can begin (Juffer, Bakermans-Kranenburg & Van Ijzendoorn 2008, 2014).

In service evaluations and training feedback, professionals in the local authority report that they have gained an enhanced understanding of the value of individual attention and child-led play. Clinicians have also reported that this observational approach, where time is taken to become familiar with child and carer, provides an invaluable training experience. A manual is now in preparation for the WMP approach (Wakelyn in preparation). As a next step, we are exploring applications of the approach as a preventative intervention with teenage parents.

Conclusion

The WMP approach aims to promote child-led play in foster placements by encouraging foster carers to provide children with their undivided attention in a quiet environment at regular times during the week, and to reflect with another professional on the atmosphere of the child's play. Facilitating child-led play allows children to develop trust in their carer's attentiveness and receptiveness and to begin to express themselves and explore the world around them. Sharing observations between foster carers and clinicians facilitates a child-centred focus in professional meetings and guides what can be regarded as good practice with the child in foster care. This is further enhanced by providing foster carers and other professionals involved in foster care work with training workshops and forums which draw from child development and attachment research (First Step 2016).

Play is recognised as one of the first steps children take towards coming to know themselves and to know others. Children in foster care may have experienced traumas that have robbed them of opportunities to explore through safe play. 'Watch Me Play!' offers children the opportunity to regain a sense of personal agency and to explore their world and their relationships with the confidence that their experiences and communications can be taken seriously and held in mind.

Acknowledgements

I am grateful to the children, foster carers and social workers whose eloquence about their experiences has inspired this work, and to my colleagues and supervisors. I also thank the editors for helpful comments and suggestions for this chapter.

References

Alvarez, A. & Phillips, A. (1998) 'The importance of play: A child psychotherapist's view.' *Child Psychology and Psychiatry Review 3*, 3, 99–104.

Ayling, P. & Stringer, B. (2013) 'Supporting carer-child relationships through play: A model for teaching carers how to use play skills to strengthen attachment relationships.' *Adoption and Fostering 37*, 2, 130–143.

American Academy of Pediatrics (AAP) Committee on Drugs (2012) 'Neonatal drug withdrawal.' *Pediatrics 101*, 6, e540–e560.

Anda, R.F., Felitti, V.J., Bremner, J.D., Walker, J.D. *et al.* (2006) 'The enduring effects of abuse and related adverse experiences in childhood: A convergence of evidence from neurobiology and epidemiology.' *European Archives of Psychiatry and Clinical Neuroscience 256*, 174–186.

Bick, E. (1964) 'Notes on infant observation in psychoanalytic training.' *International Journal of Psychoanalysis 45*, 558–566.

Birk Irner, T. (2012) 'Substance exposure in utero and developmental consequences in adolescence: A systematic review.' *Child Neuropsychology 18*, 6, 521–549.

Brandon, M., Glaser, D., Maguire, S., McCrory, E., Lushey, C. & Ward, H. (2014) *Missed opportunities: Indicators of neglect – what is ignored, why, and what can be done?* Research report, November 2014. London: Department for Education, Childhood Wellbeing Research Centre: DFE-RR404 443-7. Retrieved 05/02/19 from www.gov.uk/government/publications/indicators-of-neglect-missed-opportunities.

Bratton, S., Landreth, G., Kellam, T. & Blackard, S.R. (2006) *Child Parent Relationship Therapy (CPRT) Treatment Manual: A 10-Session Filial Therapy Model for Training Parents.* New York: Routledge.

Browning, A.S. (2015) 'Undertaking planned transitions for children in out-of-home care.' *Adoption and Fostering 39,* 1, 51–61.

Cohen, N.J., Lojkasek, M., Muir, E., Muir, R. & Parker, C.J. (2002) 'Six-month follow-up of two mother-infant psychotherapies: convergence of therapeutic outcomes.' *Infant Mental Health Journal, 23,* 4, 361–380.

Dozier, M., Lindehiem, O., Lewis, E., Bick, J., Bernard, K. & Peloso, E. (2009) 'Effects of a foster parent training program on young children's attachment behaviors: Preliminary evidence from a randomized clinical trial.' *Child and Adolescent Social Work Journal 26,* 4, 321–332.

Elliot, A.J. & Reis, H.T. (2003) 'Attachment and exploration in adulthood.' *Journal of Personality and Social Psychology 85,* 2, 317–331.

Emanuel, L. (2006) 'The Contribution of Organisational Dynamics to the Triple Deprivation of Looked-After Children.' In J.Kenrick, C. Lindsey & L. Tollemache *Creating New Families. Therapeutic Approaches to Fostering, Adoption and Kinship Care.* London: Karnac.

Ferguson, H. (2017) 'How children become invisible in child protection work: Findings from research into day-to-day social work practice.' *British Journal of Social Work 47,* 4, 1007–1023.

First Step (2016) 'Under 2 Questionnaire.' Unpublished service questionnaire.

Fraiberg, S. (1982) 'Pathological defenses in infancy.' *Psychoanalytic Quarterly 51,* 612–635.

Gerhardt, S. (2004) *Why Love Matters: How Affection Shapes a Baby's Brain.* London: Brunner Routledge

Goodman, R. (1997) 'The Strengths and Difficulties Questionnaire: A research note.' *Journal of Child Psychology and Psychiatry 38,* 581–586.

Goodman, R., Renfrew, D. & Mullick, M. (2000) 'Predicting type of psychiatric disorder from Strengths and Difficulties Questionnaire (SDQ) scores in child mental health clinics in London and Dhaka.' *European Child & Adolescent Psychiatry 9,* 129–134.

Halton, W. (1994) 'Some Unconscious Aspects of Organizational Life.' In A. Obholzer & V.Z. Roberts (Eds) *The Unconscious at Work. Individual and Organizational Stress in the Human Services.* London: Routledge.

Hardy, C., Hackett, E., Murphy, E., Cooper, B., Ford, T. & Conroy, S. (2013) 'Mental health screening and early intervention clinical research study for under 5-year-old children in care in an inner London borough.' *Clinical Child Psychology and Psychiatry 20,* 261–275.

Houzel, D. (2010) 'Infant observation and the receptive mind.' *Infant Observation 13,* 2, 119–133.

Juffer, F., Bakermans-Kranenburg, M.J. & Van Ijzendoorn, M.H. (Eds) (2008) *Promoting Positive Parenting: An Attachment-Based Intervention.* New York: Taylor & Francis.

Juffer, F., Bakermans-Kranenburg, M.J. & Van Ijzendoorn, M.H. (2014) 'Attachment-Based Interventions: Sensitive Parenting Is the Key to Positive Parent–Child Relationships.' In P. Holmes & S. Farnfield (Eds) *The Routledge Handbook of Attachment: Implications and Interventions.* London: Routledge.

Klee, L., Kronstadt, D. & Zlotnick, C. (1997) 'Foster care's youngest: A preliminary report.' *American Journal of Orthopsychiatry 6,* 2, 290–299.

Lanyado, M. (2003) 'The emotional tasks of moving from fostering to adoption: Transitions, attachment, separation and loss.' *Clinical Child Psychiatry and Psychology 8*, 3, 337–349.

Lerner, C. & Barr, R. (2015) 'Screen sense: Setting the record straight. Research-based guidelines for screen use for children under 3 years old.' *Zero to Three 35*, 4, 1–10. Retrieved 08/09/2015 from https://eric.ed.gov/?id=EJ1125470

Main, M. & Solomon, J. (1986) 'Discovery of a New, Insecure-Disorganized/Disoriented Attachment Pattern.' In M. Yogman & T.B. Brazelton (Eds) *Affective Development in Infancy*. Norwood, NJ: Ablex.

McCrory, E., De Brito, S. & Viding, E. (2011) 'Heightened neural reactivity to threat in child victims of family violence.' *Current Biology 21*, 23, R947–948.

Meakings, S. & Selwyn, J. (2016) '"She was a foster mother who said she didn't give cuddles": The adverse early foster care experiences of children who later struggle with adoptive family life.' *Clinical Child Psychology and Psychiatry 21*, 4, 509–519.

Needell, B. & Booth, R.P. (1998) 'Infants entering foster care compared to other infants using birth status indicators.' *Child Abuse and Neglect 22*, 12, 1179–1189.

Neil, E., Beek M. & Schofield, G. (2018) *Moving to adoption: The development and piloting of a practice programme*. Research Briefings, Centre for Research on Children and Families, University of East Anglia.

Pallet, C., Blackeby, K., Yule, W., Weissman, R. & Scott, S. (2000) *Fostering Changes: How to Improve Relationships and Manage Difficult Behaviour: A Training Programme for Foster Carers*. London: BAAF.

Panksepp, J. (2007) 'Can PLAY diminish ADHD and facilitate the construction of the social brain?' *Journal of the Canadian Academy of Child and Adolescent Psychiatry 16*, 2, 57–66.

Rhode, M. (2007) 'Infant Observation as an Early Intervention.' In S. Acquarone (Ed.) *Signs of Autism in Infants. Recognition and Early Intervention*. London: Karnac

Robertson, J. & Robertson, J. (1989) *Separation and the Very Young*. London, Free Association.

Rustin, M.E. (2014) 'The relevance of infant observation for early intervention: Containment in theory and practice.' *Infant Observation 17*, 2, 97–114.

Rustin, M.J., Rustin, M.E, Miller, L. & Shuttleworth, J. (1997) *Closely Observed Infants*. Bristol: Classical Press.

Schore, A. (2001) The effects of early relational trauma on right brain development, affect regulation and infant mental health. *Infant Mental Health Journal*, 22, (1–2), 201–269.

Slade, A. (1994) 'Making Meaning and Making Believe: Their Role in the Clinical Process.' In A. Slade & D. Wolf (Eds) *Children at Play: Clinical and Developmental Approaches to Meaning and Representation*. New York: Oxford University Press.

Sunderland, M. (2007) *What Every Parent Needs to Know. The Incredible Effects of Love, Nurture and Play on Your Child's Development*. London: Dorling Kindersley.

Trevarthen, C. (2001) 'Intrinsic motives for companionship in understanding their origin, development, and significance for infant mental health.' *Infant Mental Health Journal 22*, 1–2, 95–131.

Trowell, J. & Rustin, M.E. (1991) 'Developing the internal observer in professionals in training.' *Infant Mental Health Journal 12*, 3, 233–246.

Tustin, F. (1986) *Autistic Barriers in Neurotic Patients*. London: Karnac.

Urwin, C. & Sternberg, J. (2012) *Emotional lives. Infant Observation and Research*. London, Routledge.

Wade, J., Biehal, N., Farrelly, N. & Sinclair, I. (2010) *Maltreated children in the looked after system: a comparison of outcomes for those who go home and those who do not*. London, Department for Education/University of York Social Policy Research Unit. Retrieved 05/02/19 from www.education.gov.uk/publications/eOrderingDownload/ DFE-RBX-10-06.pdf.

Wakelyn, J. (2011) 'Therapeutic observation of an infant in foster care.' *Journal of Child Psychotherapy 37*, 3, 280–310.

Wakelyn, J. (2012) 'Observation as a therapeutic intervention for infants and young children in care.' *Infant Observation 15*, 1, 49–66.

Wakelyn, J. (in preparation) *'Watch Me Play!': A Manual*.

Ward, H., Munro, E. and Dearden, C. (2006) *Babies and Young Children in Care: Life Pathways, Decision-Making and Practice*. London: Jessica Kingsley.

World Health Organization (WHO) (2006) *Mental health and psychosocial well-being among children in severe food shortage situations*. Department of Mental Health and Substance Abuse (MSD). Retreived 05/02/19 from www.who.int/nutrition/publications/emergencies/WHO_MSD_MER_06.1/en.

Winnicott, D.W. (1951) 'Transitional Objects and Transitional Phenomena.' In *Through Paediatrics to Psychoanalysis: Collected Papers*. London: Karnac.

Winnicott, D.W. (1986) 'The Concept of a Healthy Individual.' In *Home Is Where We Start From*. Harmondsworth: Penguin (first published 1965).

CHAPTER 5

Keeping the Child in Mind When Thinking About Violence in Families

ANGELIQUE JENNEY

Introduction

It is of great concern that seeing and working with infants as little but sentient people has not yet translated to mainstream child and family services. This includes the lack of translation in the family violence sector. Bunston, Franich-Ray & Tatlow (2017) argue that in regards to the considerable problem of family violence, it seems that the child/adolescent mental health sectors have turned a blind eye. They cogently argue violence is not only a precursor to child mental health problems, but at the same time it is underexamined and profoundly absent from mental health diagnostic discussions. Further, Bunston *et al.* (2017) interrogate the basis of many classifications of the *Diagnostic and Statistical Manual of Mental Disorders (DSM-5)* (American Psychiatric Association 2013), finding an inadequate examination of family violence as a determinant of child mental health problems. Having a more central infant/child perspective could make a significant difference in addressing violence in families. Child maltreatment risk exists where infants directly witness, or are in proximity to, adult caregivers engaged in domestic violence (Carpenter & Stacks 2009; Edleson 1999; Holt, Buckley & Whelan 2008; Jaffe, Wolfe & Wilson 1990; Kimball 2016). Concerns about such exposure to family violence have led child protection services in Canada and the USA to receive an increase in the number of reports for children subjected to violence between caregivers (Edleson, Gassman-Pines & Hill 2006; Alaggia *et al.* 2007). By taking a more trauma-informed perspective to working with infants and young children, we could make a significant difference in their lives.

This chapter provides: 1) an overview on the relevant literature regarding infants and trauma, and the evidence for greatly needed therapeutic interventions; 2) an example of therapeutic group work, with a mother and her baby who have experienced trauma, illustrating the difficulties encountered by both clients and staff when delivering a program within the context of a child protection service; and 3) the ongoing challenges of keeping the baby at the forefront of intervention are explored.

Exposure to violence and the impact on the infant/young child

Tronick & Beeghly (2011) have articulated that an infant's capacity for meaning making in such an environment influences the development of good mental health. Specifically they argue:

> Infants make meaning about their relation to the world of people and things and about themselves. Of course, their meaning-making is non-symbolic and radically different from the representational meaning made by older children and adults, but it is meaning nonetheless.

Thus, we need to appreciate that the infant not only has capacity for meaning making but that this may also impact on their development. Furthermore, this occurs within the context of witnessing violence against their primary caregiver.

Exposure to violence may result in trauma symptoms in young children, such as gaze aversion, regression, emotional dysregulation, developmental delays and sensitivity to conflict becoming more identifiable (Bogat *et al.* 2006; DeJonghe *et al.* 2005; Kitzmann, Gaylord & Kenny 2003; Osofsky 1995, 1999). Easterbrooks and colleagues (2018) explored the effect of intimate partner violence (IPV) of first-time adolescent mothers and their children under the age of 2 years and found that impacts were similar regardless of whether the perpetrator was the mother or father. They also concluded that both psychological and physical IPV (minor and severe) were associated with compromised toddler development.

Past and current experiences of adversity, such as domestic violence (DV), may profoundly influence parent–child attachment, particularly due to difficulties with maternal sensitivity, responsiveness and attunement (Appleyard & Osofsky 2003; Casanueva *et al.* 2008; Letourneau, Fedick & Willms 2007). Fraiberg, Adelson and Shapiro (1975) coined the poetic term "ghosts in the nursery" for the enduring impact of these maternal (and paternal) histories of trauma. These "ghosts" may continue to haunt developing caregiver–child relationships unless skilled interventions are offered (Fraiberg *et al.* 1975; Malone *et al.* 2010).

When an infant's parent/caregiver experiences, or is the perpetrator of, interpersonal violence, the impact may be felt for years to come. This includes DV in the parent's childhood, adulthood or just prior to conception. Caregivers may have been subjected to violence years before becoming a parent, whether from intergenerational trauma experiences, socio-political violence, or the result of sexual violence resulting in pregnancy. When the caregiver's experience is considered, we now know we need to take into account how this experience impacts and impinges directly on their infant. Many researchers are engaged in disentangling the process of how the intergenerational transmission of trauma occurs between fathers/mothers and their children. Two American studies offer important messages for those working with family violence: Cohen, Hien and Batchelder (2008), in a study of 176 mothers, found "cumulative maternal trauma was a significant predictor of abuse potential, punitiveness, psychological aggression, and physical discipline, even after controlling for demographic and diagnostic variables"; Schechter and colleagues (2008) studied 41 mother–infant dyads in a clinical sample and found that "the more severe and symptomatic mother's PTSD was, the more likely she was to maintain a physical and/or psychological distance from her young child". Both authors explore how the inability of a parent to contain a child's emotions, particularly involving normal developmental behaviours (such as temper tantrums and separation anxiety), may act as additional stressors. For example, it is not uncommon for us to hear a mother, with a trauma history, describe her child's temper tantrums as frightening, feeling she needs to protect herself from her child. Such early traumatic experiences may lead a mother to misattribute meanings to her child's behaviours, believing that somehow they are malevolent or dangerous to her (Huth-Bocks *et al.* 2004; Malone *et al.* 2010).

It is understood that fear caused by, and generated by, abusive partners during and post-relationship influences the caregiver–infant relationship. Main and Hesse (1990) found these ways of relating were often directly related to the infant's experience of being with a frightened/frightening caregiver. An example of this is a caregiver who is being assaulted while holding their baby in their arms. When this happens this parent is often in high distress, unable to keep their baby safe (by falling or dropping the baby) or even at the point of acting protectively (running away and leaving the baby, or fighting back). Furthermore, abusive partners harm children in various ways: through neglectful, inconsistent or irresponsible parenting; exposing the child to new threats of violence (toward their parent or a new partner); and even psychological, physical or sexual abuse (Bancroft & Silverman 2002). We advocate that support programs should be available for violent parents as crucial interventions to improve the lives of their young children (Bunston 2013; Labarre *et al.* 2016; Scott & Crooks 2004).

The term infant-led or child-led practice was originally signaled by Australians Paul and Thomson-Salo (1997) and further consolidated by fellow Australian Bunston (2002, 2008). This approach means keeping the infant/child's experience at the centre of casework. As many interventions in the DV sector still work only with adult survivors of abuse, DV professionals may erringly over rely on caregiver accounts, which often leave the child out of the narrative and, as a consequence, out of consideration for intervention.

Early intervention: Mothers in Mind™

Trauma-informed practice is a critical component of our work, and several principles have been adapted from the literature (British Columbia Provincial Mental Health and Substance Use Planning Council 2013; Elliott *et al.* 2005) and are embedded within the intervention to: 1) create safety; 2) recognize the impact of trauma and minimize risk of retraumatization; 3) explore intergenerational, historical, cultural and gender factors influencing parenting; 4) focus on healing through healthy relationships, peer support and maximizing choice; and 5) focus on strengths for both mother and baby.

Mothers in Mind™ is an early intervention, community-based program focused on promoting the safety and well-being of vulnerable children under the age of 4 years. The model provides intervention to mothers and children together; in particular, those affected by family violence and involved with child protective services. The goals of the Mothers in Mind™ program are to improve outcomes for young children by:

- providing mothers with access to trauma-informed parenting information, while connecting with other mothers who have had hurtful experiences in their lives

- strengthening mothers' self-care, self-compassion and stress management skills in relation to parenting

- supporting the mother–child relationship through enhancing sensitivity and responsiveness to children and strengthening feelings of parenting self-efficacy.

The program has been adapted and offered in diverse settings, including women's shelters/refuges and children's mental health agencies and was recently implemented directly within a child protection agency in Toronto, Canada.

Relationships: Moments of connection and disconnection

The intervention focuses on two core Attachment Theory concepts: connection and disconnection. Using a trauma-informed lens, the program revolves around strengthening such moments of relationship connection when things go well, and recognizing and repairing the frequent and normal moments of disconnection, also called "mis-attunements."

The process of intervention

Our Mothers in Mind™ group facilitators include staff from the community agency and one facilitator from the Child Protection Service (CPS). Our example below regards delivering a program that is within the context of a CPS. Mothers are informed that the goals of the program are keeping children with their families. They explain that Mothers in Mind™ is not a CPS group, but with CPS involvement they can learn how the CPS also aims to support mothers and babies growing in families together. We clarify with parents that our notes are not a part of the CPS file. This approach promotes not only our relationship-building with vulnerable mothers but also collaboration between services of protection and services with therapeutic aims. Following a new referral, staff members contact the parents, provide further program information and arrange to meet to consider whether the pair is ready to participate.

The following case example describes our work and process of intervention.

■ Case example ■

The referral

The mother, Amhika[1] (28 years), and baby, Gurit (8 months), were referred by the family's CPS worker due to concerns of domestic violence perpetrated by Gurit's father, Abbot (35 years). A second child, Daniel (3 years), was removed from the family home a year previously. Alerted by a police report, the CPS were concerned about possible impacts on the infant.

Following the removal of the first child, Daniel, from the home a year earlier due to physical abuse by Abbot, the CPS remained involved. The father's violence was a major concern, and since the CPS viewed that neither the father nor mother were able to keep Daniel safe, he was placed in foster care just before his second birthday. Amhika became, pregnant shortly after Daniel was removed. Following a very serious physical assault by her husband, she was hospitalized in the final trimester of her pregnancy. Gurit was born nine weeks premature and due to developmental immaturity and concerning low birth weight, both mother and baby remained in hospital for six weeks. The CPS— acting on their assessment of risks for the newborn baby—made plans for baby Gurit's removal. However, the father, due to fears of criminal charges, fled the country. This then made it possible for Gurit to be discharged from hospital into her mother's care, and plans to reunite Daniel with his mother and sister began. The CPS's concerns about Amhika's ability to manage both her children (i.e. a new baby and a toddler) led to temporarily delaying Daniel's return to the home. At the point when the CPS made a referral to our program, six months later, Amhika was doing well with her daughter and thus a reunification for Daniel was planned to occur in three months. Amhika and Gurit then attended the Mothers in Mind™ program at the agency.

---

1   In order to protect confidentiality, a composite case study from program participants is used. Names are fictional: Amhika is an Indian word for "Mother," Gurit, is Hebrew for "innocent child," Daniel means "lost child" and Abbot is the Hebrew word for "father."

First: The child and family meeting

An adequate play space supports the work, by being child-friendly and welcoming. Clay, coloured pencils and paper, as well as water, tissues and developmentally appropriate toys—all examples of tactile expressive arts materials—are available to support emotional regulation and grounding.

In the first meeting, Nadia, our Mothers in Mind™ facilitator, is with the CPS worker and Amhika and Gurit in the CPS building. Amhika enters the room clutching little Gurit, now 8 months old, tightly against her chest. Amhika, giving an icy look to both workers, takes the seat closest to the door. As introductions take place, Amhika is asked to introduce her baby, and herself, and Gurit is directly included in all conversations.

The CPS worker tells the story of Amhika and Gurit's involvement with the agency and expectations for her attendance in the program. The impact on Amhika is immediate and she hangs her head as personal details of her life are discussed. Gurit begins to squirm and fuss, but Amhika does not loosen her grip on her. Nadia gently interrupts the CPS worker and reminds her that there will be time for Amhika to tell her story in her own time when she feels comfortable to do so. She makes a point of asking Amhika what goals she might have for herself and her daughter, and specifically to ponder what Gurit might get out of attending as well. Amhika is further reminded that participation in the program is voluntary and she is reassured that if she joins the program she can decide what information is shared with the CPS (outside of any actual child protection concerns). Amhika looks up, surprised that her views are valued; her body relaxes a bit, which allows Gurit to free one chubby little arm and bring her fist to her mouth. The brief involvement of the CPS worker in the interview process is to clarify service expectations, as well as being an opportunity to confirm that conversations with the CPS will occur only with Amhika present. Amhika relaxes when the CPS worker leaves. Nadia again reminds her of her choices throughout the process. Nadia reiterates the questions that she will begin to ask and takes a moment to check-in with Amhika about Gurit's comfort (e.g. "Before we begin, does Gurit need to be fed/changed? Would she like a toy?"). She also invites Amhika to raise any questions or concerns she might have at this stage. Amhika asks about confidentiality, as she's worried about information being shared with her CPS worker. Reassured, Amhika becomes both teary and angry as she describes Daniel being taken from her and her experience of leaving Gurit in the hospital. Her grip on Gurit tightens as she speaks, and the baby begins to actively struggle and fuss. Nadia feels the urge to reach out and release the pressure on the baby, worrying that Gurit cannot breathe properly due to the tightness of the hold. As Amhika becomes more agitated, her grip tightens and Gurit's sounds become distressing. Nadia gently looks at the baby and says: "Your Mommy doesn't want to lose you, and she's holding you tightly to let you know how much you mean to her." Amhika looks down at the baby, sees the distress, loosens her grip, and moves the baby to a more comfortable position. Tears are rolling down her cheeks as she speaks soothingly to the baby in their mother tongue. Amhika looks back at the facilitator, and says: "I don't want to come to this program; I know they only want to take her away from me. They've had Daniel for so long; I don't think he even knows I'm his mother anymore."

The assessment determined that Amhika and Gurit were very suitable for the program. However, Amhika advised that she didn't trust the process or the agency. She stated that she didn't feel safe to attend, but at the same time also feared repercussions if she did not. She said the whole experience felt like a trap and wondered why she couldn't just be left alone with her family. Nadia needed to work hard in order to engage Amhika in determining how best to make the environment a safe one. This was the opportunity to talk about Amhika's fears and also the painful dilemma she found herself in. Eventually, Amhika reluctantly agreed to come to the first session.

Thomson-Salo and Paul (2014) point out:

> The significance of the infant is constantly being denied, as though somehow you can understand what is going on in the baby just by listening to the mother…the essential element is to make a link with the baby and the rest follows. (p.267)

This program offers an opportunity to talk, think and reflect on the experiences of violence and trauma and what this may mean for both mother and child. In the case example, once the therapeutic relationship had been established, the facilitator could begin to gently explore experiences of the violent context surrounding the conception and birth of Gurit and what that may have meant for them both. One would also want to explore thoughts and feelings around the father and her son, and his early experiences of abuse and his absence from his family.

Asking about the child's developmental history (e.g. "Tell me a little bit about how this baby came to be"), followed by questions that explore a mother's history, furthers an understanding of the dyad's present circumstances (e.g. "What were your own experiences of being parented? How would you like to parent differently now?").

Explicit details about specific traumas are not necessary, but the impact is explored (e.g. "I'm terrified to leave my child alone"). The intention is to discover therapeutically useful information in the least intrusive way.

The program

The therapeutic model involves a closed group with a minimum of ten sessions offered, which may be extended to 12 sessions if needed (e.g. with child protection clients). The model requires 2–3 facilitators for a maximum of 6–8 mother–child dyads. Sometimes this constitutes quite a large group of 12–16 individual clients, plus the staff. We are aware that the inclusion of too many people may create chaos and reduced safety, particularly for distressed children, thus diluting direct dyadic interaction.

The therapeutic stance of our group work model is to provide consistency; which includes our facilitators, our structure and routine. Each session contains familiar stages: Free Play; Welcome Circle; Talk, Play & Connect, Integration of Self-Compassion; Goodbye Circle; and Weekly Follow-Up. As each mother–child pair arrives, they are introduced to the other people in the room and the theme for each week is explained; they are also made aware of the availability of snacks and toys, and the provision of a quiet space if babies need feeding or changing.

Free Play allows children to have time to freely transition into the group. It also makes a space for those families arriving late, to limit the stress of a disruptive late entry.

> Amhika and Gurit arrive fifteen minutes late for the first session. Amhika lifts Gurit out of the stroller and carries her around the room. Gurit is looking around, wide-eyed and curious. Amhika finds a space on the floor with a pillow and gently places Gurit on it. She looks around her at the other mothers and children who are playing and looks around for a suitable toy for Gurit. Nadia, in an attempt at engaging the dyad within this new space, brings over a set of colourful plastic stacking cups. Amhika looks at them with disapproval, goes back to the stroller and pulls out a well-worn stuffed dog, clearly a loved toy for Gurit, who immediately puts the dog's ear into her mouth and settles easily as Welcome Circle time begins.

Welcome Circle is the next part of the structured and predictable beginning. Musical instruments for the children to play with offer a chance for a lively connection between feelings and body. To conclude Welcome Circle time a facilitator reads a children's story, therapeutically aligned with the weekly topic (e.g. Session 3 on Managing Stress and Other Challenging Feelings incorporates a book called *Calm-Down Time*). This leads to the next component.

Talk, Play & Connect introduces the concept of self-compassion to improve resilience and reduce post-traumatic stress disorder (PTSD) symptomology (Barlow Goldsmith, Turow & Gerhart 2017). For example, the compassion quote for Session 3 is "I am not alone in this. This will pass." Affirming quotes or phrases are written on note-cards or bookmarks, and given to participants to take home.

> When the facilitators introduce the topic of challenging feelings, Amhika bravely states that she is worried that because Daniel is in foster care, other group members might judge her. Other mothers talk of their anxious feelings about their children being removed by the CPS.
>
> In a later session, Amhika shares that the Free Play part of the group is particularly stressful for her. She remembers the first group session, with the discussion of the value of play and differentiated adult-led from child-led play. Amhika looks at Gurit in her arms and says she feels she doesn't know how to play with her child. Gurit looks back at her intently, her face mirroring her mother's sadness. Amhika recalls having had no toys in her childhood home and asks how other mothers learned what their children like to play with. Some mothers share their children's favourite toys, and there is shared laughter about some of the choices. Gurit hears her mother's laughter and a smile lights up her face. Amhika looks down at her incredulously and asks: "Are you smiling at me?" She then exclaims to the group: "She never smiles!" Nadia smiles back warmly, saying: "I guess she likes the sound of your laughter, and I think she likes seeing you smile too!" Amhika beams with this new knowledge and begins to engage in some lovely back and forth playful interactions with Gurit.

The Goodbye Circle offers an infant-sensitive ritual for goodbyes and departures that assists clients in closures and the transition to leaving us. Often, children find this difficult and protest as it seems they quickly become aware that in this space their mothers feel safe, sometimes even more playful.

We also offer a weekly follow up outside of the group to discuss anything the mothers felt uncomfortable raising within the group.

Amhika gets Gurit ready for the trip home by placing her gently in the stroller, saying: "Well, we made it through another week, and we even had some fun, didn't we?" She then turns to Nadia: "I still don't know if we are coming back next week, but today was okay." Nadia simply smiles back at her, and replies: "Coming to the group will always be your choice, Amhika. We loved having you, and it was wonderful to see you and Gurit really enjoying each other. Would it be okay if I gave you a call later this week to check-in and see how you are?" She then looks at Gurit and says: "You have a gorgeous little smile, don't you? I hope we see it again soon." Gurit responds with another partial smile, grips her stuffed dog and brings the well-worn ear once again into her mouth.

The aim of the therapeutic intervention is to build a secure relational base both with the facilitators and also between all the mothers and infants. From this secure base we can actively learn more deeply about the mothers and their children, and also about the missing or damaged, or dangerous, fathers. We are interested in the mothers' achievements, hopes and dreams as well as the need to help them explore the impact of traumatic experiences on parenting. The overall goal is to help them strengthen relationships with their children. By learning to observe their children, and explore and talk about feelings, we support parents in order to help their children develop. We help parents know their own responses and reactions and feelings, and manage their own and their children's feelings.

Amhika and Gurit did continue to come to the group each week. However, we could see that Amhika could not let Gurit explore the room with the other babies and their mothers, preferring to keep her close at all times.

Each time Gurit attempted to make her way over to a tempting wall of toys, Amhika gently steered her back or picked her up and put her onto her lap. Gurit, however, watched the other children and her eyes flit back from one exciting toy to another. Nadia decided again to bring over the plastic stacking cups. She knelt and put them in front of Gurit, while saying: "Everyone is playing with something. You look like you might want to try too?" Gurit looked curiously toward the cups and reached her little hand out for one. Amhika angrily swept the cups out of the way exclaiming: "Why would she want to play with these stupid plastic cups? You don't think my daughter deserves a real toy?" The facilitator was startled by this sudden aggression. Gurit too became wide-eyed and completely froze while looking at her mother. The facilitator took a moment and asked herself what could be happening in this moment. What has caused this moment of disconnection? Given that this response is out of character for Amhika, Nadia reflected on previous weeks and about what she knew about Amhika. Is something in Amhika's past or present experiences of violence at the root of her behaviour? Nadia remembered Amhika talking about the fact they didn't have toys in her childhood home and being forced to play with whatever was around the house. Nadia made eye contact with Amhika and tentatively wondered: "I guess these plastic cups seem just like something that would be lying around a household; they don't seem like a real toy, something you didn't have yourself and really want for Gurit. Maybe we could look together for something else that you think she would like better?" Amhika looked down, nodded and began to weep silently. Gurit made a corresponding whimpering sound and without looking at her, Amhika pulled her into her arms. Nadia said: "I'm sorry that my choice of toy was insensitive to your experiences; these cups are usually really popular with little ones; let's try to find something else."

This vignette, illustrating mis-attunement between facilitator and participant, was ultimately transformative; creating meaning from the distress. This example demonstrates the importance of the facilitator sensitively experiencing, processing her own and the mother's emotions, and holding the anxiety. This led to an empathic reconnection and eventual repair. Both Amhika's aggression and her weeping are understood as coming from her own deprivation, found in the meaning of "just household cups." Such unexpected therapeutic opportunities arise and illustrate how past and present often interact.

Several weeks later, Amhika picks up the set of cups herself, gives them to Gurit and watches. Gurit looks at them, tentatively reaches out for one and brings it back to her mouth. She then bangs it onto another cup, which tumbles over and rolls a little bit out of reach. Gurit's eyes widen again and she looks at her mother. Amhika rolls the cup back, much to Gurit's delight—she smiles and lets out a giggle. Amhika sees Nadia watching and says: "Well, you were right, she does seem to like them." Nadia laughs and takes the opportunity to describe what Gurit might like about them: their shape, texture and the fact that they can stack, nest or roll. She talks about normal child development and what Gurit is learning in this moment. Amhika seems open and somewhat relieved, remarking: "It's like it's simple, but also hard."

This final session of the program ends with thinking about how to promote nurturing of both children and mothers. They reflect on the importance of self-compassion for both mothers and children, celebrating the group's end, reflections and looking ahead. Mothers are asked to share with us their reflections on their time in the program and to tell us how the program might be improved for future mothers and babies.

> Amhika and Gurit's relationship blossomed over these weeks together, and things were going well for both of them. Amhika joyfully shared in the final group that Daniel was coming home after a gradual increase in his visits. "You know, I've been using lots of the things I've learned in this group to make things better for him—I think about what he's feeling all the time and I try to give him those feelings of safety that you are always talking about. It's really important." She asks if she might be able to come back and do the group again with Daniel next time.
>
> Amhika could finally describe what it was that so frightened her in attending: "I've got to be honest: I thought this whole group was a trick by my worker to take Gurit away from me forever. All this time I was so angry at her and afraid, and it turns out she was trying to help me from the beginning!" She laughs a bit sadly: "It's hard to trust people when you've been through what I have—but I'm learning."

This example of a troubled mother and her baby is a realistic portrayal of challenges encountered by both clients and staff when delivering a program that is within the context of a Child Protection Service. The very meaning of child protection involvement may evoke an intense fear in mothers toward program staff and the power they have to influence their lives, remove their children, blame and judge. Any lack of trust and fear needs to be acknowledged and addressed, and actively worked with throughout the group if both mother and baby are to feel safe enough to grow together. Winnicott's (1960) famous quote, "There is no such thing as an infant...without maternal care one would find no infant," is profound.

It is in this vein that one must consider the key principles of this work: Child safety and well-being cannot be separated from caregiver safety and well-being. Attending to the needs of the infant in the context of the relationship with the abused or abusing caregiver is a challenge that can only be met through constant reflective practice.

In the family violence sector, the belief has been that if caregivers are assisted, then their children will ultimately be supported well. However, experience proves this to be a dangerous fallacy. We must never lose sight of the child, as Thomson-Salo and Paul (2014) observe: "We all miss the baby and have to keep working on it" (p.278). When it comes to considerations of exposure to violence, focusing on the signs of violence in the form of a child's physical exposure or actual witnessing can be privileged over considering the damaging impacts of prolonged periods of fear, uncertainty and caregiver unavailability on the infant–caregiver relationship. Without the continual privileging of the infant's experience, interventions will necessarily fall short of being the infant-centred work that can truly promote change.

References

Alaggia, R., Jenney, A., Mazzuca, J. & Redmond, M. (2007). 'In whose best interest? A Canadian case study of the impact of child welfare policies in cases of domestic violence.' *Brief Treatment and Crisis Intervention 7*, 4, 275–290.

American Psychiatric Association (2013) *Diagnostic and Statistical Manual of Mental Disorders (5th ed.) (DSM-5)*. Washington, D.C.: American Psychiatric Publishing.

Appleyard, K. & Osofsky, J.D. (2003) 'Parenting after trauma: Supporting parents and caregivers in the treatment of children impacted by violence.' *Infant Mental Health Journal 24*, 2, 111–125.

Bancroft, L. & Silverman, J.G. (2002) *The Batterer as Parent: Addressing the Impact of Domestic Violence on Family Dynamics* (1st ed.). Thousand Oaks, CA: Sage Publications.

Barlow, M.R., Goldsmith Turow, R.E. & Gerhart, J. (2017) 'Trauma appraisals, emotion regulation difficulties, and self-compassion predict posttraumatic stress symptoms following childhood abuse.' *Child Abuse and Neglect 65*, 37–47.

Bogat, G.A., DeJonghe, E., Levendosky, A.A., Davidson, W.S. & Eye, A.V. (2006) 'Trauma symptoms among infants exposed to intimate partner violence.' *Child Abuse and Neglect 30*, 109–125.

British Columbia Provincial Mental Health and Substance Use Planning Council (2013) *Trauma-informed practice guide*. Retrieved 05/02/2019 from http://bccewh.bc.ca/wp-content/uploads/2012/05/2013_TIP-Guide.pdf.

Bunston, W. (2002) 'One way of responding to family violence: "Putting on a PARKAS".' *Children Australia 27*, 4, 24–27.

Bunston, W. (2008) 'Baby lead the way: Mental health groupwork for infants, children and mothers affected by family violence.' *Journal of Family Studies 14*, (2–1), 334–341.

Bunston, W. (2013) '"What about the fathers?" Bringing "Dads on Board" with their infants and toddlers following violence.' *Journal of Family Studies 19*, 1, 70–79.

Bunston, W., Franich-Ray, C. & Tatlow, S. (2017) 'A diagnosis of denial: How mental health classification systems have struggled to recognize family violence as a serious risk factor in the development of mental health issues for infants, children, adolescents and adults.' *Brain Sciences 7*, 133, 1–26.

Carpenter, G.L. & Stacks, A.M. (2009) 'Developmental effects of exposure to intimate partner violence in early childhood: A review of the literature.' *Children and Youth Services Review 31*, 831–839.

Casanueva, C.E., Martin, S.L., Runyan, D.K., Barth, R.P. & Bradley, R.H. (2008) 'Quality of maternal parenting among intimate-partner violence victims with the child welfare system.' *Journal of Family Violence 23*, 413–427.

Cohen, L.R., Hien, D.A. & Batchelder, S. (2008) 'The impact of cumulative maternal trauma and diagnosis on parenting behavior.' *Child Maltreatment, 13*, 1, 27–38.

DeJonghe, E., Bogat, G.A., Levendosky, A.A., von Eye, A. & Davidson, W.S. (2005) 'Infant exposure to domestic violence predicts heightened sensitivity to adult verbal conflict.' *Infant Mental Health Journal 26*, 3, 268–281.

Easterbrooks, M.A., Katz, R.C., Kotake, C., Stelmach, N.P. & Chaudhuri, J.H. (2018) 'Intimate partner violence in the first two years of life: Implications for toddlers' behaviour regulation.' *Journal of Interpersonal Violence 33*, 7, 1192–1214.

Edleson, J.L. (1999) 'Children's witnessing of adult domestic violence.' *Journal of Interpersonal Violence 14*, 8, 839–870.

Edleson, J.L., Gassman-Pines, J. & Hill, M.B. (2006) 'Defining child exposure to domestic violence as neglect: Minnesota's difficult experience.' *Social Work 51*, 2, 167–174.

Elliott, D.E., Bjelajac, P., Fallot, R.D., Markoff, L.S. & Glover-Reed, B. (2005) 'Trauma-informed or trauma-denied: Principles and implementation of trauma-informed services.' *Journal of Community Psychology 33*, 4, 461–477.

Fraiberg, S., Adelson, E. & Shapiro, V. (1975) 'Ghosts in the nursery: A psychoanalytic approach to the problems of impaired infant–mother relationships.' *Journal of the American Academy of Child and Adolescent Psychiatry 14*, 3, 387–421.

Holt, S., Buckley, H. & Whelan, S. (2008) 'The impact of exposure to domestic violence on children and young people: A review of the literature.' *Child Abuse and Neglect 32*, 797–810.

Huth-Bocks, A.C., Levendosky, A.A., Theran, S.A. & Bogat, G.A. (2004) 'The impact of domestic violence on mothers' prenatal representations of their infants.' *Infant Mental Health Journal 25*, 2, 79–98.

Jaffe, P.G., Wolfe, D.A. & Wilson, S.K. (1990) *Children of Battered Women*. Newbury Park: Sage Publications.

Kimball, E. (2016) 'Edleson revisited: Reviewing children's witnessing of domestic violence 15 years later.' *Journal of Family Violence 31*, 625–637.

Kitzmann, K.M., Gaylord, A.R. & Kenny, E.D. (2003) 'Child witnesses to domestic violence: A meta-analytic review.' *Journal of Consulting and Clinical Psychology 71*, 2, 339–352.

Labarre, M., Bourassa, C., Holden, G., Turcotte, P. & Letourneau, N.L. (2016) 'Intervening with fathers in the context of intimate partner violence: An analysis of ten programs and suggestions for a research agenda.' *Journal of Child Custody 13*, 1, 1–29.

Letourneau, N.L., Fedick, C.B. & Willms, J.D. (2007) 'Mothering and domestic violence: A longitudinal analysis.' *Journal of Family Violence 22*, 649–659.

Main, M. & Hesse, E. (1990) 'Parents' Unresolved Traumatic Experiences Are Related to Infant Disorganized Attachment Status: Is Frightened and/or Frightening Behavior the Linking Mechanisms?' In M.T. Greenberg, D. Cicchetti & E.M. Cummings (Eds) *Attachment in the Preschool Years*. Chicago, IL: University of Chicago Press.

Malone, J.C., Levendosky, A.A., Dayton, C.J. & Bogat, G.A. (2010) 'Understanding the "ghosts in the nursery" of pregnant women experiencing domestic violence: Prenatal maternal representations and histories of childhood maltreatment.' *Infant Mental Health Journal 31*, 4, 432–454.

Osofsky, J.D. (1995) 'The effects of exposure to violence on young children.' *American Psychologist 50*, 9, 782–788.

Osofsky, J.D. (1999) 'The impact of violence on children.' *The Future of Children 9*, 3, 33–49.

Paul, C. & Thomson-Salo, F. (1997) 'Infant-led innovations in a mother–baby therapy group.' *Journal of Child Psychotherapy 23*, 2, 219–244.

Schechter, D.S., Coates, S.W., Kaminer, T., Coots, T. *et al.* (2008) 'Distorted maternal mental representations and atypical behavior in a clinical sample of violence-exposed mothers and their toddlers.' *Journal of Trauma and Dissociation 9*, 2, 123–147.

Scott, K.L. & Crooks, C.V. (2004) 'Effecting change in maltreating fathers: Critical priniciples for intervention planning.' *Clinical Psychology: Science and Practice 11*, 95–111.

Thomson-Salo, F. & Paul, C. (2014) 'Some Principles of Infant–Parent Psychotherapy.' In C. Paul & F. Thomson-Salo (Eds) *The Baby as Subject: Clinical Studies in Infant–Parent Therapy*. London: Karnac Books.

Tronick, E. & Beeghly, M. (2011) 'Infants' meaning-making and the development of mental health problems.' *American Psychologist 66*, 2, 107–119.

Winnicott, D.W. (1960) 'The theory of the parent–infant relationship.' *International Journal of Psycho-Analysis 41*, 585–595.

CHAPTER 6

'Murder in Their Family'

Making Space for the Experience of the Infant Impacted by Familial Murder

KATHY EYRE, NICOLE MILBURN AND WENDY BUNSTON

Introduction

Ebony was only 2 years old when her father murdered her mother, then shot himself dead in the family home. Ebony was found some hours later, shut in her bedroom, playing with her dolls. Her maternal grandparents took on her care and decided to migrate from Europe to Australia some 24 months later. Ebony's grandparents spoke little of her father, a great deal about her mother and never about the true circumstances of how they died. When one of the authors met Ebony, she was 16 years old. Her grandparents described her as a very studious girl who had many friends. Ebony appeared to have been thriving despite her early, catastrophic loss. Was it coincidence that a week after extensive media coverage of the murder/suicide of a high-profile Melbourne couple, Ebony was admitted to an adolescent mental health in-patient unit? Ebony had attempted suicide and presented as almost catatonic. Might there have been a triggering relationship between the murderous events reported in Melbourne at this time, Ebony's early life experiences and her breakdown in adolescence?

What might happen for infants, now and in their future, when they are exposed to, and impacted by, one family member killing another? This chapter explores our therapeutic work with infants and young children who have experienced murder in their family. Sadly, our involvement with Ebony and other children gives us the confidence to claim that it is imperative to begin making space for the experience of the infant, and that this needs to happen as soon as possible.

This chapter is written in three sections. The first section argues there has been little recognition of the number of infants who have been impacted by the murder of a family member, and notes neurodevelopmental research regarding the infant's possession of early embodied physiological memory. The importance of holding and claiming the infant's experience as paramount in working with families after there has been a murder is highlighted. The second section focuses on current research and what we believe are important practice principles underpinning this work. It also describes the difficulty adult caregivers have in finding words to explain to infants and children what has happened when there has been a murder in their family. The third section goes on to offer examples of our direct work with infants and children.

Section 1: what we know

It is difficult to ascertain just how many infants have been affected by familial murder per year. For example, in Australia, homicide rates, victim, perpetrator and family constellation numbers are recorded. What is not recorded, however, are the numbers of infants in these families (Cussen & Bryant 2015); nor do figures about the infant surface in the collection of other data sets. For example, UK investigations into the experience and background of children who experience bereavements commence only from age 5 onwards (Fauth, Thompson & Penny 2009) and a preliminary analysis of the 1970 British Cohort Study into childhood wellbeing did not identify babies who experienced murder in their families (Parsons 2011). *The World Report on Violence Against Children* published by the United Nations identifies when children themselves are killed but not the incidence or experience for infants and young children when murder occurs for one or more of their family members (Pinheiro 2006). This omission continued in the recent UNICEF report on violence in the lives of children and adolescents (UNICEF 2017), with no mention made of the incidence or impact of familial murder on the infant themselves and their subsequent caregiving experience or circumstances.

Such absences in recording render infants as invisible victims and support our contention that there is a lack in thinking about babies and very young children affected by family murder. These infants must be counted to acknowledge that they are impacted, and significantly, to ensure that appropriate services can be developed and provided. Anecdotally, it appears that infants are over-represented in families who have experienced murder. For example, one of the authors examined the raw data for the service she works for, which provides therapeutic services for child protection clients. She found that of those 365 children who had suffered a violent death in their family during their lifetime, more than half of the young clients were known to be under 5 years of age (Milburn 2018).

The failure to include infants as those impacted in the statistics related to familial murders supports a prevailing, and often mistaken, protective response: that these very young children are too young to remember and/or are better served by not being involved. Current neurodevelopmental research supports the need to recognize and respond to early childhood trauma (Rifkin-Graboi, Borelli & Enlow 2009; Schore 2016; Siegel 2015; Van der Kolk 2014). What we know is that the infant brain reaches 95 percent of its adult size by the time a child is 3 (Perry *et al.* 1995). The infants' neurological development occurs as part of a complex relationship between the child's biology, physiology and genetics, plus the 'outside environment'. The family environment is part of the wider environment for infants, which also includes nutrition, housing, culture and health care. Perry *et al.'s* (1995) pioneering work has helped articulate the profound effect of the 'relational milieu' on the young infant's brain.

We now have scientific evidence that early brain development for all children is interdependent with their early relationship experience (Schneider 2015; Schore 2016; Siegel 2015; Van der Kolk 2014). A good example of how the developing brain is influenced by, and interdependent on, those around us is the research on voice recognition in babies soon after birth. Most newborns demonstrate that they consistently recognize their parents' voice(s) in preference to the voices of strangers (Nugent *et al.* 2012; Stern 2003; Van der Kolk 2014). This suggests that the newborn hears their parents' voices whilst in utero, encodes this sensory experience and is then able to access this encryption within hours of their birth (Stern 2003; Van der Kolk 2014).

Relational health is pivotal to recovery from trauma and can mitigate the effects of adverse events in early childhood (Hambrick, Brawner & Perry 2018). Working from this perspective can be complex and taxing, as adult family members and professional colleagues alike may argue against including the infant in working through the experience.

As mentioned previously, a prevailing, and often mistaken, protective response is that very young children are too young to remember and/or are better served by not being involved.

Section 2: how we think

Our thinking builds on the pioneering work of others around grief, loss and the capacity for very young children to be impacted by the death of loved ones (Bowlby 1980; Furman 1964; Lieberman *et al.* 2003), in particular where that death is as a result of murder (Harris-Hendriks, Black & Kaplan 1993; Lieberman, Ghosh Ippen & Van Horn 2015; Pruett 1979). This approach recognizes that the very young child does develop ideas around death, that sorrow is felt (Bowlby 1980; Furman 1964) and that such loss risks developing into traumatic grief where 'children whose loved ones die under traumatic circumstances develop trauma symptoms that impinge on the children's ability to progress through typical grief processes' (Mannarino & Cohen 2011). Our work with infants and very young children is built on the premise that:

1. The infant has their own subjective experience of the murder, whether they were present or not.

2. Their experience exists whether it is acknowledged and attended to by others, or not.

3. If not acknowledged or attended to, there are likely to be adverse consequences for the infant's capacity to integrate and make sense of their experience.

4. The denial of their experience creates a fundamental disconnect and deceit between reality-as-experienced and reality-as-told.

5. The denial of the infant's subjective reality can be 'crazy-making' (as perhaps was Ebony's experience, described above).

6. The infant is entitled to be an equal participant in the therapeutic work undertaken to address the trauma associated with such a profound event (Harris-Hendriks *et al.* 1993; Paul & Thomson-Salo 2014).

Recovery from trauma

Thinking about and acknowledging the reality of the infant's experience after violence is fundamental to therapeutic approaches for traumatized infants (Bunston 2017; Bunston *et al.* 2016; Lieberman *et al.* 2015; Sadler, Slade & Mayes 2006). Hearing the story and imagining it from the infant's perspective grounds our therapeutic practice by focusing on the infant's sense of reality. We carefully and thoughtfully, but unapologetically, represent the infant's experience in the therapeutic relationship with the family. Leading evidence-based practice in this field proposes that we specifically hold that the infant must have the unspeakable put into words (Lieberman *et al.* 2015). With sensitive therapeutic support, this can be achieved. The task for those of us engaged in this work is to mitigate the risk of aligning with the defensive, egocentric or otherwise inaccurate narrative voice of some family members (Jones & Bunston 2012; Lieberman *et al.* 2015).

An infant-led group intervention, the 'Peek-a-Boo Club ™', was developed in Melbourne, Australia, and provides therapeutic support for infants and mothers impacted by family violence (Bunston, 2006, 2008). A second group, 'Dads on Board ™' has been designed for infants and their fathers post-violence (Bunston 2013b). The therapeutic thrust of both is to create a 'safe enough' space where the 'unthinkable' can be thought about and spoken about in a way that gives the infants permission to have their experience validated. Both these interventions have been evaluated and found to be effective in attempting to both redress and prevent future relational disruptions (Bunston 2006, 2008, 2013b; Bunston *et al.* 2016). Jones and Bunston (2012) note:

> Children live, see, feel, and introject these experiences, whether (they) are talking about the violence or not. The group experience enables each attachment figure's capacities to hold their infant in mind, supporting them to create a congruent and meaningful account in a way that is particular to themselves and their child.

The case example below illustrates the most common dilemma we have found in undertaking this work. This involves the difficulty the adult carer has in finding words to explain the circumstances and enormity of such a horrendous loss for their infant, let alone for themselves:

John (20 months)

John's mother stated that she felt completely at a loss as to how to speak to her son about the murder of the child's father. The toddler would ask 'Where's Daddy?' and wander around their home searching for him, finding him only in photographs. The mother told John that part of Daddy was in an urn on a shelf. How does a toddler make sense of the idea that this is their Daddy? This mother was unable to bring herself to say the word 'dead' and could find no other way to help her son make sense of Daddy's absence. The therapist reflected the child's question of 'Where's Daddy' and gently wondered with the mother about the communication of 'Where's Daddy? I can't find him' and how difficult that was for the child. Hearing and thinking about what the infant or young child may be trying to tell us is critical to our ability to give something truthful and reliable back to them (Morgan 2014).

John, as seen above, was initially given no answer to his question of 'Where's Daddy?' Sometimes infants and young children are given an incorrect answer to this question, such as 'Away on holiday', but the communication of words often doesn't match the tone, intonation and facial expressions accompanying the content of what is being communicated to the child. The child picks up that something big has happened, which often matches their experience of the trauma, and becomes confused. The confusion risks being embedded in their implicit memory and carried within as a powerfully impeding unconscious and unprocessed trauma. Connecting with the infant or child's experience requires us, as the therapist/worker, to being open to what the infant's behaviour and actions may be communicating and possibly reflecting about their underlying thoughts and feelings. This can then aid our ability to support the caregiver's capacity to find words to make sense of what has happened in their communications with the infant.

Section 3: what we do

Contemplating the child's experience, although often painful, is fundamental to working therapeutically with infants or small children who have experienced murder in their family. This requires a safe space and the establishment of a strong therapeutic alliance. This section will focus on the practice of working with infants who have lost family members to familial murder. Common practice issues will be identified and, where possible, case examples used to illustrate some of the ways in which the 'how we think' is actualized in the 'what we do'.

Not always knowing

We have often found there is no complete story about what infants or young children see, hear, smell, taste or feel when they are present during the murder of a family member or members. For therapists/ workers and other family members, this absence is compounded when little is known about what the infant's life was like before the event. Of the multiple tragic consequences of one parent killing the other, there may be the loss of stories, rituals and memories for the infants left behind. There may be no one left who has a good knowledge of the infant's life, their developmental history or the quality of their relationship with either parent. Even in cases where the infant has a surviving parent, another relative or caregiver they may not have been an integral part of the infant's life, and may be unable to fill the gaps in the 'before' story.

Exacerbating the trauma where one parent kills the other is the fact that the infant effectively loses both parents, as few parents who kill avoid prosecution and imprisonment. Being in a position of not knowing is difficult for all concerned, and for those of us who do this work it must suffice to be able to reach a place where we have a 'good enough' understanding. The risk of the therapists and caregivers becoming immobilized or caught up in needing to know can be unhelpful for the child. In situations where the story is not fully known, the infant's experience can be pieced together 'well enough' by close observation of their behaviour. This requires a willingness to consider the behaviour as a communication and may be confronting for caregivers. The following example describes how a foster carer who was being offered therapeutic support managed such a situation.

▨ Isac (3 years) ▨

Isac was found by police next to his mother's body. She had been stabbed repeatedly, but police were unsure whether the boy had witnessed the stabbing or had come to her side some time afterwards. One day, his foster carer gave him a drink of apple and cranberry juice, which he promptly squirted all over the kitchen. He had a very blank look on his face while he did this and became very distressed when his carer tried to stop him. This very thoughtful carer was able to put some words to his experience, saying 'the red stuff was squirting everywhere'. He looked at her and collapsed into her arms, sobbing uncontrollably.

Supporting the caregiving system

The infant is never the only person whose life has been irrevocably changed. As professionals, our work with other family members, and our knowledge and appreciation of their grief is important. We need to get to know them under tragic circumstances. We need to gauge their emotional and mental states, and, overall, the family's functioning. We may also be involved in evaluating who might be most available to help the child's recovery and, conversely, who may hinder this process. Infants develop their sense of self in relation to their caregiving world and are highly dependent on these relationships. As such, success in our therapeutic endeavours is reliant on this work being a shared process.

When family members are in great distress, there is a danger of losing sight of the infant's best interests. Families are often torn apart by such tragedies and see preventing the child(ren) from having contact with (or even talking about) certain members of their family as protective. This is especially so in cases where one parent has murdered the other. We take the stance that imperative to infant's healing is respecting that the infant is the result of both parents and has the right to be supported in making meaning of their individual relationships with both parents. However, we understand that sometimes this is not possible (Fraiberg, Adelson & Shapiro 1975; Lieberman *et al.* 2005; Jones & Bunston 2012).

▪ Bea (4 years) and Jane (2 years) ▪

The mother of Bea and Jane took the life of their brother Roger (5 years) when she was suffering from a psychotic episode. The mother's daughters, who remained in the care of their father, were prevented from seeing their mother as her mental health was assessed and treated. The media took a strong negative stand against the mother, running an emotionally charged and concerted campaign to prevent her from having any contact with the two young girls. Despite understanding the emotional outrage expressed by the media, the children's mental health workers assessed that preventing the girls from having contact with their mother was not aiding their recovery. In the court, they presented evidence about the perspective of the girls, their psychological needs and a therapeutically supported access plan. The plan provided infant-led relational work, which gradually allowed them contact and provided them with good relational repair work with their mother. It was important they be given an ability to see their mother as only their mother, not as a 'monster mother'. The work involved creating a therapeutic alliance with their mother: assessing individually what and how much Bea and Jane needed; providing guidance on how to restore the mother–daughter relationships, only ever to be on a visitation basis; and helping the girls process the loss of Roger and their mother. This all took great courage and effort on everyone's part, and ultimately sitting with some things that might never make sense.

Another complexity faced in this work with infants is how to intervene when their ongoing care is in the hands of family members who cannot bear to know the truth.

▓ Zahir (4½ years), Abraham (3 years) and Rachel (13 months) ▓

Work was undertaken with Zahir, Abraham and Rachel when they saw their father murder their mother. The father, however, had insisted to police that the murderer was the mother's ex-boyfriend. He claimed that this other man had broken into the house while he, the father, was out. The three children were placed with their paternal family. The evidence that the father committed the murder was unequivocal and he was incarcerated. However, the paternal family believed the father was incapable of such an act. This was highly problematic for the children, who were reliving the trauma every time they saw their father and being told by their family that their memories and fears were unfounded.

This type of family denial can lead to an emotional disconnect between the children's experience and what they are told by their carers. Such 'disconnects' can compromise children's mental and emotional capacity for recovery and healing. Furthermore, they impede developing a relationship predicated on trust. Over time, other memories may surface, and the loss of trust can become a further, subsequent relationship trauma.

In this case, it was helpful for us to understand that the father's family members needed to defend themselves against the awful reality and shame of what their beloved family member did. We work from a stronger base if we have the capacity to keep in mind the distress and trauma of the whole caring system. We were able to provide a separate therapeutic space that honoured the children's truth without compromising their relationships with their caregiving environment. This was delicate work supported by our regular supervision sessions. We believe it is only possible to do this demanding work well by accessing ongoing, reflective supervision (see Chapter 2).

Honouring the infant's experience of their relationship with the person who has murdered

It can often be very complex and difficult for professionals and their systems to tolerate and support the relationship between the infant and the parent/attachment figure who has committed the murder. This relationship has its own unique history, which others may not understand, condone or wish to support. However, for the infant it has a meaning and function that we need to know about if possible and need to respect. Attention must always be given to concurrent physical and emotional safety assessments, as in some cases conditions cannot be created that are sufficiently safe for children to see parents who have murdered.

▪ Peter (3 years) and his father

The father of Peter, who had been extremely violent towards his mother over several years and ultimately killed her, also read to him every night, was proud of him and told him he loved him. As adults and professionals, we can quickly assess the dangers such a confusing relationship can have for the toddler over time. Yet, to deny or disregard the toddler's potential love, mixed with fear for his mother, confusion about how Daddy could be both a 'good and bad' father, despite what he has done, replicates a 'killing off' of complex feelings. Those who engage in this difficult work need to be supported to think through how not to expect this toddler to extinguish the feelings, love and need for his father. The work also needs to involve coaching the father to understand the infant's perspective and for him to be utterly vigilant about how he refers to the mother in the infant's presence.

Sometimes our own responses to the abusive violence of a parent get enacted by our need to kill off this relationship. This poses more damage to the infant by needing them to deny what might be their mixed feelings and risks leaving the toddler alone to deal with the enormity of this complex relationship. By respecting their connections, ensuring any contact is safe and supporting the child, in their own time and way, to make sense of their relationship with their parent who kills, we can offer infants far more powerful and healthy healing experiences.

Wider systemic issues

Most infants and young children referred to services after a traumatic death accumulate a large system of professionals, including police, child protection, sometimes (but unfortunately not always) infant or child mental health services, the justice system and sometimes the media. It can be very helpful for at least one person in the care team to understand systems theory so as to consider potential difficulties from a meta-perspective, such as splitting, parallel processes and mirroring of the dysfunction that might be occurring in the family system. As infant mental health workers, we have found that the guidelines outlined below contribute to more productive and cohesive teamwork:

- establishing regular meetings of all professionals

- ensuring the meeting has a chair person and a minute-taker and that the minutes are distributed

- establishing a clear purpose for meeting and providing an agenda for every meeting

- establishing an understanding of professional roles and responsibilities and clear and transparent communication about the limitations of these.

Following these guidelines can help reduce feelings of anxiety and lessen the need for individual workers to defend themselves by developing alliances or encouraging divisions. Similarly, although we are involved with the family for professional reasons, we have emotional responses to our work and acknowledging the emotional toll of such work is important.

Intervening to create safety

In the immediate aftermath of the event it is essential to ensure that the child knows who will care for them. The question may arise as to who should do the telling? Families and systems are in shock, which impedes reflective thinking and the capacity to process. It is not uncommon for professionals involved to be asked to help do the telling. Such requests need careful consideration. It is important to consider whether having a stranger tell children such awful news will hamper the child's ability to hear what is being said. A middle path might consist of joining together with family members to help them to talk to the children, or joining with the authorities who make the request. Police involvement can be a positive. It can be very helpful in some circumstances for small children to be told by police that the person who committed the violent act is locked up and will be punished.

Contact with parents

Any contact with parents who have committed violent crimes needs to be carefully managed to ensure it is in the child's best interests. Communication with the child may be face to face or through emails, letters or phone calls, if not safe or possible in person. In whatever form, it needs to be carefully monitored as physical and emotional safety are paramount. Equally, contact should not be forced when any young child clearly expresses anxiety or fear of the offending parent, but should be managed carefully to prevent traumatic or phobic avoidance. We need to advocate for the psychological needs of the developing child, and not the needs of the parent.

Developing a trauma narrative

It is incredibly important to develop 'trauma narratives' for the infant or child that are factual and use plain language to match the child's level of understanding. These can be built upon as the child matures (Lieberman *et al.* 2003; Lieberman *et al.* 2015). Below are three trauma narratives from our work.

> Dad was so sick and he could not think properly and he got very, very angry. He hurt Mum so badly that the doctors couldn't make her better and her body

stopped working. That's why you can't see her any more. Dad still loves you and is very sad about what he did.

Dad and Mum loved each other once but stopped being friends and had a lot of fights. One day their fighting got so bad that Mum was killed and her body stopped working. Dad felt so bad about this that he stopped his body working too. They didn't want to leave you; they just didn't know how to stop fighting. They are happy that you're living with Grandma and that she'll take care of you.

Mum got so angry that she couldn't find a way to talk about it, and she hurt your brother so badly that his body broke and couldn't be fixed. A special talking doctor has been helping Mum to find her words so that she can talk about her angry feelings. She's much better now and the doctor is helping her make sure it never happens again.

Where possible, the trauma narrative can be developed with family members. However, sometimes families cannot find words to capture what has happened in a way that will make sense to the infant. In these instances, the professional may need to assist in the development of a narrative for what has occurred.

Targeting the intervention

The child is sometimes, but not always, the target of intervention. The reactions of pre-verbal children are not always readily understood, and adults are not always aware of the suffering of infants. A worker can evaluate an infant's reaction by both considered observation, and by questioning other professionals directly involved.

The family is usually a target for intervention, although it is important again to consider the what, when and why of intervention. It is helpful to think of the intervention in terms of a number of episodes; for example: a first episode might take place in the immediate aftermath where the family can be helped to find words for the tragedy. A second episode, not necessarily immediately after the first, might focus on the relationship between the infant and the surviving parent or new caregiver. A third episode might consist of support to resume contact with the offending parent. Each episode should be closely monitored and supervised, and outcomes measured. Sometimes, referrals to other psychotherapy services are important for the adults in the family system.

The immediate aftermath of a murder is not always the time for infant mental health services to become directly involved, but their contribution to the understanding and management of the situation through a professional team is always useful. This approach can very effectively support the professionals already involved, with more intensive services offered when required.

Focusing on outcomes

Interventions should always include a focus on goals and measures of outcomes (i.e. what we are trying to achieve, and how we will know when the work is done). Typically, in our experience, the practitioner's goals for the infant are not always fully met before the family or another agency decides the work is done. The practitioner may need to sit with a number of questions: Was it good enough? If not, is there a way that more work can be done? If it can't happen now, can we lay the groundwork for another episode later?

It is normal for practitioners to wish for everything to be 'back on track' for the infant exposed to tragedy. Maintaining hope is crucial for the work. The sad reality is that the tragedy will remain part of the family's experience in this generation and for generations to come. Sometimes the professional system can become anxious when an episode of clinical care comes to an end. There is often the belief that the children can never move on from the traumatic experience and will require lifelong therapy. This may be more of an expression of the system's unconscious anxiety about the case being closed than that of the child and/or family.

Reflective supervision and support

Vital to this model of therapeutic work is having access to regular, reflective supervision to unpack, recognize, manage our reactions, and 'to understand ourselves as part of not separate to the…process' (Bunston 2013a, p.183). We are just as likely as others to enact unhelpful and defensive unconscious material in our actions and words, with clients as well as other professionals. Reflective supervision operates as our secure and safe space to think about how we feel, act and use ourselves to bind together the messy and confronting aspects of this work (see Chapter 2).

Ending the work

There are differing reasons for bringing therapeutic work to a close: The work may naturally finish; families move; a parent or family member may insist that it is time for the child to move past the trauma, despite the recommendation of the worker; the young child themselves may no longer want involvement. Planned or unplanned, the development and functioning of the infant or child in their relationship environment should remain the primary consideration. Are the caregivers able to help the child keep the memory of the lost person alive in a positive way and assist the child work through traumatic or sad memories when they arise? If outcome measures have been used, is progress evident?

The process of ending is a therapeutic episode in itself, where the original loss of the loved/hated one is reworked in the loss of the therapeutic relationship. It is important, whenever the work closes, to openly discuss with children and families any underlying anxieties they may have about 'going it alone'. The loss of the containing, supporting and reflective space provided by a therapeutic worker can be felt enormously by caregivers. Ending therapeutic work is often an important step in 'putting the past in the past' and moving on into a life where tragedy is not the defining narrative. A therapeutic letter can help mark this ending and recognizes that this is an important step in the healing journey. At the same time, it is important to recognize that as children develop and their cognitive capacities increase, the desire for further therapy to rework their understanding of the trauma may re-present.

A final word

What we learn from infants and their families overcoming trauma stays with us forever and has a profound impact on us professionally and personally. We discover much about resilience and courage—our own and that of the infants and families we work with. We also learn about the importance of authenticity, emotions, relationships and developing coherent and truthful narratives. Providing a safe space for holding the enormity of these complex feelings is crucial to bringing about positive change regardless of what therapeutic work we may be engaged in.

References

Allen, J.G., Fonagy, P. & Bateman, A.W. (2008) *Mentalizing in Clinical Practice*. Washington D.C.: American Psychiatric Publishing Inc.

Bowlby, J. (1980) *Attachment and Loss: Volume 3*. London: Penguin.

Bunston, W. (2006) 'The Peek a Boo Club: Group work for infants and mothers affected by family violence.' *The Signal 14*, 1, 1–7.

Bunston, W. (2008) 'Baby lead the way: Mental health groupwork for infants, children and mothers affected by family violence.' *Journal of Family Studies, 14*, (2–1), 334–341.

Bunston, W. (2013a) 'The group Who Holds the Group: Supervision as a Critical Component in a Group With Infants Affected by Family Violence.' In L.M. Grobman & J. Clements (Eds) *Riding the Mutual Aid Bus and Other Adventures in Group Work*. Harrisburg, PA: White Hat Communications.

Bunston, W. (2013b) '"What about the fathers?" Bringing 'Dads on Board™' with their infants and toddlers following violence.' *Journal of Family Studies 19*, 1, 70–79.

Bunston, W. (2017). *Helping Babies and Children (0–6) to Heal After Family Violence: A Practical Guide to Infant- and Child-Led Practice*. London: Jessica Kingsley Publishers.

Bunston, W., Eyre, K., Carlsson, A. & Pringle, K. (2016) 'Evaluating relational repair work with infants and mothers impacted by family violence.' *Australian & New Zealand Journal of Criminology 49*, 1, 113–133.

Cussen, T. & Bryant, W. (2015) 'Domestic/family homicide in Australia.' Australian Institute of Criminology. Retrieved 17/01/19 from www.aic.gov.au/media_library/publications/rip/rip38/rip38.pdf.

Fauth, B., Thompson, M. & Penny, A. (2009) *Associations between childhood bereavement and children's background, experiences and outcomes*. London: National Children's Bureau. Retrieved 17/01/19 from http://citeseerx.ist.psu.edu/viewdoc/download?doi=10.1.1.584.6512&rep=rep1&type=pdf.

Fraiberg, S., Adelson, E. & Shapiro, V. (1975) 'Ghosts in the nursery.' *Journal of American Child Psychiatry 14*, 3, 387–421.

Furman, R.A. (1964) 'Death and the young child.' *The Psychoanalytic Study of the Child 19*, 1, 321–333.

Hambrick, E., Brawner, T. & Perry, B. (2018) 'Examining developmental adversity and connectedness in child welfare-involved children.' *Children Australia 43*, 2, 105–115.

Harris-Hendriks, J., Black, D. & Kaplan, T. (1993) *When Father Kills Mother: Guiding Children through Trauma and Grief*. New York: Routledge (reprinted 2000).

Jones, S. & Bunston, W. (2012) 'The "original couple": Enabling mothers and infants to think about what destroys as well as engenders love, when there has been intimate partner violence.' *Couple and Family Psychoanalysis 2*, 2, 215–232.

Lieberman, A.F., Compton, N.C., Van Horn, P. & Ghosh Ippen, C. (2003) *Losing a Parent to Death in the Early Years: Guidelines for the Treatment of Traumatic Bereavement in Infancy and Early Childhood*. Washington, D.C.: Zero to Three.

Lieberman, A.F., Ghosh Ippen, C. & Van Horn, P. (2015) *Don't Hit My Mommy!: A Manual for Child–Parent Psychotherapy With Young Children Exposed to Violence and Other Trauma* (2nd ed.). Washington, D.C.: Zero to Three.

Lieberman, A.F., Padrón, E., Van Horn, P. & Harris, W.W. (2005) 'Angels in the nursery: The intergenerational transmission of benevolent parental influences.' *Infant Mental Health Journal 26*, 6, 504–520.

Mannarino, A.P. & Cohen, J.A. (2011) 'Traumatic loss in children and adolescents.' *Journal of Child & Adolescent Trauma 4*, 1, 22–33.

Milburn, N. (2018) 'Working with child survivors following filicide in a family' (data set prepared and presented by M.Frederico, A. Jackson, M.A. Hameed & A. Cox), Berry Street Take Two, Melbourne, Australia. Unpublished report. Retrieved 17/01/19 from www.childhoodinstitute.org.au/sites/default/files/2018-06/Working-with-child-survivors-following-filicide-in-a-family_0.pdf.

Morgan, A. (2014) 'What I Am Trying to Do When I See the Infant With His or Her Parents.' In F.T. Salo & C. Paul (Eds) *The Baby as Subject* (2nd ed.). Melbourne: Stonnington Press.

Morgan, A. (2014) 'What I Am Trying to Do When I See the Infant With His or Her Parents.' In F. Thompson Salo & C. Paul (Eds) *The Baby as Subject: Clinical Studies in Infant–Parent Therapy*. London: Karnac.

Nugent, J.K., Keffer, C.H., Minear, S., Johnson, L.C. & Blanchard, Y. (2012) *Understanding Newborn Behavior and Early Relationships: The Newborn Observations (NBO) System Handbook*. Baltimore, MD: Brookes Publishing.

Parsons, S. (2011) *Long-Term Impact of Childhood Bereavement: Preliminary Analysis of the 1970 British Cohort Study* (BCS70). CWRC working paper. Retrieved 17/01/19 from https://assets.publishing.service.gov.uk/government/uploads/system/uploads/attachment_data/file/181353/CWRC-00081-2011.pdf.

Paul, C. & Thomson-Salo, F. (Eds) (2014) *The Baby as Subject: Clinical Studies in Infant–Parent Therapy*. London: Karnac.

Perry, B., Pollard, R., Blakley, T., Baker, W. & Vigilante, D. (1995) 'Childhood trauma, the neurobiology of adaptation, and "use-dependent" development of the brain: How "states" become "traits".' *Infant Mental Health Journal 16*, 4, 271–291.

Pinheiro, P.S. (2006) *World Report on Violence Against Children*. Geneva: UN.

Pruett, K.D. (1979) 'Home treatment for two infants who witnessed their mother's murder.' *Journal of the American Academy of Child & Adolescent Psychiatry 18*, 4, 647–657.

Rifkin-Graboi, A., Borelli, J.L. & Enlow, M.B. (2009) 'Neurobiology of Stress in Infancy.' In C.H. Zeanah (Ed.) *Handbook of Infant Mental Health* (3rd ed.). New York: Guilford Press.

Sadler, L.S., Slade, A. & Mayes, L.C. (2006) 'Minding the Baby: Mentalization-Based Parenting Program.' In J.G. Allen & P. Fonagy (2006) *Handbook of Mentalization-Based Treatment*: Chichester: John Wiley.

Schneider, W. (2015) *Memory Development From Early Childhood Through Emerging Adulthood*. Cham, Switzerland: Springer International Publishing.

Schore, A.N. (2016) *Affect Regulation and the Origin of the Self: The Neurobiology of Emotional Development*. New York: Routledge.

Siegel, D.J. (2015) 'Interpersonal neurobiology as a lens into the development of wellbeing and resilience.' *Children Australia40*, Special Issue 02, 160–164.

Stern, D.N. (2003) *The Interpersonal World of the Infant: A View From Psychoanalysis and Developmental Psychology*. London: Karnac Books.

UNICEF (2017*) A Familiar Face: Violence in the Lives of Children*. Retrieved 23/07/18 from www.unicef.org/publications/files/Violence_in_the_lives_of_children_and_adolescents.pdf.

Van der Kolk, B. (2014) *The Body Keeps the Score: Brain, Mind, and Body in the Healing of Trauma*. London: Penguin.

CHAPTER 7

Homelessness in Infancy

Finding 'Home' for Babies in Crisis Accommodation after Family Violence

WENDY BUNSTON

It was 7pm and Johan looked terrified. He was surrounded. He had no way out, so, he went in, inside himself. I wondered how many times that day this little 4-month-old baby had needed to do this: retreat inside himself to manage. He had started his day at 7am being awoken by police and child protection workers arriving at the door. They had received an anonymous tip-off that Johan's father was breaching an intervention order which prevented him from having contact with Johan and Johan's mother, Sally. As child protection had assessed that Sally was complicit in breaching the intervention order, they were removing Johan from her care. Johan was taken from the only home he had known and by a worker unfamiliar to him, and then was driven, without his mother, to the local court house. His mother was told to follow them to court if she wished to appeal their decision and she immediately caught a taxi to the court house. Whilst little Johan and his mum caught sight of each other during the day, they were forbidden anything more than a glimpse.

Johan remained in the care of strangers for 4 hours. The judge made her deliberation: If Johan's mother Sally would agree to leave her public housing flat, not have any contact with her current violent partner and go into crisis accommodation, she and Johan could be reunited. This decree meant a different home urgently. They arrived at a crisis accommodation service by taxi that evening. There were forms to fill out and questions to be answered. An exhausted Sally sat patiently as all the rules and conditions of the accommodation service were explained, and Johan cuddled into his mother's lap and found the first moments of peace he had experienced all day. However, these moments were short-lived. Another family staying at the shelter had arrived back after a day out. Johan was suddenly surrounded by more strangers. Two of these were toddlers. They were fascinated by Johan and wanted to say hello, to cuddle him. His defeated mother simply smiled. Johan did not. When the other family left to prepare their dinner, Johan and Sally were ushered out of the warmth of their small shared unit and into the cold evening air. They were taken to select food from the store room. Johan was deposited into a staff member's arms whilst Sally selected food for dinner. After dropping this food back into the refrigerator in their unit, Sally begged for permission to quickly run to the shops nearby to buy cigarettes. Johan protested loudly as he was helped into a borrowed jacket and bundled into his pram. He soon quietened, Sally attributing this to the movement of the pram. Johan's face told another story. He was exhausted, and his eyes, so very close to shutting, remained just slightly open, peering out through two small slits. He remained alert to any further potential dangers. When he and Sally returned, his mother placed him in his carry cot and sat this on one of the two single beds in their allocated room. She stared into space, whilst Johan in his cot remained frozen – his eyes still staring through two small slits. It was 12 hours after his day had started and Johan looked terrified

What constitutes homelessness for the infant? The above account is taken directly from data I collected for research regarding the experiences of infants and their mothers in women's refuges and shelters following family violence (Bunston 2016). Johan and Sally became officially homeless that evening in that they were forced to leave their home and enter crisis accommodation. However, Johan became homeless that very morning when he was taken from his mother. The service system intending to address the safety concerns about Johan in fact took away his emotional home; his mother. For this 4-month-old baby, the sudden and repeated separations from his mother, the bombardment of new smells, noises, child protection procedures, strange people and strange places stretched him and his mother beyond their capacities. Whilst child protection and the police took action to ensure Johan's physical safety, how it was executed caused much undue emotional trauma.

Sally was Johan's safe place, and their relationship was his home. It was his mother's ongoing relationship with his father which made Johan, in the context of family violence, unsafe. Multiple times that day Johan had been taken from his distressed mother. This had equally traumatised Sally. Such demands and expectations on infants create frightening and even terrifying experiences and produce outcomes clearly at odds with the intention to protect the child at risk.

Introduction

Whilst infants and young children make up the highest numbers of children who enter refuges, shelters and crisis accommodation services with their mothers following violence (AIHW 2012, 2018; Shinn 2010), they are the least researched, written or thought about (Bunston 2016). Traditional definitions of homelessness have emerged from research which has focused on single adults, and/or parent(s) who have children who accompany them (Bassuk *et al.* 1996; Buckner, Bassuk & Zima 1993; Chamberlain & MacKenzie 2006; McFerran 2007; Wenzel, Leake & Gelberg 2001). These definitions emphasise the physical deprivation of housing that is deemed appropriate for that society (Bassuk *et al.* 1996; Chamberlain & MacKenzie 2006). Only recently has the experience of children who experience homelessness been of increased interest (Buckner 2008; Edalati, Krausz & Schütz 2016; Gewirtz, Hart-Shegos & Medhanie 2008; Shinn *et al.* 2015). The helping professions' current captivation with early brain development and impacts of trauma on the formation of neural pathways has led to a recognition more generally that the infant is impacted by exposure to familial violence and external adversities such as homelessness (Ahlfs-Dunn & Huth-Bocks 2014; Graham, Fisher & Pfeifer 2013 Margolin & Vickerman 2007; Perry 2001; Schechter & Willheim 2009; Schore 2015; Teicher *et al.* 2003; Van der Kolk 2014). This chapter will contemplate the experience of the infant who is homeless. This will be done through:

- exploring what the infant/young child may experience as home

- presenting the findings of my research with infants in crisis accommodation settings

- considering how the homelessness/housing sector might think about, respond to, and learn from, the infant and their families regarding what they consider to be home

- Discuss how 'infant- and child-led practices' may inform a model of working within the homelessness and crisis accommodation sector.

The chapter will conclude with some suggested ways of directly engaging with infants in crisis accommodation settings and recommending some resources I believe are helpful.

The homeless infant

The housing sector has long held a notion that children only accompany the parent(s) who are homeless and as such are not specifically entitled to, or require, their own sector response (Buckner 2008; Glennen 2011). To conceptualise a sensitive service response to the preverbal infant remains a conundrum for the homelessness sector. This is in part due to a continued preoccupation with the physical provision of housing and services. Australian practitioner Karen Glennen (2011) argues that 'perhaps we need to get rid of the word "home" from the word homelessness; it resonates with many as the bricks and mortar solution'. She goes on to add that we need to:

> Look beyond 'the house' and think about 'the home' for infants. Distinguish between physical structural shelter and emotional shelter and acknowledge the needs for both infants [and] children. Acknowledge the capacity of parents in crisis and support them in parenting as their most important role, and acknowledge the life circumstances of the caregiver but equally recognise and enhance their capacities to be there as mother/carer in the first instance. (Glennen 2011)

Equally passionate about the need to consider the homeless infant, and to recognise their sensate and emotional states, American Anne Smolen (2003) explored the developmental consequences for babies born to mothers who live on the streets. She described these infants as being born into loss, leaving behind the perfect and protected environment of the womb:

> From the beginning of life these babies encounter an unbearable cycle of nowhere to go, no place to call home, no safe sanctuary, only the feeling of 'falling forever'… The infants to whom I am referring are rarely held. Their mothers' gaze looks outward, searching for a place to sleep for the night and concentrating on finding their next meal. These mothers avoid looking into their infants' eyes because they will see only a reflection of their own inadequacy… The babies of whom I am speaking are born into a void. There is no physical structure to provide a stimulus barrier and the mother is unable to perform this function for her child. (p.250)

Smolen (2003) asks how such beginnings impact the infant, and how such loss shapes their developing sense of self and their world, and their capacity for resilience. She captures the need for the creation of an internal home for the infant. This is the home that all infants need – one which is created through relationship.

As I wrote some years ago:

> The physical needs of the infant notwithstanding, it is the warmth of the parent's arms, breath, eyes, face and presence that does more to provide the infant with a sense of safety than does the structure of the building they are living in. (Bunston 2011)

It is acknowledged that infants and children who are not homeless may also feel lost in a void, through a lack of emotional connection and an impoverishment of stable and secure attachments. How the experience of the infant who does not have access to secure physical shelter differs is the additional environmental stresses that being homeless incurs and the increased threat of external dangers.

Researching the experience of the infant in crisis accommodation

Research undertaken for my PhD (Bunston 2016) involved collecting data through conducting Infant Observation sessions with ten infants, and interviewing ten mothers and 13 crisis accommodation staff. Eight women's refuges (shelters) in three countries (Australia, England and Scotland) were visited for the purpose of exploring the experiences of infants in these settings. My research was concerned with the ways in which refuge was provided to, and experienced by, pre-verbal infants who, because of family violence, entered women's refuge accommodation with their mothers. I used an 'infant-led' qualitative research approach, utilising Infant Observation techniques (Bick 1964; Datler *et al.* 2014; Rustin 2009; Urban 2000), and drew on a constructivist grounded theory methodology in its implementation and analysis (Charmaz 2014).

My research found that infants in refuges were not seen as being capable of possessing their own subjective experiences; consequently, they were often lost from view. The provision of refuge to the infant was considered, both by staff and the mother, to be the mother's responsibility. However, the mother's capacities were considerably impacted not only by their current trauma but many past traumas. Direct assistance was only given to an infant experiencing obvious difficulties. This assistance was sought externally, and from specialist workers. In very remote areas, however, such services were not available. In general, adults in the refuges appeared to find it too painful to see or even think of the infant as sentient humans impacted by experiences of trauma. Refuge staff did not lack empathy. Their response appeared more as an absence of thought about the infant; serving possibly to defend themselves from compassion fatigue.

Additionally, there appeared to be little space to allow for the child's feelings towards the now 'absent' father, or to make sense of this complex relationship. Might it be possible to contemplate how fathers or other significant male family members may be recognised as significant attachment figures? Could the inclusion of sensitive male staff members employed in such settings have a role in healing and recovery for those who have experienced male-perpetrated violence?

Each mother interviewed in my research left their violent partner to ensure the safety of their child(ren). Some had remained in relationships with violent partners for a considerable time before falling pregnant or giving birth to their child; this then served as the catalyst for their leaving. This is an important finding, as it speaks to the high motivation these mothers had to protect their infants. How these mothers conceptualised safety did, however, appear to be more associated with physical, rather than emotional, safety. On analysing the data collected from my Infant Observation sessions (see Chapter 2 for some more information on Infant Observation), I found that the majority of, but not all, infants appeared to be most at home when held by their mothers, either in their arms or on their laps. Similarly, when mothers and/or staff engaged with the infant by directly relating to them – looking, talking and responding to them – the infants presented as seeming most settled and safe.

An example of an infant finding home

Aesha (6 months), and her mother, Aahna, had only arrived at this particular women's shelter the previous day. The two of them were attending their first 'house meeting', with around a dozen women present and several infants and toddlers either with their mothers or running around the room. Thus, this dyad encountered approximately 18 unknown individuals, as well as staff. The setting was very noisy, and it seemed hard to distinguish whose baby belonged to whom. Aesha sat in her pram next to her mother. One of the other mothers asked to see Aesha and she was passed along a row of women sitting on a couch. As Aesha was moved from woman to woman, she seemed to progressively withdraw from the noisy space and impinging demands made by each woman as she was passed along, and she gradually shut down, frightened. When she was eventually returned to Aahna, and was placed on her lap, her mother also appeared to have shut down, somewhat, overwhelmed by this boisterous meeting. Aesha sat on her mother's lap but remained staring outwards. Earlier, I had been introduced to the shelter's collective of women and children as a researcher. As I observed this sequence, I wondered if Aesha, given her state of mind, even registered that she had been reunited with her mother. Neither of them looked at or communicated with the other. Following this large group meeting, I again met with this baby and mother in their small bedsit. It was as though Aesha had come alive. Aesha sat in a little baby rocker, and her mother was talking and singing with her as she was cooking their lunch. When Aahna left her cooking and sat down next to her daughter, chatting with her and asking her questions, Aesha's eyes lit up and she became increasingly vocal, as if telling her mother a story.

Aesha found home not in where she was but in who she was with. Her mother looked forward to getting to know the other women in the refuge, despite being initially overwhelmed by the busyness of their first house meeting. Aesha needed a gentler introduction to the house where they had come to live and to remain near her mother. Aesha feeling at home began with her mother and what their relationship offered. This does not preclude being introduced to other residents in a 'house meeting'; rather, we need to work out how this might be done in a way that considers how the infants might experience such spaces. How we reflect on the world from the infant or young child's perspective offers tremendous opportunities to de-escalate their stress and accelerate their healing.

The infant holding hope

Nearly all the mothers in my research felt great hope for their infant and saw that their relationship with their baby provided them with the chance to create a different future. A key conclusion was that greater attention needs to be given to the infant and mother relationship if this hopefulness is to be supported and grown, and their experience of entering refuge/shelter is maximised (Bunston 2016). Furthermore, the infants' subjective experience and their individual needs are important to acknowledge in order to bring about their healing from trauma. It is necessary to recognise that the infants, whilst intimately connected to their mothers are also separate from them.

It is worth noting that none of the women in the study identified themselves as coming from a same-sex relationship. This, as with previous research I have undertaken (Bunston & Glennen 2008) as well as through my ongoing work in the crisis accommodation sector, leaves me to wonder; just where do these women and their children go for support? Are these women not disclosing their sexual orientations for fear of not being welcomed into women's refuges?

Creating home for the infant

We can help build a home for the homeless infant through making them feel safe, or at least safer than they may have previously felt. Being in a motel, a shelter, a house, couch surfing, sleeping rough in a car, irrespective of the environment the infant feels safe when they can actively seek out and/or maintain ready access to a familiar person, and that person responds protectively. Most often this is their mother. But sometimes it is not. Within crisis accommodation services, mothers themselves can remain feeling frightened, and physically and emotionally wounded, and may not be emotionally available to their infant. Whilst some workers may feel hesitant to do so for fear of undermining the mother, infants may need us to step into the breach.

Infants urgently need responsive, nurturing interactions. Not to provide this as professionals is rendering them invisible and, worse still, neither needing nor worthy in and of themselves as requiring attention. The infant is not only entitled to be engaged with, as is any client, but developmentally must also have caring relational reciprocity from others in order to grow their mind, their sense of self and their capacities. All workers, not just those identified as children's workers, need to respond to the infant, talk to them and think about the experience of the infant. They can best do this with and alongside their mother. On some occasions this may not be possible, (e.g. when a mother attends court, or is in hospital). In such instances an infant case management plan would require a very small number of staff, who are ideally already known to the baby, to act as back-up carers. Safety for an infant is by necessity relational and physiological, and felt within the context of a responsive and attuned caregiving environment. In ordinary circumstances, when frightening things happen, the caregiving environment becomes activated, to protect as well as soothe. It is the active use of the relationship which brings calm to quell distress. Donald Winnicott (1960) proposed that maternal care needed to be simply 'good enough', offering regularity of responsiveness, being there for their infant when it really counted and showing attentiveness that enabled the infant to feel that their safe place was with their parent.[1]

Creating an environment of refuge

The need for refuge is as old as time itself (Rabben 2012). This recognises not only our shared humanity, but that we all need access to refuge at times of threat or distress. Finding refuge is not simply physical but, more importantly, a state of mind (Stevenson 2010). There is no other time where access to refuge and protection is so critically important than during the formative stages of infancy (Schechter & Willheim 2009; Siegel 2012; Teicher 2002). In ordinary circumstances the transition to early motherhood and/or parenthood brings much emotional turmoil. Infants and their parents are often finding their way in uncharted waters. Throw in family violence, and the mother may not have the capacity to be the infant's life-line. Furthermore, where do men and their children who may be subjected to family violence take refuge, when their partner (either female or male) is violent?

I began this chapter by giving an account of Johan and his mother Sally's experience of entering the crisis accommodation sector. How might they have had a different experience? Perhaps this might be an example:

> Johan started his day being awoken by the police and child protection workers acting on an anonymous report that he and his mother Sally were living in dangerous circumstances. Johan and his mother were reassured they would remain together, and then they were taken together to court, to await a judge's deliberations. If Johan's mother would agree to leave her housing commission flat, not have any contact with her current violent partner, and go into crisis accommodation, she and Johan could continue to remain together. They arrived at the crisis accommodation shelter by taxi that evening. As they were both exhausted and overwhelmed, staff decided to delay filling out all but the

---

1   See www.youtube.com/watch?v=ZaZkvvB367I for an introduction to the work of Donald Winnicott.

most important forms until mother and baby were more settled. Staff made Johan and Sally feel welcome and enquired about what they might need whilst they were settling into the crisis unit. Age-appropriate toys were made available to Johan, and the ones he chose were his to keep. Making a space for infants can include giving small toys that are not then removed from them. He was noticed and included in all the discussions which helped settle his mother and reinforced that this was a place where people could support her to support him. He cuddled into his mother's lap and together they found the first real moments of peace they had experienced all day. As there was another family staying in their unit shelter, staff decided to protect the dyad from more intrusions and proposed that they keep Johan and Sally's bedroom door shut. Staff explained to the other family sharing the unit that Johan and his mother needed rest and that introductions would be made the next day. Staff asked Sally what she would like from the store room for dinner and arranged to bring this to the unit. Sally begged for permission to quickly run to the shops nearby to buy cigarettes. Staff encouraged Sally to stay resting with Johan after their big day and organised for cigarettes to be purchased. Johan and Sally remained sitting in their warm bedroom, recovering from their distressing day and protected by staff attending to their need for recovery.

This description is the ideal but not always possible. If you think it through, it is not a lot more than what a good enough maternal figure might offer (i.e. some boundaries around protecting the infants, children and mothers from unnecessary stresses, extra support to provide/purchase dinner/cigarettes, and the system having an important healing role as a benevolent container of distress for the infant) if and when parents cannot do it alone. Thinking about the youngest of clients, the infant is, and needs to be, the priority.

Staff need more support to enable them to have the time and space in their minds and in their practice to attend to families' emotional and psychological needs. Staff directly talking with the infant, gently and tentatively wondering aloud what they might be feeling, telling us and wanting from us, can be revelatory for some mothers, even those who are highly distressed.

Reflecting on what is home

Why is this gentle, reflective work so very important to the infant's rapidly developing mind? If continually flooded with powerful chemical reactions as a result of their internal biochemical response to stress, threat and trauma, then the sensitive, still-forming neural pathways are impacted (Schechter & Willheim 2009; Schore 2015). Thinking about the quality of the internal home the baby needs means making concerted efforts to provide for them relationally. An example of this is shown in the re-imagining of how different Johan and Sally's experience of entering crisis accommodation might have been, and how staff can create small relational overtures right from the beginning.

Staff can introduce themselves and have a small toy as a beginning of an exchange. This builds and co-creates a feeling of safety in the infant/family relationship before, during and after working with them. Regular reflective supervision sanctions a time to reflect on staff's feelings about what is needed, and to help calm and regulate themselves emotionally, particularly when families have fled urgent, dangerous and frightening experiences (see Chapter 2). In the process of offering only housing safety, Johan experienced continuous relational disruptions and abandonment by his mother for four long hours, terrifying him rather than tending to him.

Reflective practice privileges the capacity to 'be with' the traumatised infant, child and mother over the compulsion 'to do' things for them (Bunston 2017). Refuges (and shelters) have become more bureaucratised, and the expectations of practical, concrete Key Performance Indicators (KPIs) or outcomes measures seem to be more important than the unique relational opportunities these very early and fragile moments present in aiding the infant/child and mother's recovery. This risks any KPIs achieving lasting success.

Recognising, reflecting on and respecting culture

Aboriginal and Torres Strait Islander women, infants and children, as well as men, are over-represented in Australian homelessness statistics, incarceration, and children in out-of-home care. Cultural respect for First Nations people in Australia has been a long time in coming. The 'ethics of recognition' inherent in acknowledging the 'personal and communal subjectivity for Indigenous Australians' is documented by Australian academic Kay Schaffer (2004). The recognition that the dispossession caused by colonisation, and the 'stolen generation' (where the Australian government deliberately removed children from Aboriginal families) has created enormous inter-generational loss and cultural subjugation (AIHW 2012, 2018; HREOC 1997; Read 1981/2006). Whilst inequalities, such as have been experienced by many indigenous Australians, have had impacts on their ability to care for children, just as many First Nation peoples are more than capable of caring for their own children, children of their kin, and of their community (Kruske *et al.* 2012; Lowell *et al.* 2015).

It may also come as no surprise to learn that women and children from non-English-speaking backgrounds are also over-represented in crisis accommodation services (Chamberlain & MacKenzie 2006; Rog & Buckner 2007; Shinn 2010). Once again, workers need more time, resources and organisational support in educating themselves about the cultural imperatives for each family.

Creating a feeling of home through a model of infant- and child-led practice

Taking an approach that is context sensitive and led by the infant and child's needs sees an emphasis on prioritising the emotional basics, ensuring that the feeling of being at home comes before anything else (Bunston 2017). This approach recognises that the emerging subjectivity and neural development of the infant and child happens in the context of their primary and environmental relationships. What happens now in the infant/child's and mother's relationship is integral to this and shapes the rest of the infant's life. The mother, herself in recovery from relational trauma, needs here-and-now support of her relationship with her child as a template for the rest of their lives together.

An infant- and child-led practice model within crisis accommodation rests on a culture of:

- Reflection – supporting the infant/child and mother to de-regulate down from a traumatic non-thinking (and reactive) state through the provision of a calm, attentive, relational entry into refuge.

- Respect – demonstrating a gentle capacity for discovering the infant and mother's sense of self post-trauma, through following their lead and supporting their child/mother attachment.

- Relationship – using the power of the infant/mother attachment to enhance and strengthen their bond and facilitate the potential healing of the mother's own early childhood traumas.

- Recovery – using a therapeutic infant–child environmental approach to bring emotional/psychological healing to women, mothers and infants and children as a precursor (and/or in tandem) to attending to the physical and practical elements of providing refuge.

(Bunston 2018)

As further noted in Bunston (2018), the model requires:

- *Reflective supervision*: Providing refuge staff with regular monthly reflective (group) meetings facilitated by a clinically trained infant and child mental health practitioner (or equivalent) who is also knowledgeable about family violence.

- *Re-designing outcomes measures:* Measures such as KPIs need to be realigned with training in, and a focus on, relational outcomes. For example, it might include a preliminary assessment of the infant–child and mother attachment and support for a reduction in traumatic responses and increase in relational repair. This can only happen if the model of practice and context allow staff time for reflective supervision and educational support in order to know how to support relationship-building opportunities.

- *Resources*: Adequate staffing levels and resources at high-risk entry points (such as refuge/shelter) for women and mothers who, with their children, seek to leave violent relationships. It also demands more attention in relation to men. How do we create refuges for fathers? How do we employ male staff and recognise the powerful healing that good, healthy male relationships bring?

- *Recognition:* Refuge work is complex, demanding and generally underpaid, but full of committed, hardworking and dedicated staff. Just as the families and individuals who require refuge/ shelter are often hidden from the general community, so too are the staff who work in these settings. Staff who work in a refuge and/or support families within a refuge are most often the 'hidden' players in family violence work. These staff need to be celebrated! We need to provide them with recognition, ongoing access to appropriate professional development and employment structures that support what they do. Refuges/shelters having to exist on 'hand to mouth' budgets promote vulnerable and uncertain employment. The staff are the very scaffold which effectively holds a refuge together, not the building. They need a voice if they are to enable infants/children and mothers to find their voice.

Building home in refuge

Women's refuges (and the subsequent creation of crisis accommodation services for women and children) were born out of the women's movement (Women's-Liberation-Halfway-House-Collective 1976). They have a rich and important history of responding to those in our community who, up until the 1970s, were not recognised by society generally or by governments formally, as deserving of, or even entitled to, refuge as a consequence of men's violence (Schechter 1982; Theobald 2009, 2012). Underestimating what is needed in women's refuges, and privileging a bureaucratic response to the vulnerable infants, children, mothers and women who enter refuge is not good enough (Arnold & Ake 2013; Ferraro 1983; Finley 2010; Lehrner & Allen 2009). Furthermore, exclusion of the provision of services for fathers seeking refuge with their children, and recognising that good men are important for infants' healing, need urgent attention. The sector needs to access the best models of practice on offer, respecting the integrity of the infant and their culture, and attending to the importance of the emotional needs of women, men and transgender people.

Conclusion

The purpose of this chapter has been: to present an 'infant- and child-led' model of practice to facilitate healing within the context of women's refuges and crisis accommodation services; to promote the importance of culture and growing gender diversity in such settings; and, first and foremost, 'to bring the subjectivity of the infant and child alive, and the need to recognise and employ the potential, hope, and healing the new-born brings, as well as the motivation for change' (Bunston 2017, p.7). Infants and small children, as the newest members of families, are the most open to engagement and provide crucial entry points for undertaking complex therapeutic work within 'at risk' families. The quickest route to healing for the highly traumatised mother can often be through the person with whom they have the strongest attachment (albeit it positive or negative): their infant or young child, the one most ready and wanting of engagement with others.

We will now end this chapter with some tips for engaging with the infant and mother–infant relationship:

- Relate to the infant as a person, in their own right, dependent on but also separate to their mother.

- Talk gently and directly with infants, and with mothers about their infants.

- Invite mothers to wonder about their baby's communications.

- Do not overwhelm, do not underwhelm infants; wait to be invited into their space.

- Challenge the impulse to see infants as pre-verbal, and thus not communicative.

- Introduce yourself gently to the infant and ask their permission as well as their mother's permission before approaching them.

- Explain what you are doing when having any physical contact with the infant and why.

- Be relationally present 'with the infant', rather than do things to them.

- Do not underestimate the power of play and playful ways of relating.

- Reflect on what makes for a home in undertaking work with babies who are homeless.

- Make use of regular reflective supervision to think about the infant and their family.

(Bunston 2011)

Acknowledgements

I am indebted to three wise women, my PhD supervisors Professor Margarita Frederico and Dr Mary Whiteside, La Trobe University (Bundoora, Australia), as well as my 'critical friend' Dr Julie Stone, Infant, Child and Family Psychiatrist (Melbourne, Australia) in undertaking and completing my research thesis.

References

Ahlfs-Dunn, S.M. & Huth-Bocks, A.C. (2014) 'Intimate partner violence and infant socioemotional development: The moderating effects of maternal trauma symptoms.' *Infant Mental Health Journal 35*, 4, 322–335.

AIHW (Australian Institute of Health and Welfare) (2012) *Specialist Homelessness Services Collection: First results, September quarter 2011* (Cat.no. HOU 262). Canberra: AIHW.

AIHW (Australian Institute of Health and Welfare) (2018) *Family, Domestic and Sexual Violence in Australia 2018* (Cat. no. FDV 2). Canberra: AIHW.

Arnold, G. & Ake, J. (2013) 'Reframing the narrative of the battered women's movement.' *Violence Against Women 19*, 5, 557–578.

Bassuk, E.L., Weinreb, L.F., Buckner, J.C., Browne, A., Salomon, A. & Bassuk, S.S. (1996) 'The characteristics and needs of sheltered homeless and low-income housed mothers.' *JAMA 276*, 8, 640–646.

Bick, E. (1964) 'Notes on infant observation in psycho-analytic training.' *The International Journal of Psycho-Analysis 45*, 558–566.

Buckner, J.C. (2008) 'Understanding the impact of homelessness on children: Challenges and future research directions.' *American Behavioral Scientist 51*, 6, 721–736.

Buckner, J.C., Bassuk, E.L. & Zima, B.T. (1993) 'Mental health issues affecting homeless women: Implications for intervention.' *American Journal of Orthopsychiatry 63*, 3, 385–399.

Bunston, W. (2011) 'Let's start at the very beginning: The sound of infants, mental health, homelessness and you.' *Parity 24*, 2, 37–39. Retrieved 20/01/19 from http://search.informit.com.au/documentSummary;dn=908022936502962;res=IELFSC.

Bunston, W. (2016) *How Refuge provides 'refuge' to Infants: Exploring how 'refuge' is provided to infants entering crisis accommodation with their mothers after fleeing family violence.* PhD thesis, La Trobe University, Melbourne. Retrieved 20/01/19 from http://hdl.handle.net/1959.9/559171.

Bunston, W. (2017) *Helping Babies and Children (0–6) to Heal After Family Violence: A Practical Guide to Infant- and Child-Led Practice.* London: Jessica Kingsley Publishers.

Bunston, W. (2018) 'Using an "infant and child led" model of practice to facilitate healing within the context of women's refuges.' *Parity 31*, 1, 25–28.

Bunston, W. & Glennen, K. (2008) '"BuBs" on board: Family violence and mother/infant work in women's shelters.' *Parity 21*, 8, 27–31.

Chamberlain, C. & MacKenzie, D. (2006) *Counting the Homeless.* Australian Analytic Census Program, Australian Bureau of Statistics. Retrieved 20/01/19 from www.ausstats.abs.gov.au/Ausstats/subscriber.nsf/0/57393A13387C425DCA2574B900162DF0/$File/20500-2008Reissue.pdf.

Charmaz, K. (2014) *Constructing Grounded Theory* (2nd ed.). London: Sage Publications Ltd.

Datler, W., Datler, M., Hover-Reisner, N. & Trunkenpolz, K. (2014) 'Observation according to the Tavistock model as a research tool: Remarks on methodology, education and the training of researchers.' *Infant Observation 17*, 3, 195–214.

Edalati, H., Krausz, M. & Schütz, C.G. (2016) 'Childhood maltreatment and revictimization in a homeless population.' *Journal of Interpersonal Violence 31*, 14, 2492–2512.

Ferraro, K.J. (1983) 'Negotiating trouble in a battered women's shelter.' *Journal of Contemporary Ethnography 12*, 3, 287–306.

Finley, L.L. (2010) 'Where's the peace in this movement? A domestic violence advocate's reflections on the movement.' *Contemporary Justice Review 13*, 1, 57–69.

Gewirtz, A., Hart-Shegos, E. & Medhanie, A. (2008) 'Psychosocial status of homeless children and youth in family supportive housing.' *American Behavioral Scientist 51*, 6, 810–823.

Glennen, K. (2011) 'The homeless infant.' *Parity 24*, 2, 35–36.

Graham, A.M., Fisher, P.A. & Pfeifer, J.H. (2013) 'What sleeping babies hear: A functional MRI study of interparental conflict and infants' emotion processing.' *Psychological Science 24*, 5, 782–789.

HREOC (Human Rights and Equal Opportunities Commission) (1997) *Bringing them home: Report of the national inquiry into the separation of Aboriginal and Torres Strait islander children from their families.* New South Wales: HREOC Commission.

Kruske, S., Belton, S., Wardaguga, M. & Narjic, C. (2012) 'Growing up our way: The first year of life in remote Aboriginal Australia.' *Qualitative Health Research 22*, 6, 777–787.

Lehrner, A. & Allen, N.E. (2009) 'Still a movement after all these years?: Current tensions in the domestic violence movement.' *Violence Against Women 15*, 6, 656–677.

Lowell, A., Kildea, S., Liddle, M., Cox, B. & Paterson, B. (2015) 'Supporting aboriginal knowledge and practice in health care: Lessons from a qualitative evaluation of the strong women, strong babies, strong culture program.' *BMC Pregnancy and Childbirth 15*, 19, 1–12.

Margolin, G. & Vickerman, K.A. (2007) 'Posttraumatic stress in children and adolescents exposed to family violence: I. Overview and issues.' *Professional Psychology: Research and Practice 38*, 6, 613.

McFerran, L. (2007) *Taking Back the Castle: How Australia Is Making the Home Safer for Women and Children.* University of New South Wales, Australian Domestic & Family Violence Clearinghouse.

Perry, B.D. (2001) 'The Neurodevelopmental Impact of Violence in Childhood.' In D. Schetky & E.P. Benedek (Eds) *Textbook of Child and Adolescent Forensic Psychiatry.* Washington, D.C.: American Psychiatric Press, Inc.

Rabben, L. (2012) *Give Refuge to the Stranger: The Past, Present, and Future of Sanctuary.* Walnut Creek, CA: Left Coast Press.

Read, P. (1981/2006) *The Stolen Generations.* NSW: NSW Department of Aboriginal Affairs.

Rog, D.J. & Buckner, J. (2007) *Homeless families and children.* Proceedings of the Toward Understanding Homelessness 2007 National Symposium, Washington, D.C.

Rustin, M. (2009) 'Esther Bick's legacy of infant observation at the Tavistock–some reflections 60 years on.' *Infant Observation 12*, 1, 29–41.

Schaffer, K. (2004) 'Narrative lives and human rights: Stolen generation narratives and the ethics of recognition.' *Journal of the Association for the Study of Australian Literature 3*, 5–26.

Schechter, D.S. & Willheim, E. (2009) 'The effects of violent experiences on infants and young children.' In C.H.Z. Jr (Ed.) *Handbook of Infant Mental Health.* New York: The Guilford Press.

Schechter, S. (1982) *Women and Male Violence: The Visions and Struggles of the Battered Women's Movement.* Cambridge, MA: South End Press.

Schore, A.N. (2015) *Affect Regulation and the Origin of the Self: The Neurobiology of Emotional Development.* New York: Routledge.

Shinn, M. (2010) 'Homelessness, poverty, and social exclusion in the U.S. and Europe.' *European Journal on Homelessness 4*, 1, 21–44.

Shinn, M., Samuels, J., Fischer, S., Thompkins, A. & Fowler, P. (2015). Longitudinal impact of a family critical time intervention on children in high-risk families experiencing homelessness: A randomized trial. *American Journal of Community Psychology, 56*, 3–4), 205–216.

Siegel, D.J. (2012) *Developing Mind: How Relationships and the Brain Interact to Shape Who We Are* (2nd ed.). New York: Guilford Press.

Smolen, A.G. (2003) 'Children born into Loss: Some developmental consequences of homelessness.' *Journal for the Psychoanalysis of Culture and Society 8*, 2, 250–257.

Stevenson, A. (Ed.). (2010) *New Oxford American Dictionary* (3rd ed.). New York: Oxford University Press.

Teicher, M.H. (2002) 'Scars that won't heal.' *Scientific American 286*, 3, 68–75.

Teicher, M.H., Andersen, S.L., Polcari, A., Anderson, C.M., Navalta, C.P. & Kim, D.M. (2003) 'The neurobiological consequences of early stress and childhood maltreatment.' *Neuroscience & Biobehavioral Reviews 27*, (1–2), 33–44.

Theobald, J. (2009) 'Constructing a feminist issue: Domestic violence and the Victorian refuge movement.' *Parity 22*, 10, 12–14.

Theobald, J. (2012) 'Collaboration, confrontation and compromise.' *DVRCV Quarterly, Autumn*, 1, 9–12.

Urban, E. (2000) 'Infant observation, experimental infant research and psychodynamic theory regarding lack of self/other differentiation.' *Infant Observation 3*, 2, 64–79.

Van der Kolk, B. (2014) *The Body Keeps the Score: Brain, Mind, and Body in the Healing of Trauma.* London: Penguin.

Wenzel, S.L., Leake, B.D. & Gelberg, L. (2001) 'Risk factors for major violence among homeless women.' *Journal of Interpersonal Violence 16*, 8, 739–752.

Winnicott, D.W. (1960) 'The theory of the parent–infant relationship.' *International Journal of Psychoanalysis 41*, 585–595.

Women's-Liberation-Halfway-House-Collective (1976) *HERSTORY of the Halfway House 1974–1976.* Melbourne: Sybylla Cooperative Press Ltd.

Handy resources

Refuge for Babies in Crisis Manual: www.dvrcv.org.au/sites/thelookout.sites.go1.com.au/files/Refuge%20for%20Babies%20Manual%20FinalWEB.pdf or

Watch, Wait, Wonder: http://shop.savethechildren.org.au/shop/item/watch-wait-and-wonder-dvd-only

Still Face Experiment: www.youtube.com/watch?v=apzXGEbZht0

Zero to Three: https://www.zerotothree.org

World Association of Infant Mental Health: https://waimh.org

Safe From The Start: www.salvationarmy.org.au/safefromthestart

PART 3

Culture and the Infant

CHAPTER 8

Self-Determining Support for Indigenous Children in Australia

The Bubup Wilam Case Study

ANGIE ZERELLA, LISA THORPE, LUELLA MONSON-
WILBRAHAM AND KERRY ARABENA

Introduction

Bubup Wilam, meaning 'Children's Place' in Woiwurrung language (the Indigenous Australian language spoken by the Wurundjeri people of the Kulin Nation[1]), is the name of an Aboriginal Child and Family Centre in Melbourne, Australia. Bubup Wilam supports the education, health and wellbeing of about 100 Aboriginal children each year, aged 6 months to 6 years, and their families, many of whom face challenges and complexities in their everyday lives. The centre emphasises a strength-based approach to learning and wellbeing that promotes high expectations and supports the self-determination and aspirations of the children and families it works with and learns from.

Bubup Wilam ensures that Aboriginal identity is embraced, and the children and families have a strong sense of who they are, where they come from and to whom they belong. Using both Aboriginal and mainstream pedagogical approaches, Bubup Wilam supports children to be strong in 'both ways' – strong in their Aboriginality and strong in mainstream skills and knowledge – and thus well prepared for life beyond Bubup Wilam.

---

1   The Kulin Nation is the collective title of the five language groups which are made up of the traditional owners of the land in the Port Phillip region of South Central Victoria, Australia.

This chapter outlines the practices used by Bubup Wilam to build a place for Aboriginal children where they can grow strong, make choices and develop relationships. The rights-based principles which guide this work will be explained and illustrated through examples taken from the work with the children themselves. These rights include: the right to self-determination; the right to grow in culture; the right to know who you are; the right to be calm; the right to speak, be heard and understood; and the right to be strong.

Building strengths

Longstanding, historical transgenerational trauma and ongoing institutional racism within Australia increase the likelihood that Aboriginal and Torres Strait Islander children and their families deal with complex trauma and vulnerabilities (SCRGSP 2016). These include issues such as family violence, suicide and self-harm, child protection notifications, children in out-of-home care, housing crises, incarceration, drug and alcohol challenges and unemployment.

The Australian government is struggling to address the life disparities or 'gap' between non-Indigenous and Aboriginal and Torres Strait Islander peoples, referencing Indigenous children as 'the most vulnerable group of children in Australia' (COAG 2009). Data from the Australian Early Development Census[2] also reveals that 'Indigenous children in 2015 were twice as likely as non-Indigenous children to be developmentally vulnerable in one or more social, health and educational domains, and up to four times more likely to record difficulties in the areas of language and cognition' (DET 2016).

While the children and families with whom we work face many significant challenges, the moment they walk through Bubup Wilam door we see them as strong and resilient. Challenges are addressed through a strengths-based lens, where the aim is to work through the trauma, not be defined by it. This allows the strength of children and families to shine.

Bubup Wilam operates from a philosophy of Aboriginal community control, decision making and self-determination through employing

---

2   The Australian Early Development Census (AEDC) is a nationwide data collection of early childhood development across five developmental domains at the time children commence their first year of full-time school. (Results of 'developmentally vulnerable' are those who measure in the lowest 10 per cent.) See www.aedc.gov.au/about-the-aedc.

an Aboriginal CEO, Aboriginal staff and an Aboriginal board of management. Aboriginal self-determination serves as the heartbeat of our practice and is evident in all that we do. Bubup Wilam's curriculum states that self-identity, self-esteem, self-belief and self-regulation all underpin the bigger self of self-determination.

Self-agency

Young Aboriginal children and their families are the key stakeholders at Bubup Wilam, and it is their involvement in making their own choices and setting their own goals which is seen as the indicator of success. Martin (2017) explains that the voices of young Indigenous children and their families in the early childhood education space are often displaced by a narrative of deficits, not achievements, where inadequate development, homes or parental skills are seen to predominate. The things children and parents see as important or special about early education are often not recognised.

Fleer (2004) explains that 'families having a voice' means a dismissal of Aboriginal stereotyping, an enabling of agency and sense of power as involved and respected knowledge-holders, and the building of trust through collaborative processes. Children and families have a strong voice at Bubup Wilam and are positioned as holders of diverse and valuable knowledge. This approach aligns with international evidence (Preston *et al.* 2011), incorporating strategies that privilege Aboriginal pedagogy, promote language and culture, provide qualified Aboriginal teachers, and empower parents and community to participate in governance and everyday activities.

An additional core element of Bubup Wilam's approach is a focus on social justice, and advocacy for the rights of Aboriginal children and their families. Hard, Press and Gibson (2013) argue that 'intentional' early childhood leadership[3] can generate socially just educational spaces that redress inequality. The Aboriginal and non-Aboriginal leadership at Bubup Wilam melds two worlds of knowledge to 'embrace diversity and actively confront inequality in order to change the traditional

---

3   Hard, Press and Gibson (2013) describe 'intentional leaders' as courageous decision makers who work collaboratively towards collective goals and challenge assumed knowledge, power relations and practices of oppression.

constructions on education and afford access and opportunity' (Hard, Press & Gibson 2013).

Building relationships

Bubup Wilam has developed an innovative award-winning[4] training model to deliver the Certificate III and Diploma of Early Childhood Education and Care on site. The training is designed and delivered by Aboriginal people who have worked through their own trauma, putting them in a unique position to support the healing journey of others. The training also aims to build workforce participation and sustainability, and to develop the career goals of Aboriginal people.

This approach is not task-focused but is responsive to needs and building relationships. Time is made available to get to know people and respond to any situation which may arise. The centre offers a non-judgemental safe space where people are respected and given honest responses.

Having rights

Having 'rights' may be something non-Indigenous peoples can take for granted. Our 'rights-based' principles are presented below, and while not the sum of our work, they give insight into the values that underpin our work. A holistic approach ensures that the principles do not act in isolation; rather they support interrelated ways of learning and connecting, and 'facilitate the goal of wholeness to which Indigenous knowledge aspires' (Battiste 2002).

Right to self-determination

Self-determination is about ensuring the children's rights to be strong in identity, to be in control of themselves and to be key leaders in the organisation and as future Elders and leaders of their communities. Bubup Wilam is supporting children and families to advocate for equity, social justice and their distinctive rights as the First Peoples of Australia. Changing the future for our children means gifting them

---

4   Bubup Wilam's training model was awarded the best in the state of Victoria and one of the top three in the national Australian Medium Employer of the Year category in 2016.

with the knowledge and skills for making their own choices and striving to realise their own dreams. Instilling our children with a belief in self-determination helps them grow up knowing that they can do anything, voice their needs and access things as others do.

■ 'These children get it' ■

Aboriginal advocate Clinton Pryor, known as the Spirit Walker, recently visited the centre while walking in protest at the injustices faced by Indigenous Australians. His long Walk for Justice began in Perth, Western Australia, and he was heading to Australia's capital city, Canberra, to speak to the Prime Minister, stopping off at Aboriginal communities and gathering additional messages along the way.

The children were very excited to meet Clinton, as they had been following his journey; and as advocates for their people and themselves, they understood what he was walking for. The children drew pictures and gave messages to Clinton to take with him, including: 'Our Elders should be the boss of the country', 'Don't put our people in jail', and 'Tell the truth'.

One of our children drew a picture of people behind bars and outside of this she drew police. She showed her picture to Clinton and quite forcefully told him to tell the Prime Minister that he needed to stop putting our people in jail, and that the Elders were the boss of the country, not him. 'Our Elders know what our country needs', she said.

Clinton was amazed at all he heard and said to the staff: 'These children get it.' In response to the children's strength and advocacy, he presented them with a boomerang that he had made in his country, along with a pair of shoes he had walked in. He told the children that his Elders were teaching him about how hard things were and that we always need to respect the hard fight of our Elders and continue the fight for them. The children then invited Clinton to march with them outside the building. He got out his Spirit Walker banner and joined the children in an impromptu demonstration march, shouting out 'It always was, always will be, Aboriginal Land!'

Right to grow in culture

The Bubup Wilam model does not teach but surrounds the children with their culture. Opportunities are constantly provided for children to co-create environments and systems of care that nurture culture as an experience, an aspiration, an identity and a way of communicating about how to respectfully engage with the world.

▓ 'Culture sings to them, and it shows them their heartbeat' ▓

All the children participate in the daily ritual of the flag-raising ceremony and take turns to collect the flag from a display box, carrying it over their shoulders ensuring that it doesn't touch the ground. Another group of children call the community at Bubup Wilam to the ceremony by chanting 'Flag raising, flag raising', while playing clapsticks. Even children who are not yet verbal hum and attempt to say the words as they join in the chant, and then join in the 'Acknowledgement of Country' that follows, to show our respect to the traditional Aboriginal owners of the land.

Recently, visitors came to tour Bubup Wilam and a 3-year-old child who is relatively new to the service wanted to support staff in taking the tour. When she went past the flag display box, she noticed that the flag had not yet been raised. She quickly grabbed the flag, put it around her neck without it touching the ground and grabbed a pair of clapsticks. She then requested that the door to the kindergarten room be opened for her and walked in on her own, playing her clapsticks and chanting 'Flag raising, flag raising'. She then acknowledged country for everyone. This is so important for her as she lives with her non-Aboriginal father and he brings her to Bubup Wilam for her connection to her identity. He is so proud of her and how much she is teaching him about who she is.

On another occasion a Wiradjuri artist made and presented the children with clapsticks. He stayed for the morning, teaching them to use them, beginning a learning journey of how clapsticks work and where they are from. The children were shown how to get different sounds out of the clapsticks and how to hold them. Culture is an engagement of all the senses. The beautiful smell of the wooden clapsticks stayed on their hands the entire day. After he left, the children spoke about having to respect these clapsticks 'as they are a special gift from Wiradjuri country'. We found a special basket to put them in. The children were then teaching each other about how to respect and use them, remembering they sound like their heartbeat, and that you need to hold them softly, so they can make the best sound. Playing clapsticks is an opportunity for the children, and the Aboriginal artist who guided them, to live and revitalise culture.

Everyone also takes part in the weekly smoking ceremony, which brings strength and healing to the children. This takes place outside in our sacred space, where there is a permanent fire-pit area. Eucalyptus leaves are collected and placed in the fire-pit, where they are lit to create smoke. The children then move around the fire, bringing the smoke into themselves by drawing it up with their arms. A fire is also often lit outside for both warmth and cooking. The fire is calming and nurturing for the children and it is important that they know how to be safe around fire, as it is a part of their cultural life.

Being on country is also an important part of a child's right to grow in culture, as it ensures that children have a direct opportunity to learn about respecting the country they are on and their custodianship rights and responsibilities to look after it. Bubup Wilam's 'Connection to Country' program enables the 3- and 4-year-old children to be in a bushland space for five hours each week to explore and build their own unique relationship with Aboriginal land. They learn about the foods and medicines that grow in the bush and are free to explore and connect with the land, test themselves and take risks.

▓ 'Looking after the land and each other' ▓

The children have been learning about Bunjil, the Wedge-Tailed Eagle, who is the spirit creator of Wurundjeri land, the land the children are on. They have been creating clay sculptures, drawing, reading stories and acting them out.

When out on country the children remind each other when needed: 'You are not respecting Bunjil because you are not respecting the land'; 'we need to do the right thing on this land for the Wurundjeri people and for Bunjil'; 'remember Bunjil is watching us to make sure we are looking after the land.'

We have one child who is Wurundjeri, and when one of the children dropped rubbish on the ground during lunch another child got up and went over to them and said: 'You are not respecting J's country. This is her land, you know, and you are not looking after it for her.'

On another visit the children also discussed not bringing anything back from country because it belongs to that land and should not be removed. On returning to Bubup Wilam that day, one of the children went outside and grabbed a large stick that was on the ground. She painted it red, yellow and black like the Aboriginal flag. She then told her educator: 'This is a stick from

Wurundjeri country. It needs to stay here at Bubup Wilam because it belongs to this land and can never be taken away.' We hung the stick up in our foyer with her words beside it to respect her and showcase her knowledge and respect for country.

Families are owners and participants in all of that Bubup Wilam offers, and are deeply engaged in the service, including as teachers of culture.

Caring across generations

A grandfather of one of the children taught the children a song for their graduation ceremony to celebrate their achievements at the centre before they leave to start school. The children could barely wait for him to come and perform with them; and his granddaughter said: 'This is my poppy' and proudly showed him off to the other children. The children recorded the song in a studio and were proud to know that the song was originally written for some of their parents when they were young. The parents became very emotional on receiving their children's recording and seeing their pride as they sang these songs.

Bubup Wilam's philosophy of instilling and strengthening children's strong sense of Aboriginal identity is about knowing who you are, who you are connected to, and who your mob is. Your mob is the land you are from, and the group or nation of people of that land which you are connected to by ancestry. Every child has a wooden block with their name and the name of their mob on it, which they carry from room to room. Each room is named after one of the five Kulin Nations[5] that are closest to the centre. An Indigenous language map of Australia, with a picture of each child, is in every room and used as a teaching tool. Outside the rooms, for all to see, is a large map with photographs of all the children and string connecting them to where they are from. Children learn the colour of their mob, and, together with their family, can see the connections our Aboriginal children have across Australia.

---

5   The five language groups of the Kulin Nations are Boonwurrung (Boon-wur-rung), Dja Dja Wurrung (Jar-Jar-Wur-rung), Taungurung (Tung-ger-rung), Wathaurung (Wath-er-rung), and Woiwurrung (Woy-wur-rung) commonly known as Wurundjeri.

'Pride in who she is and how she is connected'

The children are very proud of who they are and who they are connected to. On Remembrance Day we spoke to the children about the Aboriginal soldiers who fought for us in the First World War. One child's great-great-great grandfather fought in the war and she had great pride in learning about this and learning about him. As a part of her learning, she painted an amazing picture that showed him and his friends all holding Aboriginal flags to respect him as an Aboriginal man, and then underneath painted five poppies that showed his respect for the non-Aboriginal soldiers who fought with him.

The picture was a remarkable depiction of solidarity and showed her pride in who she is and how she is connected. She proudly stated that her great-great-great grandfather was the same mob as her and he fought for their land. This developed an even deeper connection for her and the struggle for her people's rights – a legacy that she already talks about continuing.

Right to be calm

It can be taken for granted by many people in mainstream society that feeling calm, or returning to a state of calm after stress, is a common experience. Children living with ongoing trauma and chaos cannot simply self-regulate, as their brain's normal state is one of alarm (Perry 2006). At Bubup Wilam, we purposefully create a state of calm to reduce stress, so children can be available to learn new things, and develop an embodied memory of what it feels like to be calm and access this bodily memory when life becomes chaotic. Providing calm relational experiences aims to build new neural pathways that regulate emotions in a healthy way (Siegal 2012), which is especially important during the first 1,000 days of life during early brain development (Schore 2015; Shonkoff 2004).

This is more than just a matter of providing an environment to be calm; it is a right to experience what it is like to be calm that underpins our work. We teach children to self-regulate, broaden their emotional range and make their own choices on how to best nurture themselves in an environment that is not overstimulating or overwhelming.

■ 'She is learning empathy and self-regulation'

It took a long time for one of our children to transition from the Boon Wurrung (infant) room into the next room when she turned 2. We wondered if this was due to the connection she had with her educators or whether it was due to her comfort in being with the younger children. As an infant she seemed to understand when other babies became distressed, alerting an educator if they were not getting to a baby who needed them quickly enough.

Now she is 4 years old and still likes to go back to the Boon Wurrung room, either for a short visit or for the day. She is given the freedom to go there and care for the babies when she needs to. She was visiting the room when visitors took a recent tour of Bubup Wilam, and when asked what she was doing in the infants' room she stated: 'Oh I'm working in here today, and they need my help. I'm working in the babies' room today.' She was sitting with a baby, feeding it at the time.

Bubup Wilam supported this little girl to develop at her own pace, and her empathy for others provided her with a sense of belonging and purpose. She found pride in being allowed to have some responsibility and being given choices. The babies' room offered her a place where she found nurturing, learnt to read herself and know the days when she felt she needed some quiet time, aiding her own capacity for self-regulation.

The rooms at Bubup Wilam are deliberately decorated with muted colours and minimal stimuli to help establish calm and self-regulating processes. Additionally, a high staff-to-child ratio gives educators time to help children learn to slow down and support children to work through situations and emotions. The children are learning that emotions are not bad things and that it is okay not to be happy sometimes, as well as learning that there are different ways to deal with disappointment.

When a child becomes overwhelmed and can no longer self-regulate their emotions, educators step in and support the child to take deep breaths, offer physical comfort by rubbing their arms or legs (or cuddling younger children), and speak softly to let them know they are safe and that we will remain with them until they feel calm. If they are physically lashing out, we carry them safely to our Zen room, where adults remain with the child and talk them through the self-regulation process. Once calm, we talk to the child and, together, develop strategies for the future and remind them of these strategies in their everyday play.

Right to speak, be heard and understood

Some children at Bubup Wilam experience expressive and receptive language challenges and have been assessed by mainstream professionals as having language or developmental delays. This led us to question how such standardised thinking was applied to all children and if it was truly representative of the way Aboriginal children communicate. While a speech therapist is on site to support children with serious language delays, the therapist also works collaboratively with educators and families to maintain the right of children to communicate in their own way. Western communication relies largely on verbal communication, which is different to Aboriginal ways of communicating and learning (Yunkaporta 2009) and does not capture the nuanced ways our children express themselves and effectively get their messages across.

This led Bubup Wilam staff to develop their own 'Ethics of Communication' program. This respects Aboriginal children's right to be heard, rather than simply measured, and supports them to find their own voice and gain the communication skills needed to help them transition to school. This involves a child's right to communicate: the right to speak, the right to be heard, the right to be understood and the right to understand.

Children need to feel safe, secure and supported and to know that adults will respond to their needs when they request it. This applies especially to children who carry trauma or live in chaotic environments. When babies cry, for example, they are responded to immediately and priority is given to enabling their feelings to be understood. A staff member will sit with them and support them in finding their own way back to feeling calm.

Art as a form of communication is an integral part of the Bubup Wilam program. Children can express themselves and their story through their art, and their understanding becomes visible to others.

'Telling her story through art'

A 6-year-old child struggled to communicate verbally and required extensive speech intervention. Due to this, her cognitive abilities were often underestimated. Through art, she found a medium to express her knowing about the world, and to showcase her incredible and well-developed conceptual understanding.

After the children had been engaging in a long-term learning encounter regarding the invasion of Australia by Captain Cook in 1788, this child wanted to do a drawing. She was having an emotional day and things were overwhelming for her. Art for her was not only a form of communication but also a way for her to self-regulate her emotions. We took her into a quiet space on her own and she was given a large canvas to use to express herself.

Over time she worked on her painting when she needed time out and didn't give up until it was completed. She began by drawing a large circle and inside drew many shapes which then became Aboriginal flags. She drew two horizontal lines across from each side of the circle to make the whole picture an Aboriginal flag. On the right she drew another shape with dotted lines leading to the larger circle; and on the left she wrote 'Aboriginal Land'.

She explained her art work to her educators. The circle in the middle represents her world. The flags represent the many mobs in Australia, all under one flag as it is all Aboriginal land. The shape in the right corner was the *Endeavour* (Captain Cook's ship), and the dotted lines represent his voyage to Australia and back to England. In the bottom of the ship are children – they are the children he had stolen from their families.

She said: 'Captain Cook came to steal our land and he stole the children and took them away. But he really didn't steal our land because it's still here and it's still ours – it always was and always will be Aboriginal Land!'

Right to be strong

Mainstream data and narratives about Aboriginal peoples are largely negative and focus on what is lacking and fails, rather than focusing on the strengths and values that Aboriginal people bring to society (see Fogarty *et al.* 2018). Bubup Wilam is a strong, visible face of the Aboriginal community. It is not entrenched in a negative welfare context; it is situated in community, in a beautiful building architecturally designed to meet the needs of the centre.

When children have strong culture, and when they are nurtured and free to feel calm, they have a strong base from which to learn. Children are supported to define and protect their own boundaries and develop positive ways of being in relationships that can carry them into adulthood, where they do not need to please others at the expense of their own rights, or demand things of others that disrespect the rights of others.

Children leave Bubup Wilam knowing who they are and who they are connected to, and proud and strong in their Aboriginal identity. Our transition to the primary school program, in partnership with families and local schools, is about building skills and self-belief in children that supports them to be ready for school. School principals and teachers report back to Bubup Wilam that our children are excelling at school, that they are starting school on a par with, or ahead of, their peers, and that they are leaders, innovators and keen, self-directed learners.

▰▰ 'Strong Aboriginal children with strong voices for change' ▰▰

One of our children, who now attends a Catholic school, didn't think it was right that the school prayed to God every day but didn't know how to acknowledge the country they were on. He took it upon himself to facilitate an Acknowledgement to Country every day in the classroom before prayer. He also gets up every Monday in front of the whole school and acknowledges country at the full school assembly. This child is 5 years old!

His mother also shared that when he was saying his prayers at bedtime with her he prayed for his mob. He told his mum he wanted to use the money he had saved in his money box to 'feed the mob' who were living on the street in Fitzroy, a suburb of Melbourne. He then went and got donations of food and he ran a barbecue on the street for the Aboriginal people, so they could have a feed. He also did an acknowledgment of country for them all by himself.

A child who has just started her first year at school came back to visit Bubup Wilam. She told us, 'My school is alright but I miss Bubup Wilam. Don't worry though, I only have to just go to school for a few years and then I will come back to Bubup and be a teacher to teach the kids how to look after country!'

Another of our children, now at school, was worried about a homeless person she saw in the street, and so went and told the school principal that something needed to be done about the issue of people being homeless. Together they ran a project to support the cause. She is a quiet child with a strong voice who knows she has a right to be heard and respects the rights of others. Again, this was a child of only 5 years of age!

Transferable learning

Bubup Wilam delivers an Aboriginal cultural model of early years learning focused on supporting children's leadership and capacities through safe spaces, child-led practice, engaging community members and operating in a culture of expectation for excellence and the right to be strong. Bubup Wilam's knowledge of cultural ways of knowing can empower practitioners, children and families to break cycles of trauma and do more than survive, but thrive.

The rights-based principles of practice discussed in this chapter offer transferable learnings based on children and families' right to:

- Self-determination – children are self-determining contributors and seekers of knowledge who can make decisions in their own way.

- Grow in culture – culture protects children when they can learn in culture, engage in what their culture means and understand how it connects people and place in positive ways.

- Know who you are – supporting a child's identity, enabling them to know who they are and who they are connected to, empowers them to move forward as a strong and proud person.

- Be calm – slowing down and being calm can help create an environment free of stress and chaos, where children can take control and learn to self-regulate their emotions

- Speak, be heard and understood – practise an ethics of communication with children that ensures an educator or practitioner has asked: 'Did I give this child an opportunity to convey a story in their own way, did I hear and understand their story in the way they intended, and when I speak with them do I wait to ensure they understand?'

- Be strong – every child is seen as a strong child who is not defined by the challenges they face and is capable of building and learning skills. Every parent can be supported to parent well and be supported to ask for help if challenges arise, through the building of honest relationships. With access to quality and contextually appropriate training, every educator or practitioner can build skills to model strong practices and relationships.

Above all, the key to the success of Bubup Wilam is the strong voice and leadership of Aboriginal people. The Aboriginal community of Bubup Wilam is truly committed to delivering a place for children within which they can thrive, paving the way for a different future for this generation of Aboriginal children, and for the generations to come.

References

Battiste, M. (2002) *Indigenous knowledge and pedagogy in First Nations education: A literature review with recommendations.* Prepared for the National Working Group on Education and the Minister of Indian Affairs and Northern Affairs Canada (INAC), Ottawa.

COAG (Council of Australian Governments) (2009) *Closing the Gap: National Partnership Agreement on Indigenous Early Childhood Development*. Canberra: COAG. Retrieved 20/01/19 from www.federalfinancialrelations.gov.au/content/npa/education/national-partnership/past/ctg-early-childhood-NP.pdf.

DET (Department of Education and Training) (2016) *Australian Early Development Census National Report 2015*. Canberra: Commonwealth of Australia.

Fleer, M. (2004) 'The culture construction of family, involvement in early education: Some Indigenous perspectives.' *Australian Educational Researcher 31*, 3, 51–68.

Fogarty, W., Lovell, M., Langenberg, J. & Heron, M.J. (2018) *Deficit Discourse and Strengths-based Approaches: Changing the Narrative of Aboriginal and Torres Strait Islander Health and Wellbeing*. Melbourne: The Lowitja Institute.

Hard, L., Press, F. & Gibson, M. (2013) '"Doing" social justice in early childhood: The potential of leadership.' *Contemporary Issues in Early Childhood 14*, 4, 324–334.

Martin, K.L. (2017) 'It's special and it's specific: Understanding the early childhood education experiences and expectations of young Indigenous Australian children and their parents.' *Australian Educational Researcher 44*, 89–105.

Perry, B. (2006) 'Applying Principles of Neurodevelopment to Clinical Work With Maltreated and Traumatized Children: The Neurosequential Model of Therapeutics.' In N. Webb (Ed.) *Working With Traumatized Youth in Child Welfare*. New York: Guilford Press.

Preston, J.P., Cottrell, M., Pelletier, T.R. & Pearce, J.V. (2011) 'Aboriginal early childhood education in Canada: Issues of context.' *Journal of Early Childhood Research 1*, 1, 3–18.

Schore, A. (2015) 'Plenary Address, Australian Childhood Foundation Conference Childhood Trauma: Understanding the basis of change and recovery early right brain regulation and the relational origins of emotional wellbeing.' *Children Australia 40*, 2, 104–113.

Shonkoff, J.P. (2004) *Science, Policy, and the Young Developing Child: Closing the Gap Between What We Know and What We Do*. Chicago, IL: Ounce of Prevention Fund.

Siegal, D. (2012) *The Developing Mind: How Relationships and the Brain Interact to Shape Who We Are* (2nd ed.). New York: Guilford Press.

SCRGSP (Steering Committee for the Review of Government Service Provision) (2016). *Overcoming Indigenous Disadvantage: Key Indicators 2016*. Canberra: Productivity Commission.

Yunkaporta, T. (2009) *Aboriginal pedagogies at the cultural interface*. Professional Doctorate (Research) thesis, James Cook University, Australia. Retrieved 20/01/19 from http://eprints.jcu.edu.au/10974.

Infants and Young Children in the Aftermath of the Great East Japan Earthquake, Tsunami and Fukushima Daiichi Nuclear Power Plant Accident

HISAKO WATANABE

Introduction: a triple disaster

The Great East Japan Earthquake and Tsunami (GEJET) and ensuing hydrogen explosions in the Fukushima Daiichi Nuclear Power Plant (FDNPP) in March 2011 devastated the Tohoku (northeastern Japan) region, yielding an unprecedented triple disaster in human history. The forms of trauma and its course of recovery differed amongst individuals and in the three major afflicted regions. While the people in Iwate and Miyagi regions suffered from the massive trauma of a tsunami and earthquake, those in Fukushima prefecture, Tohoku region, were shattered by the living hell created by the man-made nuclear disaster compounding the catastrophic natural disaster. In this chapter the author explains her participation in establishing post-disaster child care and what she and colleagues were able to do to be in touch with the non-verbal infants' feelings in Koriyama, Fukushima prefecture, and in Miyako, Iwate region.

The projects which operated in the cities of Koriyama and Miyako shared similar infant mental health principles, and embraced a child-sensitive, reliable, and relationship-based approach. They were conducted with a basic approach of *primum non-nocere* (first do no harm) (Call 1979), respect for the local culture and a commitment to ongoing outreach support. Tohoku citizens are culturally known, in general, to be sincere, persevering, sensitive and reserved, and the project was reported back to us as being positively received by them. In Miyako, the project enhanced incentives in local workers for building competency in recovery and support for the survivors of the natural disaster, leading to the creation of a sustainable system of child mental health. In Koriyama, a rigorous effort was made to address the harmful effects of any stigma and fear associated with the aftermath of the radiation effects, by developing numerous creative intervention activities. One such project was named PEP Kids Koriyama, PEP for "pep" meaning "Cheer up!" It became the largest popular public indoor playground for children in Tohoku region.

The post-disaster care project began when two child psychiatrists, Hiroko Suzuki and the author of this chapter, Hisako Watanabe, were contacted by their colleagues, Kimiko Toyoshima and Shintaro Kikuchi, two pediatricians who were based in two of the locations where the disaster had hit. Both Suzuki and Watanabe could hear the strained tones in their colleagues' voices and how they conveyed fear of further imminent dangers and a plea for help. Intuitively they knew that they should go to these disaster-stricken areas, to see for themselves what had happened and meet with their colleagues face to face (Papousek & Papousek 1987).

Suzuki learned that her colleague, Toyoshima, one of the only two pediatricians in the whole area of Miyako city, had lost numerous acquaintances in the community. Suzuki tried to reach out to Toyoshima in Miyako, while Watanabe rushed to Koriyama to check on her young colleague, Kikuchi. This marked the start of their long-term "pro bono" commitment to the children of Tohoku, which evolved into naturalistic research study on the aftermath of the GEJET (Anthony 1975).

Marginalized children in the disaster regions

Children in the disaster regions tended to be inadvertently neglected, exposed to turmoil and left behind while parents and other caretaking adults were overwhelmed by the unpredicted disaster. How could we revive intimate secure relationships among children, families and their community so that they as a whole would feel connected, reunited, relieved and resolved to proceed a long recovery process, sharing compassion, warmth and gratitude for being alive?

At this juncture, primitive feelings were aroused in everyone. Everyone felt like a hopeless baby born into a frightening world, in the throes of massive disasters. Infant mental health has to do with interaction in the early stage of life to form a secure attachment which involves survival measures entailing mutual joy and reciprocity. As John Bowlby (1951), Selma Fraiberg (1983), Katherine Barnard (1974) and other pioneers of infant mental health emphasized, the early secure relationship is the necessary crucial element for child development; and so is building harmonious, reliable and consistent relationships.

The victims of Tohoku were in dire need of a secure base. For people having to cope with a sudden loss of daily life, family members, relatives and friends, what was needed was a simple, tangible, useful approach. We had to create a way to strike a chord with those in supporting roles as well as the victims themselves. We resorted to the essence of infant mental health which focuses on the effect of relationships on relationships. We had to unite the potential power of the Japanese community living along the 500 km coastline of Tohoku.

Wisdom of Nakai, survivor of Hanshin-Awaji Earthquake

On March 15, 2011, the *Asahi Shimbun* newspaper featured an article by a psychiatrist, Hisao Nakai, who lived in Kobe and was a survivor of the 1995 Hanshin-Awaji earthquake. The article struck a chord in Watanabe and prompted her to take a copy to Kikuchi. In the article Nakai encouraged the readers to see the world through the eyes of the victims of the massive disaster. His message, which became a reference for basic principles of disaster care for Watanabe and her team, could be summarized as follows:

- Hold the plight of the victims in your mind.

- To be forgotten is the worst blow to the victims.

- Just listen quietly to their breathing and sighs that convey their unspeakable internal truths.

- Don't intrude with questions and jargon, which are what the victims deplore the most.

- Convey utmost respect and trust that they will eventually recover.

- Warm meals and comfortable places to sleep are crucial.

- Respond swiftly to the survivors within 50 days.

Koriyama city on March 21, 2011

On March 21, 2011, 10 days after the disaster, Watanabe and her colleague reached the Kikuchi clinic in Koriyama. The streets were empty, with radioactive rain silently falling. The citizens had been warned never to open windows or dry clothes outside. In the first moments of reunion, Shintaro Kikuchi and his father, Tatsuo Kikuchi, recounted their experience. On March 11, soon after the earthquake struck, their clinic was shattered, the sky darkened and suddenly snow began to fall. They thought the end of the world had come.

With a population of around 300,000, the city of Koriyama was the second largest commercial city in Tohoku, and was positioned 50 km to the west of FDNPP (Kikuchi & Kikuchi 2011). More than 2,000 evacuees fled from the nuclear plant zones into Koriyama. However, Koriyama itself was contaminated by north-westerly winds carrying radioactive materials. When radioactive plumes reached Koriyama, stigma about the radiation quickly followed. For example, vehicles with Fukushima license plates were refused entry into other cities out of fear of radioactive contamination, and there was blatant victim-blaming and ostracism. Some previously active children who had fled to other regions to stay with relatives became quiet and withdrawn. Their bewildered mothers mistook the changes in their children's behaviors as improvements.

This alerted Shintaro Kikuchi to the need for immediate effective measures to prevent children from developing post-traumatic stress and other emotional disorders. He sought Watanabe's advice and she encouraged him to swiftly create a safe haven for children where they felt at home in the arms of their parents and able to play with peers. She advised him to look out for things Koriyama had traditionally excelled in, things that were traditional and enjoyable. Kikuchi realized that Koriyama had a long tradition of picture book reading, similar to library 'story time.' There was a good children's library and hundreds of volunteers already trained in picture book reading in the community. Therefore Watanabe and Kikuchi went to the office run by the Department of Mother and Child Health in Koriyama to implement this reading activity right away. On the way they visited evacuation centers, one of which was in the upper floors of Koriyama Children's Care Center. Watanabe assumed that the local people might be feeling vulnerable and would be suspicious of her. Her initial endeavor was to become a secure base for the local people and to find ways to connect with them and the victims.

A vigilant and tense baby evacuee

In the evacuation centers, Watanabe observed mothers desperately hugging and rocking their babies. Following a chance meeting with a baby girl and her mother, she quickly sensed the reality of the risks for the babies living in the aftermath of these disasters. It had become apparent that there was an urgent need to empower mothers and help them restore their own maternal role as a secure base for their infants and children.

This chance meeting with a baby evacuee occurred at the evacuation center in Koriyama, where the third floor of this building had been allocated to mothers with infants and young children. These families had fled from a coastal village near the exploded atomic plant. One of Watanabe's colleagues had inadvertently peeped into a room and was met with the fearful eyes of a mother. This mother then cautiously emerged from the room but remained vigilant and looked at them with suspicion. Her baby girl was tied to her chest and kept a close eye on her mother's face.

Watanabe greeted them, saying: "I am sorry we have frightened you... How old is your baby?" The mother softened and replied: "Two months old." The author complimented the mother, remarking, "What a lovely girl!" and the baby turned to look at Watanabe. The baby's curiosity towards the stranger, who talked in melodious tones, revealed the baby's healthy intersubjectivity, an infant's inherent ability to perceive and receive the intensions of another (Malloch & Trevarthen 2009). As Watanabe playfully greeted the baby girl with smacking lips, she chuckled with joy. Watanabe interacted more and the baby burst into unexpected laughter. Watanabe realized she might have gone too far in engaging the baby in this way, and feared she may have alienated the mother by too swiftly engaging in play in such fragile circumstances. So, trying to mend this perhaps mis-timed interaction, she added: "How lucky you are to have a mum who holds and hugs you day and night. That's why you can laugh like this!" The mother's eyes welled with tears, and the baby looked intently at her. The mother nodded soothingly and the baby snuggled into her breast. How sensitive and attuned the baby was to her mother's emotional state, detecting the slightest tension and anxiety in her!

Infants are affected by insecurity and threats; they do not have words or verbal explanations to understand. Without adequate support and intervention, traumatic emotional states are internalized and remain active within the implicit, neuro-physiological memories laid down in early childhood, risking the development of anxiety, depression, post-disaster traumatic stress disorder and other developmental difficulties (Lyon-Ruth 2017; Reddy 2008; Van Horn 2011).

This exchange with a baby and her mother led Watanabe to instigate action which facilitated public health nurses to intervene swiftly and effectively to mitigate the anxieties of mothers with young children. These children could not wait, and the establishment of a secure base for them in their relationship with their mothers became a priority for the supporting professionals. The following day, all the public facilities for children in Koriyama were opened and welcomed children with accompanying adults.

Children's laughter as they were reunited with peers and provided with a safe place to explore after such a prolonged confinement at home made people feel relieved and not so isolated. The parents' own relief at being reconnected with their community and their happiness at feeling supported in turn would have supported infants as they would certainly have sensed their parents' pleasure. Many parents were in tears. The local administrators acknowledged the power of children in reviving vitality affect and hope in the community.

Application of infant mental health principles in the immediate aftermath

The nature and the scale of the GEJET and FDNPP disasters defied any easy solution and there was no manual to help tackle the difficulties. The focus needed to be on how to retrieve people's sense of agency and morale. *Primum non nocere* (first do no harm) (Call 1979) and conveying utmost respect to the survivors echoed with Nakai's message in the newspaper article. As infant mental health professionals striving to offer a supportive presence, Watanabe and her team explored how to approach and engage the survivors. What would help create a viable environment with mutually rewarding relationships that felt safe, validating and emotionally accessible in the local community? What could become a sustainable secure base that facilitated mobilization of competences in the individual and the community?

In Fukushima, the chaos was aggravated by incessant aftershocks and fears of radiation contamination. Pediatricians and local child professionals were disaster victims as well—they were toiling day and night to restore life in a community where not even basic needs were being met. The primary role of outside supporters like Watanabe and her colleagues was to ensure that local interventions were carried out safely and adequately. To revive and enhance the morale and sense of agency in the people of the disaster areas, they drew on the principles of infant mental health, which dealt with containing primitive anxieties.

Neuroscience and gene-environment researchers have found that the brain of a fetus and an infant are vulnerable to impact by maltreatment and malfunctioning environments that fail to respond to their needs (Aitken 2008; Fonagy *et al.* 1991; Grossmann & Grossmann 2005; Malloch & Trevarthen 2009; Nelson, Fox & Zeanah 2014; Panksepp 1988; Rutter 1972; Rutter *et al.* 1999; Stern 1985). They have also extensively clarified the powerful effects of relationships (Lyon-Ruth 2017). With actual photos and diagrams, Watanabe and colleagues used the metaphor of a fetus in the womb as a nurturing environment to illustrate the importance of basic trust in any relationship. (In the past, such metaphors had been useful in discussing the care of vulnerable children.) The people in Tohoku, in the throes of primitive anxieties, were receptive to this metaphor for trust. It evoked a sense of security and hope, and helped people to overcome uncontrollable fear. A universal image for reciprocal interaction and empathic support would yield a sense of unity, structure and value for positive self-identity (Stern 1985).

The establishment of the Koriyama City Post-Disaster Childcare Project

Dr. Kikuchi immediately summoned all the professional childcare leaders to set up a project named Koriyama City Post-Disaster Childcare Project (KCPCP). The aim was to create a "New Normal" for the children of Koriyama. Local administrators, public health nurses, pediatricians, social workers, clinical psychologists, nurses, daycare workers, teachers, librarians, physiotherapists, speech therapists, school teachers and others got together. He envisioned the three principles of the project as:

- unity

- structure

- continuity.

A project team was formed. This worked in harmony like an orchestra under his command. With such leadership, the team powerfully carried out numerous activities to counteract, empower and enliven devastated adults in the community. During the spring of 2011, for 12 months after the disaster, outdoor activity was strictly forbidden in schools, kindergartens and day nurseries for fear of radioactive contamination. For two consecutive summers, young children under five were allowed only 15–30 minutes of outdoor play each day. Adults were tense as aftershocks were frequent, making children nervous and fearful. For the first time ever, the residents of Koriyama felt besieged by invisible and odorless radiation.

KCPCP activities included the following: "Story time" was carried out in several places across the city. In the first year of the aftermath, 150 sessions were conducted for 3,900 parents and children. During each session, a trained story time volunteer read picture books while a public nurse carefully and silently observed to see if some mothers and children needed special attention and care. KCPCP made it a rule to put the baby–mother relationship at the center of its efforts and give all the credit to the mother for any successes and positive moments the dyad experienced. As part of the team's approach for the local support of parents, it produced 50,000 fliers for mothers with infants and young children, which the local city department distributed. The two-page fliers contained the following messages with colorful pictures:

- Mother is the one who can best soothe her child.

- Contain your child's worries by trying the following:

    - Embrace and hug your child.

    - Listen to your child.

    - Tell your child: "It is not your fault."

    - Tell your child: "It is OK to be scared. I will find a way to make you feel safe."

- Tell your child: "It is OK to be baby-like. Come and cuddle with me."

- Tell your child: "If you have a tummy ache and headache, I will hold you till they go away."

The fliers were written in a way to convey hope to anxious parents confined indoors with aftershocks, and to reassure them that their distressed children could be supported and settled. This, we explained, would happen when the parents assured their children simply by embracing and responding to them. We reinforced that, as parents, they had already known how onto hold their child in the acute stress immediately after the earthquake. It empowered mothers and fathers to feel that they were already doing things well and that their physical and emotional presence was mostly what their young child needed and whenever their children were stressed.

This was intended to acknowledge the existing strengths many of these parents already had and to reinforce the importance of supporting their infant/child's attachment to them. This gave parents a renewed sense of agency and confidence. They were already doing so much right, but this disaster had figuratively and literally rocked their foundations and shaken their beliefs in themselves.

A 5-month-old boy named Ta

Ta lived in Miyako, which was assaulted by the tsunami. He was caught in the Great Eastern Japan tsunami but had miraculously survived. One year and 3 months later, in June 2012, he was found to suffer from lack of speech and eye contact, with an overall developmental delay. Pediatrician Dr. Kimiko Toyoshima was his doctor. Ta and his family were cared for by her team of local health visitors. Seeing the boy deteriorating, she asked Watanabe to visit Miyako and meet the infant at the Toyoshima clinic.

Ta was born healthy as the first child. His father worked far away, while his mother remained at home. Ta was irritable and cried all the time. On March 11, 2011, Ta, at 5 months old, was with his mother when they were swallowed by the tsunami. He was tied to his mother's chest with a sling. When the waves receded, he gave a loud cry, which brought his mother and maternal grandmother back to consciousness. Miraculously the three had survived. They were whisked away to an emergency center in an inland city hospital by helicopter. Two weeks of thorough examinations revealed no problems. On the day of discharge, they were bombarded by a hoard of journalists at the hospital exit. They hailed this infant as the "miracle baby" but proceeded to frighten him with their flashing camera lights.

The three returned to Miyako to find their house washed away and the city a pile of rubble. Ta's mother had to live with her mother, with whom she had been at odds, in a narrow and uncomfortable temporary shelter. The grandmother had lost her husband in the tsunami and clung onto the little infant Ta. Ta's father, as mentioned, was away in a remote town. When Watanabe first saw Ta, at the age of 1 year and 2 months, Ta was mute, withdrawn and avoided her gaze. Both he and his mother appeared to have a low-key affect; with faces like emotionless masks. Ta was positioned on his mother's back in a traditional "onbu" sling. Watanabe greeted him but he avoided her gaze while his limbs bounced in a lively way.

Watanabe carried out a crisis intervention in infant–parent psychotherapy (Fraiberg 1987). She gently invited avoidant, unresponsive Ta to play with a toy on the floor. His mother untied her sling. He was immediately attracted to a window pane and waved his right palm in an autistic-like manner. The author continued to elicit his interest with her soft, rhythmical, melodious overtures and guided him to new toys (Trevarthen 2001). Gradually he became aware of them and started to grasp the toys one by one. He scanned Watanabe's face, first with fleetingly, then with a longer gaze. Meeting her welcoming eyes, he started to utter sounds and showed clear, fleeting readiness to engage in a relationship. All this while, he never showed any referencing to his mother. She sat on the floor with an apathetic face, depressed, anxious and exhausted.

Slowly but steadily, Ta responded to Watanabe's expressive overtures with his own increasing affect, his eyes opening wider and shining with interest (Stern 1985). He began to utter sounds, which became louder, more frequent and melodious. Eventually, he smiled at Watanabe and showed her a toy. A glimmer of hope lit up in his mother's apathetic face. Watanabe pointed out how the boy clearly showed small but tangible signs of development.

Ta was warming up to Watanabe's overtures. More and more he glanced at her and when he met her smile, he gazed increasingly into her eyes. His responsiveness revealed that he had a potential for a normal range of infant inter-subjectivity. His face began to soften with joy. He became more and more responsive and started to share his play with Watanabe in joint attention and affect attunement. This revealed that he was capable of secondary inter-subjectivity, which generally becomes apparent at 7–8 months of age.

The local pediatrician and two health visitors in the room observed the changes in Ta's responses to Watanabe. The idea that Ta might suffer from autistic spectrum disorder disappeared. Ta's mother also perceived his subtle yet tangible interactions. Watanabe pointed out that although Ta might be immature for his age, this could be due to the stressful events he had been through—not only the tsunami but also a litany of new and traumatic events which had ensued post-disaster. She also pointed out that in spite of all this, Ta clearly showed numerous examples of his healthy interest in his surroundings. Clearly, he was ready to play with her, indicating a definite sign of his capacity for sociopsychological development.

Given this feedback, Ta's mother nodded with a smile for the first time and started to relax. Ta sensitively perceived his mother's change in mood. To her surprise, he rushed to her with his eyes bright and affectionately buried his face in her lap. Ta and his mother seemed to have rediscovered one another. Ta's mother's anxiety and reactive depression in the aftermath of the tsunami could have hampered a natural unfolding of their attachment relationship. At the conclusion of this intervention, she looked relieved and reassured.

Watanabe explained that Ta could have been suffering from post-traumatic stress disorder of infancy, due to the cumulative trauma of the earthquake, tsunami, hospitalization and living in temporary housing with his mother, who was also struggling with the enormity of what had happened. The overwhelming disaster, with its ensuing stressful consequences, could have derailed this mother's intuitive parenting and the boy's development, leading the dyad to certain but not intentional interactional failures (Papousek & Papousek 1987).

Following Watanabe's consultation, Dr. Suzuki offered the mother psychotherapy sessions where the she gave an account of longstanding conflicts with her own mother. The grandmother had been abandoned in early life, sent away for adoption and was an unwanted child, while her twin sister remained in the family. Because of her unresolved early life trauma and abandonment, the grandmother was apparently needy and possessive. Dr. Suzuki worked in her sessions to empower the mother and retrieve her own sense of personal agency.

Ta's father came home to Miyako, and the mother plucked up courage to ask her younger sister to take care of her mother (i.e. her son's grandmother). Without the grandmother, her family appeared to become more united. Ta's mother became more settled, whilst Ta started to catch up in his development. A younger brother was born. Ta started to attend a day nursery.

Ta's speech and social skills improved. Steadily, he grew out of his concerning initial symptoms, and his developmental problems, though continuing, improved. He was also very well cared for in his day nursery, where step-by-step, he mixed with other children. Watanabe and her colleague followed up with Ta and his family by meeting with them annually. In 2013, he was still much delayed in speech and social interaction, but his teachers were very patient with him. In 2016, six years after the first intervention, his teachers were satisfied with his remarkable improvement. They were not at all worried about him going to primary school.

In the summer of 2017, Watanabe met with Ta, his mother and his younger brother. Ta no longer had any trace of developmental deviation and had caught up completely in his development. He was a physically and emotionally healthy, adaptive school-aged boy. He played well with his younger brother. His mother was now an outgoing mother with a much-improved emotional disposition and returned my gaze with shining eyes.

The case of Ta demonstrated for Toyoshima and her team the numerous positive outcomes in treating post-traumatic stress disorder in infants. They became confident and interested in working on their skills of Infant Observation (Rustin 2009) and interaction, while also becoming interested in the psychodynamic understanding of family and community relationships They grasped the difference between pervasive developmental disorder, reactive attachment disorder and post-traumatic stress disorder of infancy (Rutter *et al.* 1999).

Reciprocal encounters for producing sustainable post-disaster care

Watanabe and her colleague acted swiftly to organize multidisciplinary post-disaster child care projects in Koriyama and Miyako. This work yielded new and sustainable child-centered mental health bases in the communities. Observing the infants in post-disaster areas, and intervening to revive positive mother–infant relationships, was based on solid infant mental health principles (Weatherston 2000).

Initially the post-disaster child mental health care in Tohoku was considered to be difficult because it is a remote, closed region with mountains, rias coasts[1] and harsh, snowy winters. The region is impoverished by a declining economy, there is an aging and diminishing population, and life still revolves around traditional filial piety and community ties. However, Tohoku was also the home to poets

---

1   A ragged coastline with numerous gulfs and peninsulas.

and writers who represented the soul of Japan. People were humbly in touch with the fleetingness of life and they cherished children in a way which impressed a foreign traveler a century ago. In 1878, a British woman, Isabella L. Bird, was the first European to go to Tohoku on unbeaten tracks, and lived among the Japanese and saw their way of life. She wrote: "I never saw people take so much delight in their offspring, carrying them about. Holding their hand" (Bird 1911, p.75).

In the face of this unprecedented disaster, Watanabe—as a Japanese woman as well as a psychiatrist—felt intuitively and professionally the need to support mothers and fathers and community care providers by enhancing their strengths, which were inherently embedded in the child-centered local culture. Also, the trust and respect that the local people and local governments showed to Kikuchi in Koriyama and Toyoshima in Miyako allowed Watanabe, who was an outsider like Bird but also an insider by language and culture, to be consequently smoothly integrated into the community.

Watanabe has no doubt that her use of the basic tenets of infant mental health became the architecture of this project. It was her understanding of how to be effective in building relationships through reciprocal interaction, compassion and meaningful encounters that opened doors for healing. This, then, became the universal echo throughout the post-disaster support. This experience of commitment to the projects in Tohoku provided her with a conviction that if people traumatized by massive disasters can retrieve some sense of agency and feelings of boosted morale, they can survive and acquire the strength they need to overcome and build resilient communities. And even more striking is the role the infant plays in bringing a sense of future and healing to such communities.

Acknowledgements

Shintaro Kikuchi, the late Tatsuo Kikuchi, Kimiko Toyoshima, Kanae Narui and Hiroko Suzuki.

References

Aitken, K. (2008) 'Intersubjectivism Affective Neuroscience and the Neurobiology of Autistic Spectrum Disorders: A systematic review.' *Keio Journal of Medicine 57*, 1, 15–36.

Anthony, J. (1975) 'Naturalistic Research: Introduction.' In J. Anthony (Ed.) *Explorations in Child Psychiatry*. New York: Plenum Press.

Barnard, K. (1974) 'A Literature Review.' In K. Barnard, K.E. Douglas & H.B. Douglas (Eds) *Child Health Assessment*. Washington, D.C.: US Department of Health, Education and Welfare.

Bird, I.L. (1911) *Unbeaten Tracks in Japan*. New York: Dover Publications.

Bowlby, B. (1951) *Maternal Care and Mental Health*. Geneva: World Health Organization.

Call, J. (1979) 'Psychiatric Intervention With Infants.' In S. Harrison (Ed.) *Basic Handbook of Child Psychiatry Volume lll*. New York: Basic Books.

Fonagy, P., Steele, M., Steele, H., Moran, G. & Higgitt, A. (1991) 'The capacity for understanding mental states: The reflective self in parent and child and its significance for security of attachment.' *Infant Mental Health Journal 12*, 3, 201–218.

Fraiberg, S. (1983) 'Treatment Modalities.' In J.D. Call, E. Galenson & R.L. Tyson (Eds) *Frontiers of Infant Psychiatry* (Vol. 1). New York: Basic Books.

Fraiberg, S. (1987) 'Pathological Defenses in Infancy.' In L. Fraiberg (Ed.) *Selected Writings of Selma Fraiberg*. Ohio: Ohio State University Press.

Grossmann, K. & Grossmann, K.E. (2005) 'Universality of Human Social Attachment as an Adaptive Process.' In C.S. Carter, L. Ahnert, K.E. Grossmann., Hrdy, S.B. *et al.* (Eds) *Attachment and Bonding: A New Synthesis*. Cambridge, MA: MIT Press.

Kikuchi, S. & Kikuchi, T. (2012) 'The medical association activity and pediatric care after the earthquake disaster in Fukushima.' *The Keio Journal of Medicine 61*, 1, 23–27.

Lyon-Ruth, K. (2017) 'The worldwide burden of infant mental and emotional disorder: Report of the task force of the World Association for Infant Mental Health.' *Journal of Infant Mental Health 38*, 6, 695–705.

Malloch, S. & Trevarthen, C. (2009) *Communicative Musicality: Exploring the Basis of Human Companionship*. Oxford: Oxford University Press.

Nelson, C.A., Fox, N.A. & Zeanah, C.H. (2014) *Romania's Abandoned Children: Deprivation, Brain Development, and the Struggle for Recovery*. Cambridge, MA: Harvard University Press

Panksepp, J. (1998) *Affective Neuroscience: The Foundation of Human Animal Emotions*. New York: Oxford University Press.

Papousek, H. & Papousek, M. (1987) 'Intuitive Parenting: A Dialectic Counterpart to the Infant's Integrative Competence.' In J.D. Osofsky (Ed.) *Handbook of Infant Development* (2nd ed.). New York: John Wiley & Sons.

Reddy, V. (2008) *How Infants Know Minds*. Boston, MA: Harvard University Press.

Rustin, M. (2009) 'Esther Bick's legacy of infant observation at the Tavistock–some reflections 60 years on.' *Infant Observation 12*, 1, 29–41.

Rutter, M. (1972) *Maternal Deprivation Reassessed*. London: Penguin Books.

Rutter, M., Andersen-Wood, L., Beckett, C., Bredebkamp, D. *et al.* (1999) 'Quasi-autistic patterns following severe early global privation.' *The Journal of Child Psychology and Psychiatry and Allied Disciplines 40*, 4, 537–549.

Stern, D.N. (1985) *The Interpersonal World of Infants: A View From Psychoanalysis and Developmental Psychology*. New York: Basic Books.

Trevarthen, C. (2001) 'Intrinsic motives for companionship in understanding: Their origin, development, and significance for infant mental health.' *Infant Mental Health Journal 22*, 1–2, 95–131.

Van Horn, P. (2011) 'The Impact of Trauma on the Developing Social Brain: Development and Regulation in Relationship.' In J.D. Osofsky, J.D. (Ed.) *Clinical Work with Traumatized Children*, New York: The Guildford Press.

Weatherston, D.J. (2000) 'The infant mental health specialist.' *Zero to Three 21*, 2, 3–10.

CHAPTER 10

Play With Us

Bringing Hope and Healing to KwaZulu-Natal's Children

RACHEL ROZENTALS-THRESHER, ROBYN HEMMENS AND JULIE STONE

Caring for the world's children is a responsibility we all share. Each of us has something unique and important to offer and we have a moral imperative to determine what that is. Elizabeth Young-Bruehl, psychoanalyst and fierce advocate for children, avowed that 'well-supported child development is the condition sine qua non [indispensable and essential condition] of all people's well being' (Young-Bruehl 2012, p.296).

This chapter takes us to the province of KwaZulu Natal (KZN) in South Africa. It describes the work of Dlalanathi, a small community development team working there with some of the province's most vulnerable, disadvantaged and marginalised children, families and communities. Play is honoured in the team's name; *dlalanathi* is the isi-Zulu word meaning 'play with us'. It also briefly describes a friendship between the Dlalanathi team and an international group of volunteers, predominantly Australian, who make up what is known as the Uthando Doll Project, so named because *uthando* is an isi-Zulu word meaning 'love'.

Setting the scene: KwaZulu-Natal's children

KZN's children are among the 250 million children younger than 5, living in low- and middle-income countries (LMICs), 'estimated to be at elevated risk' of failing to achieve their human potential 'because of stunting or exposure to extreme poverty' (Richter *et al.* 2017). They also belong to the subset of young children living in Sub-Saharan

Africa, the world's children at the highest risk of never meeting their developmental potential, where two out of three children (66 per cent), will fail to do so (Black *et al.* 2017). Children whose parents have died face even higher risks of neglect, abuse and compromised development.

As a result of the HIV and AIDS pandemic, one in five of KZN's children have mourned the death of one or both of their parents before their fifth birthday. These children are not abandoned – they are likely to live with grandparents, siblings or extended family, but in an environment of widespread unemployment, poverty and a very high burden of illness from HIV, AIDS and tuberculosis. Everyone is stretched beyond their limit.

The majority of KZN's vulnerable children live in families in informal settlements forming peri-urban communities. Most homes are without running water. Electricity is available only to those few dwellings nearest the main road. Hunger is well known to many families. Eighty per cent of KZN's young children begin school never having seen a book, a pencil or a piece of paper. There is little or no community infrastructure and very few community buildings. Cars rarely travel along the unsealed roads, which mainly serve as walking tracks. Public transport means a walk, often several kilometres, to the main road, where, if they can afford the fare, folk await the arrival of a minibus taxi to ferry them to the nearest town or hospital or clinic. If they have no money for the fare, they walk, or simply do not travel to access the support that they or their children may urgently need.

A bereavement service, as a response to a crisis

In the early years of the new century, families and communities in Sub-Saharan Africa were reeling from the widespread death and devastation of the HIV and AIDS pandemic. KZN is the South African province that has been hardest hit.

In traditional Zulu families and communities, talking with children about death was considered inappropriate. Well-intentioned adults believed that by avoiding talk about death, children would be 'protected' from pain. Children were often simply told, 'Mum has gone away for work in the city.' This left children no opening or opportunity to talk, or process their grief, when it was clear from the distress around them that Mum was never coming back.

Those left caring for grieving children, and parents who were ill and facing death, needed help to have difficult conversations with children. So, in 2000, Dlalanathi began as a bereavement service to help and support caregivers to start to have difficult conversations with children, and to help children who felt bereft and confused by what they imagined to be their parents' abandonment of them. In this context, where there are no psychologists and the few social workers are severely overworked, Dlalanathi sought to find ways to bring meaningful psycho-social support into the reach of local caring community members.

Over time, Dlalanathi's work has evolved and broadened its reach beyond parental death, to embrace the impact of trauma and loss in its many expressions and the ways in which it affects family and community life.

A wider mission: from individuals to communities and networks

Dlalanathi's central commitment has been steadfast in supporting and equipping caregivers and communities to care for their young in ways that acknowledge the child's experience, vulnerability and need for help to make sense of the world around them. So has their belief in the healing power of play and the vital role that play has in strengthening family relationships.

The chance to explore, discover, imagine, solve problems, work towards mastery of new skills, and to be delighted and bring delight to others is vital for healthy emotional growth and development. These experiences are fundamental for infants and young children to develop a coherent understanding of themselves and the world, and for them to make and maintain connection with others. Play is one of the most important vehicles through which such coherence is accomplished (Jordan 2012; Trevarthen 2001; Winnicott 1971).

As the scope of Dlalanathi's focus broadened, the work moved from working principally with individuals or small groups of children or caregivers. To maximise the impact of their contribution, Dlalanathi began working to build the capacity and competence for child-development-informed practice throughout the network of KZN's agencies and services working with children and families. Dlalanathi also created a process for working in partnership with whole communities, to help them ensure that life within their community encourages the protection of children and fosters their healthy development. According to Richter and colleagues:

> The nurturing care of young children, provided by parents, families and other caregivers is at the heart of good child development… More attention must be given to the engagement of families and communities to understand the importance of early childhood development and the crucial part they play in their children's learning. (Richter *et al.* 2017)

The evidence supporting these claims is incontrovertible (Black *et al.* 2017; Britto *et al.* 2017; Jordan & Sketchly 2009; Richter 2004; Richter & Foster 2006; Richter, Foster & Sherr 2006; Richter, Manegold & Riashnee 2004; Shonkoff & Phillips 2000).

However, in high-income countries (HIC) and LMICs alike, the importance of supporting, facilitating and encouraging caregivers to offer nurturing care to their children is not widely understood. While practical needs must be attended to, play is often dismissed as frivolous, and the child – his or her unique experience, thoughts, feelings, fears and longing – is too often simply overlooked.

All nurturing care of children is based on the principle that every child has a body, mind and spirit, which must all be attended to and encouraged for a child to fulfil his or her human potential. This principle informs all Dlalanathi's practices and process.

Irwin, Siddiqi and Hertzman (2007) say that 'the impact of play on developmental processes is universal across cultures'. Play does not belong only to children, however; it nurtures, encourages and opens up new possibilities for us all.

Every Dlalanathi intervention is designed to be experiential, playful, creative and easily accessible. The ideas can be adapted for working with a family, a small or large group. Some of the ideas have been formalised and grouped into specific programs, including Play for Communication, Play for Healing, and The Play Mat Program. A simple manual, explaining the processes and suggested activities, is given to participants when they are training to be trainers within their agencies. The Dlalanathi team also commit to providing regular mentoring, where they offer to meet new trainers, taking time and creating a space for shared reflection so that challenges, concerns and difficulties can be discussed, and success celebrated.

A source of inspiration

The evolution of Dlalanathi's work has been inspired and guided by the work of Karsten Hundeide, a Norwegian academic and clinician. Hundeide's vision embraced all the world's children. He stressed the importance of learning about and respecting local beliefs about children and child rearing practices. His key aim was to encourage and support the self-confidence and competence of caregivers, so they are better able to engage children in reciprocal and mutually enjoyable interaction (Hundeide 2001).

Together with a group of like-minded international colleagues, Hundeide developed a manual to help disseminate knowledge and skills to support children's healthy development. The International Child Development Program (ICDP) is freely available. It has informed and strengthened child-centred practice in KZN and in many other parts of the globe (Armstrong 2013; Hundeide 1991).

Three examples of activities used to engage parents, caregivers and colleagues

Many of the caregivers who take part in Dlalanathi's training are elderly, burdened, stressed and grieving. They are often illiterate and some have chronic illness. Nevertheless, caregivers courageously accept an invitation to join a Dlalanathi support group because they are concerned about the children in their care and want the best for them. This is also true for paid employees and volunteers working within the network of agencies and services for distressed families.

It is important that participants feel welcome, as they are often wary, yet also hopeful and expectant. As emphasised by Hundeide, being part of a training session or group needs to bolster participants' confidence in their capacity as caregivers or fieldworkers. The experiences are designed to encourage and equip them to discover more joy in their relationships with the children in their care, or the families in their caseload.

Each and every Dlalanathi-facilitated training or group is built around shared activities. The sessions are approximately 90 minutes. The format for each session is the same: groups, whether with colleagues or with families, begin with a simple game or play activity, followed by reflection on the experience of taking part in the activity. Reflections are then linked to the ways the participants' experience might highlight or be similar to a child's experience. Each session ends with setting a 'homework' task, to be completed before the next group session. Homework is always an activity that requires joint attention, engagement and reciprocity or two-way communication between the caregiver and one of the children in their care, or between the fieldworker and one of the families they visit.

The activities have been designed to hold both content (what they are being taught) and process (how to present the task) in a simple and coherent way. The following three simple activities each show how the linking of activity, content and process is achieved.

1. The importance of stories

Stories speak to us all. They offer a wide canvas for shared experience. Because stories have many possible meanings and interpretations, listening to a story places the authority in the listener and invites reflection. Without instructing the listener, a story can offer insight or challenge beliefs. The listener is free to choose what they take from any story.

At the beginning of the three-day Play for Communication Program, the facilitators share three simple stories with the group. The stories are chosen to resonate with the local culture and context, and are neither didactic nor instructive. The lessons and metaphors embedded in each of the stories invite reflection on positive parenting traits such as wisdom, strength, kindness or coping under stress.

Once the three stories have been told, participants are asked to pair with another group member and to tell their partner which of the three stories interested them the most, and to describe what the story meant to them and why. With no expectation that everyone will speak in the larger group, participants are then invited to share some of the ideas they discussed. Facilitators link what is offered with a few simple points about the value of stories for children's play and learning.

One of the stories, described below, is about a beautiful pot that is accidently broken. This story is taken to illustrate a framework for telling any story that can be used to tell one's own stories. The story, narrated below, carries four distinct components which can be explored. These are the womb, the wound, the work and wholeness:

- *The womb:* The ideal with which the story begins: 'Once upon a time, a woman made a beautiful pot and put it in the window for all who passed by to see…'

- *The wound:* Something goes wrong or an obstacle blocks the path: 'A great wind swept through the house, the pot fell and broke into a thousand pieces…'

- *The work:* The main character must realise something about himself or herself, access strength or knowledge from within and do something to overcome the obstacle: 'After grieving for a long time, the woman begins to gather up the broken pieces and carefully puts the pot together again…'

- *Wholeness:* This leads to a deeper understanding and growth or movement towards wholeness as the obstacle is overcome: 'The pot is restored… It looks different as the pieces have been reformed with new clay. To the woman it is more beautiful than ever… It is again displayed and admired.'

This framework offers the possibility for creating a coherent story about one's own, and one's children's, life experience. There is a promise of healing and transformation. Moving towards a more coherent life-narrative is the essence of all therapeutic endeavour – a widening of the possibilities that can be imagined for the future. By acknowledging the ideal which is lost, naming and reflecting on the wound which is painful and committing to doing whatever is necessary to bring about change, movement towards greater harmony becomes possible.

2. The healing power of touch

Day-to-day life is harsh for many families in KZN. The Dlalanathi team often observes this harshness being reflected in punitive discipline and ways of relating to children. Introducing a simple hand massage is an activity used to introduce some softening of the harshness.

The massage begins with a short visualisation on our hands and the things we do with them each day: wash, cook, carry water, collect firewood, caress, scratch, and sometimes strike or threaten violence. Participants are then asked to trace around their own hand and to decorate the tracing with five positive things about themselves and expressed by their hands. Participants then share, with one other person, any aspect of their drawing they are comfortable to talk about. The listener is asked to reflect back any strength they hear in the other's telling. Pairs then thank each other before taking some hand cream to massage into the other's hands.

After the massage, participants are asked to reflect on what they experienced, what they noticed and what, if anything, they learned about themselves. The whole group then discusses whether or not they would try this at home with a child. The aim is to connect feeling, emotion and thinking around how they might reach out to each of the children they care for and how each child might react. Caregivers are then encouraged to reflect on which of the children they find it easy to reach out to, and those they do not, and who might need them to reach out.

The homework is to give a hand massage to the child they feel most distant from, with the added request to listen to the child during the massage time, or to simply sit quietly together.

3. Joint attention: where shared play begins

Joint attention is an essential starting point for all play between two or more participants: adults in a group; caregiver with child; or children playing together. The Play Mat Program is not a training program, but an experiential group program for parents with their children, delivered by fieldworkers who have been trained by Dlalanathi. Families with children under 5, who live within easy walking distance of one another, are invited to be part of the group.

The group program is designed to help establish family play as part of the daily household routine. The importance of joint attention and engagement is emphasised by playing a game with a ball at the very beginning of the program.

The group begins by recycling plastic bread bags to create several robust baby-and-toddler-friendly balls. Group members then sit together in a large circle on the play mat to throw and catch, or pass, one of the balls.

The ball is thrown gently across the circle until everyone has received it. The name of the catcher is called with each throw. When the ball returns to the first thrower, the group tries to remember and follow the same order of throwing the ball as they try to recreate the sequence. Sometimes participants need reminding it is a game, not a test. Parents are encouraged to help the children remember the order and who they received the ball from and who they passed it to. This is played for another round. Then a second ball is introduced. It creates a new and different order. Having two balls being passed around the group makes it much harder, as now there are two different sequences to remember. Participants find the game great fun; there are peals of laughter as participants struggle to catch, throw and remember the order.

Involving the children and the adults, the group then reflects on the experience, and what it took to get the first order sorted and on the impact of the second ball. The idea of joint attention is introduced. What does it take to catch the ball? Who throws? Who catches? What do you have to concentrate on? How is this changed by the second ball? These reflections are linked to learning. What happens if child or parent is not engaged with the ball? What learning takes place?

For their homework, parents and caregivers are asked to make an effort to be more aware of actively engaging a child and joining together in an activity. Adults are encouraged to follow the child's lead, observing when the child is engaged, and when not. They are asked to notice what happens when they themselves are not engaged or paying attention, and to seek out new possibilities for joint attention within their daily routines with the children in their care.

Subsequent groups begin with feedback and reflections on the week, the last group and the homework. Caregivers and children are asked how their homework went, and whether they had noted any positive changes at home.

Some examples of Dlalanathi's practice and outcomes

When the team works directly with a community, their aim is made explicit from the outset: to encourage community members and caregivers to reflect on children and their experience; to help them discover new ways of thinking about children and to develop new ways of protecting them from the harm of abuse, neglect and exposure to violence; and honouring every child's need, and right, to be seen and heard. Dlalanathi travels to the community and regularly spends time there. It may take many visits to engage and connect with community leaders and to build a trust that allows reciprocal conversations in which the community's needs, priorities and hopes can be determined.

Dlalanathi has learnt that waiting to be invited is a critical step in community development. When the invitation comes from the community, there is a greater chance of participation and meaningful change. The development is owned by, belongs to, and is sustained by the community.

The work is intensive. Dlalanathi commits to working with a community, or group of communities in a specific geographical area, for three to four years. The exact time frame is determined by the unique needs of each community: the time that it takes for individuals and groups to embrace and take up the needs of children, youth and families, and to develop and strengthen the competencies necessary to ensure independence and sustainability.

Dlalanathi's vision is that over this time there will be the following outcomes.

1. Increased play with children at all levels of the community

Through shared play, Dlalanathi demonstrates how play encourages all aspects of children's development. When beliefs that play is a waste of time have been dispelled, play becomes a powerful way to access a freedom of expression, thought and opinion. Play helps children and those who care for them become more emotionally agile (David 2016). Play builds resilience and enriches relationships, making them more mutually rewarding and enjoyable.

Play for healing has always been central to Dlalanathi's work. In each community Dlalanathi trains local community members to run bereavement groups for children and caregivers. Play invites reflections on death and loss, and it strengthens positive ways of managing distress.

Play is not just for children; it can transform a whole family, as this *Gogo*'s experience demonstrates:

'I learned how to show my grandchildren love though play.' With tears in her eyes, this *Gogo* (grandmother) has found a way to transform resentment into delight.

When she joined a Dlalanathi-led family support group, she had no notion of playing with the grandchildren she cared for on a day-to-day basis, for she had never played as a child. She had lived with her own grandmother. Life was hard. She had to look after the cows, and never learned to read or write.

She became a mother for the first time when she was 14 and now is able to understand 'when my children were growing up I had hate in my heart and I did not have love for them; I was brutal to them'.

In the Dlalanathi group, she was given time to reflect on her life and her experience, and she learned how to play. Bringing that knowledge to her family has transformed their relationship.

'The hatred part of me is gone. Today we are a happy family. I wait in the afternoons for my grandchildren to come home from school. I know that even though I cannot read or write, I have a lot to give them. They help me have fun. Seeing them play makes me very happy.'

2. Increase in responsive care through the parenting relationship

Parenting and family care are critical for healthy child development and child protection. For many parent-figures in KZN, caring for and disciplining children who are not their own is an added challenge. Dlalanathi's work centres on strengthening relationships between caregivers and the children they care for. More respectful and reciprocal relationships between all family members facilitate optimal care and promote healthy development.

Learning to show love and give praise and acknowledgement is the base on which all learning and positive parenting is built. Yet this can be a challenge for adults who have had difficult lives themselves, and it requires a profound sense of support. For this reason, Dlalanathi's relationship-centred approach is core. Dlalanathi forms, builds and maintains relationships with caregivers, so caregivers experience what it is like to be in an affirming and encouraging relationship. Through this experience, caregivers are better able to build a positive relationship with their children, as Mr and Mrs Gwala's experience shows.

'I have been waiting for the day to tell my story', says Mrs Gwala, who with her husband, cares day-to-day for multiple grandchildren. She began the Dlalanathi family support training from a difficult emotional place, describing how she 'felt pain in my heart'. Gradually, she began to feel safe and accepted within the group, and was able to speak about things she was deeply ashamed of, after which, she says, 'I began to heal.'

This experience, she knows, has given her the skills and confidence to be a safe and accepting person, who can listen to whatever the children want to share. She now hears, accepts and resonates with their feelings: 'When they cry, I cry.'

Often, caring is seen as women's work, so when Mrs Gwala learned about a Fathers' Program that Dlalanathi was running, she said to her husband: 'You must take your friends and go to this meeting.' She was surprised when he did. The experience has transformed his relationship with the children.

'Being part of the Dlalanathi men's group taught me to listen to my children', Mr Gwala says. 'I now spend more time with them and I feel like they respect me. There is a new connection between myself and my children.' Rather than exerting his authority, he is delighted to say: 'I learn many things from them.'

Mrs Gwala confirmed this, with visible delight: 'He normally doesn't say much, but after the group sessions with Dlalanathi, he would come home and tell me and the grandchildren what he had learnt. Then he began to take responsibility at home. I bought window frames for a new room I am building, and I found my husband outside fitting them without me having to ask him! I am very proud of him... He is more confident and more willing to be part of family life.'

3. Increase in protection for children within their home and the broader community

All community members are invited to be part of Dlalanathi's Child Protection Process. It begins with raising awareness and sensitising participants to the risks and potential risks facing children in their community. Through discussion, Dlalanathi outlines the community's responsibility to safeguard and prevent neglect, abuse and harm to children. By the end of the process, all participants know how to recognise when a child's rights have been violated and what steps to take when this has occurred. Graduating participants are invited to ecome Child Protection Advocates within their community, and some volunteer for this role.

It is imperative that every effort to establish child protection within the community is practical and easy to put into action, right here and now in this house or this neighbourhood. Group time is spent reflecting on risk and the ways adults can offer care and protection. The group discusses the essential and necessary elements for a safe and sound plan of action for an identified child or children who need protecting.

Dlalanathi helps volunteer advocates to develop the confidence and skills to run groups for children, so the children have an opportunity to think about and express what makes them feel safe. Together with the children, these trained community members identify and talk about which adults in their family or community the children can count on to listen to them and to support them with their concerns.

Three volunteer Child Protection Advocates, describe how this has occurred:

'The children are relieved to be able to talk together about things that made them feel afraid', say Advocates Mbongi, Philali and Doreen. 'Some have spoken openly about physical, sexual and emotional abuse within their families.' All the children agreed that they did not like it when their parents got drunk or when they fought. They did not like being asked to go out, often at night when they feel scared, to buy alcohol or cigarettes.

These three middle-aged women are from Mpumuza, a peri-urban community 'just over the hill' from the wealthy white suburbs of Pietermaritzburg in KZN. Very soon after the turn-off from the main road, the tarmac surface gives way to potholed and rugged tracks. These tracks serve as paths for many community members who walk over the hill to supply domestic labour to the homes on the other side.

Mbongi, Philali and Doreen, the champions for child protection in their community, run groups where children come together to share their experiences of feeling safe, or not, within their families and their community. The women are themselves supported by Dlalanathi's Child Protection expert, who meets with them regularly to talk with them and to help them reflect on what is happening for the children in the community:

'Often the children share some of what has been talked about in the group with their parents when they go home. Then the parents are surprised at how much the children notice – and that some of the "top secrets" in the family are not so secret at all!'

'Our hope is that our children feel safe, that they learn right from wrong, and that they can find their voice to speak with others about what troubles them.'

Dlalanthi and Uthando, an international friendship

In 2005, two of the authors of this chapter attended a meeting of the Children in Distress Network (CINDI) in Pietermaritzburg. CINDI is an alliance of KZN agencies working together to improve the effectiveness and governance of organisations formed in response to children's vulnerability and urgent need amidst the destruction of the

HIV and AIDS pandemic. Julie Stone, an Australian infant, child and family psychiatrist, and founder of the then fledgling Uthando Project (Stone 2018), was visiting, and Rachel Rozentals-Thresher, Dlalanathi's CEO, was the Chair for CINDI's psycho-social section.

Honouring the vital role of play for children's health development, Uthando invited volunteers from HICs to make a doll for a child living in KZN in the hope of making a difference by giving the child a doll of their own, as an invitation and enticement to play. Play is the cornerstone of Dlalanathi's practice. And so a friendship began.

Since Uthando's beginning, more than 70,000 beautiful and handcrafted dolls have travelled to KZN to be used by Dlalanathi and other partner organisations in their work with vulnerable children and their caregivers. Doll-makers in Australia and other parts of the world continue to create attractive, high-quality dolls for KZN's children.

Many of the Australian volunteer doll-makers have travelled to KZN, at their own expense, to teach and share their skills with the Dlalanathi team and others. In the age-old tradition of sewing together, life stories are shared and friendships flourish. Over the years, throughout KZN, many women and men have participated in Dlalanathi/Uthando co-facilitated workshops to learn about play and to make a doll. Some participants have never before used a pair of scissors or threaded a needle. Success and delight in their creation and discovery are almost universal.

Doll-makers, aged 4–94 years, in Australia and other parts of the world, are eager to learn about day-to-day life for children and families living in KZN. As well as creating dolls and other play material for KZN's children, Uthando volunteers also become advocates for the importance of play for the health and well-being of all children. This project has also brought alive the children of KZN in the minds of many people throughout the world. The children of KZN have the knowledge that they exist in and are kept in mind by others living in far-distant places. They are not forgotten.

Caring for the world's children is a responsibility we all share. Each of us has something unique and important to offer.

Universal practice principles

- The nurturing care of young children provided by parents, families and other caregivers is at the heart of good child development.

- The nurturing care of children is based on the principle that every child has a body, mind and spirit, which all need attention and encouragement.

- Children need the adults in their world to help them make sense of their experience; to listen to their fears and to talk with them, offering age-appropriate and truthful information in answer to their questions.

- The positive impact of play on development is universal across cultures and reciprocal play strengthens relationships between children and their caregivers.

- Most caregivers want the best for the children in their care. With encouragement and some new ideas to try, harsh discipline and long-held beliefs can begin to soften and transform.

Acknowledgements

Thanks to everyone in the Dlalanathi team and the Uthando Family, and special thanks to Clare Harris for invaluable comments and suggestions. The Play Mat Program was designed and implemented in partnership with the Thandanani Children's Foundation and Singakwenza. We thank them for their creativity, generosity and lively spirit of collaboration, and for the work they do with and for children and families in KZN.

References

Armstrong, N. (2013) *ICDP in a nutshell*. International Child Development Program. Retrieved 20/01/19 from www.icdp.info/var/uploaded/2015/10/2015-10-17_01-47-10_icdp_in_a_nutshell.pdf.

Black, M., Walker, S., Fernald, L., Andersen, C. *et al.* (2017) 'Early childhood development coming of age: Science through the life course.' *Lancet 389*, 10064, 77–90.

Britto, P., Lye, S., Proulx, K., Yousafzai, K. *et al.* (2017) 'Nurturing care: Promoting early childhood development.' *Lancet 389*, 10064, 91–102.

David, S. (2016) *Emotional Agility: Get Unstuck Embrace Change and Thrive in Work and Life*. St Ives: Penguin Life.

Hundeide, K. (1991) *Helping Disadvantaged Children: Psycho-Social Intervention and Aid to Disadvantaged Children in Third World Countries*. London: Jessica Kingsley.

Hundeide, K. (2001) 'Reactivation of cultural mediational practices.' *Psychology and Developing Societies 13*, 1, 1–24.

Irwin, L., Siddiqi, A. & Hertzman, C. (2007) *Early child development: A powerful equalizer*. Geneva: World Health Organization. Retrieved 20/01/19 from www.who.int/social_determinants/resources/ecd_kn_report_07_2007.pdf.

Jordan, B. (2012) 'Therapeutic play within infant–parent psychotherapy and the treatment of infant feeding disorders.' *Infant Mental Health Journal 33*, 3, 307–313.

Jordan, B. & Sketchly, R. (2009) 'A stitch in time saves nine: Preventing and responding to the abuse and neglect of infants.' *National Child Prevention Clearinghouse 30*, 1–26. Retrieved 20/01/19 from www.aifs.gov.au/nch/pubs/issues/issues30/issues30.html.

Richter, L. (2004) *The Importance of Caregiver–Child Interactions for the Survival and Healthy Development of Young Children: A Review*. Geneva: World Health Organization.

Richter, L. & Foster, G. (2006) *Strengthening systems to support children's healthy development in communities affected by HIV/AIDS*. Geneva: World Health Organization. Retrieved 20/01/19 from www.who.int/maternal_child_adolescent/documents/pdfs/9241594624.pdf.

Richter, L., Daelmans, B., Lombardi, J., Heymann, J. *et al.* (2017) 'Investing in the foundation of sustainable development: Pathways to scale up for early childhood development.' *Lancet 389*, 10064, 103–118.

Richter, L. Foster, G. & Sherr, L. (2006) *Where the heart is: Meeting the psychosocial needs of young children in the context of HIV/AIDS*. The Hague, The Netherlands: Bernard van Leer Foundation. Retrieved 20/01/19 from www.unicef.org/violencestudy/pdf/Where%20the%20Heart%20Is.pdf.

Richter, L. Manegold, J. & Riashnee, P. (2004) *Family and Community Interventions for Children Affected by AIDS*. Cape Town: Human Sciences Research Council.

Shonkoff, J. & Phillips, D. (Eds) (2000) *From Neurons to Neighborhoods: The Science of Early Childhood Development*. Washington, D.C.: National Academy of Science.

Stone, J. (2018) 'The Uthando Doll Project: Dolls for the children of KwaZulu- Natal'. *Zero to Three Journal 38*, 4, 77–78.

Trevarthen, C. (2001) 'Intrinsic motives for companionship in understanding their origin, development, and significance for infant mental health.' *Infant Mental Health Journal 22*, 1–2, 95–131.

Winnicott, D. (1971) *Playing and Reality*. Abingdon: Routledge

Young-Bruehl, E. (2012) *Childism: Confronting Prejudice Against Children*. New Haven, CT: Yale University Press.

CHAPTER 11

The 'International Infant'

Examining the Experiences and Clinical Needs of Separated
and Reunited Transnational Infant–Parent Dyads

NATASHA WHITFIELD

In modern-day Canada, as in other countries, many immigrants live transnational lives. In this chapter I explore the ways children in these families have "transnational childhoods", living continents apart from their parents (Milan 2011; Statistics Canada 2006). Skeldon (1997) coined the term "astronaut husbands", for adult breadwinners who shuttle between continents and their families. Waters (2002), a social geographer, referred to the children of recent immigrant families with absent parents as "satellite children". Subsequently, Bohr and Tse (2009) described transnational infants affected by prolonged separations from their parents as "satellite babies". For babies, this means that parents make the choice to leave their babies and children with members of their extended family in their country of origin for a period of time (often several years), while they establish themselves overseas in their career and secure appropriate housing for their family in that country. In some cases, the babies and children are born in Canada and the parents opt to send them away to live with extended family for a period of time, with the intention of bringing them back to live with them at a later date.

In researching this phenomenon, I have met with many parents who separated from their children. These discussions revealed many factors that guided their decision to live apart from their child for a time. Among the strongest influences that led to the decision to engage in practices of parent–child separation were economic needs, career needs, and a desire to preserve the norms and tradition of their culture (Bohr & Tse 2009; Whitfield, 2008, 2014). Those who cited cultural reasons as playing a role in their decision pointed to longstanding cultural practices of having grandparents and extended family assist in caregiving and in helping raise the children during the early years. While some of these decisions to separate children from their parents, siblings, and extended family are based on cultural traditions and economic necessity, these just as often fail to alleviate stress for the family system, and in some cases lead to mental health problems for parents and children. In Canada, such separations have been seen particularly in families from mainland China, from the Caribbean, and from South Asia.

As the cultural diversity of the Canadian population has continued to grow, greater consideration is required to be more aware of cultural competency and cultural sensitivity in the context of mental health service delivery. There is widespread concern that mental health interventions for families and young children especially are still likely to be dominated by a Euro-centric/Anglo-Saxon lens and influenced by child and family life with "Western" cultural norms and values. (Bohr 2010; Liu & Clay, 2002; Sue *et al.* 1998). Accordingly, mental health professionals are increasingly required to become more culturally sensitive and to consider the cultural beliefs regarding family life when planning therapeutic interventions (Falicov 2007; Griner & Smith, 2006; Jackson, 2009; Mistry, Jacobs & Jacobs 2009).

My experiences in working with families from Chinese, African/Caribbean, and South Asian immigrant communities who experience transnational parent–child separation and reunification have revealed a number of challenges worthy of attention. Infants and young children who have been through separation and reunification experiences were noted to display concerning emotional and behavioural reactions over the course of their separation and reunification periods. Notably, parents reported that many problems began or persisted beyond the separation period, leading to increased concerns about their child's emotional and behavioural well-being.

With respect to the parents engaged in these practices, it was clear that they struggled to cope with the emotional toll of being apart from their beloved children, while also wrestling with the helplessness they felt at not having control over the quality of caregiving their children received while away, and not being able to maintain a close relationship with their child during the separation. Post-reunification, parenting difficulties were of primary concern, as parents described how they struggled with their parenting role and mourned the time they had lost with their child during the separation period. Finally, parents reported a host of other difficulties, with feelings of estrangement and distancing between parents and their children as the primary concern post-reunification.

There was also evidence of resilience in the children, parents, and parent–child relationships, with some reporting positive shifts in their children's behaviour over time, and parents noting their own ability to respond to their children's needs – making gains in their efforts to rebuild, or develop for the first time, a close relationship with their children. While the concerns cited by parents were clearly still heavy on their minds, it was heartening to find indications of positive adaptation and resilience in these children and parents, as parents described the successes they were able to achieve in rebuilding their family lives together.

The challenging experiences that families endured as a result of their separation and reunification undeniably shaped their lives in ways that left many parents with a great many more concerns than commendations about the impact it had on them, their children, and their family relationships. As research exploring the phenomenon of satellite babies and astronaut parents has suggested, these practices appear to be on the rise in immigrant families across North America. There is a need for mental health and social support, which might offer separated and reunited immigrant families the help they need to respond to their many concerns. In particular, easily accessible and culturally sensitive child care resources, parenting groups, and mental health services would be of particular benefit to these families.

It is not the role of such services to judge or discourage these parents from engaging in practices of international parent–child separation and reunification. How these services may assist these families is through offering the opportunity for parents to meet with other parents and to explore the potential benefits and challenges of these practices, and to provide support to parents before, during and after such separations and create a supported space where they themselves might make more informed decisions about what is best for their family. There are examples of such groups in communities such as the Toronto Chinese immigrant community. The Rainbow Group, for instance, has reportedly been a great resource to the families considering separation from their children and seeking information from fellow parents with whom they could connect. Furthermore, should parents then choose to engage in parent–child separation and reunification practices, their exposure to such a group, engagement in discussions about the benefits and challenges associated with family separations, and their introduction to community workers and fellow parents can provide them with valuable resources which could help them face any challenges the separation and reunification might present.

The challenges reported by these families offer some insight into the hurdles many immigrant families face in the context of parent–child separation and reunification practices. It would thus be desirable if therapeutic support and interventions could be provided routinely to parents in immigrant communities that engage in the practice of family separation. Competent therapeutic services may succeed in helping to further parents' hopes to see their children prosper and how, in such circumstances, parents might be able to creatively remain more connected to their babies. In this way, parents themselves are supported in having positive parenting experiences with their children and feeling able to meet the challenges of their parenting roles while building strong relationships with their children.

Acknowledgements

I would like to extend special thanks to my former supervisor, Dr. Yvonne Bohr, for introducing me to this important area of clinical need. I am also grateful to the following agencies for their participation in programs designed to meet the needs of these transnational families: Aisling Discoveries Child and Family Centre, the York University Psychology Clinic, and Toronto Public Health.

References

Bohr, Y. (2010) 'Transnational infancy: A new context for attachment and the need for better models.' *Child Development Perspectives 4*, 3, 189–196.

Bohr, Y. & Tse, C. (2009) 'Satellite babies in transnational families: A study of parents' decision to separate from their infants.' *Infant Mental Health Journal 30*, 3, 1–22.

Falicov, C.J. (2007) 'Working with transnational immigrants: Expanding meanings of family, community, and culture.' *Family Process 46*, 2, 157–171.

Griner, D. & Smith, T.B. (2006) 'Culturally adapted mental health interventions: A meta-analytic review.' *Psychotherapy: Theory, Research, Practice, Training 43*, 4, 531–548.

Jackson, K.F. (2009) 'Building cultural competence: A systematic evaluation of the effectiveness of culturally sensitive interventions with ethnic minority youth.' *Children and Youth Services Review 31*, 11, 1192–1198.

Liu, W.M. & Clay, D.L. (2002) 'Multicultural counseling competencies: Guidelines in working with children and adolescents.' *Journal of Mental Health Counseling 24*, 177–188.

Milan, A. (2011) *Migration: International, 2009. Report on the Demographic Situation in Canada, Component of Statistics Canada Catalogue no. 91-209-X.* Ottawa, Ontario. Retrieved 21/01/19 from www.statcan.gc.ca/pub/91-209-x/2011001/article/11526-eng.pdf.

Mistry, J., Jacobs, F. & Jacobs, L. (2009) 'Cultural relevance as program-to-community alignment.' *Journal of Community Psychology 37*, 4, 487–504.

Skeldon, R. (1997) *Migration and Development: A Global Perspective.* London: Longman.

Statistics Canada. (2006) *Immigration in Canada: A portrait of the foreign-born population, 2006 census.* (Catalogue number 97-557-XIE2006001). Retrieved 20/01/19 from www12.statcan.ca/english/census06/analysis/immcit/pdf/97-557-XIE2006001.pdf.

Sue, D.W., Carter, R.T., Casas, J.M., Fouad, N.A. *et al.* (1998) *Multicultural Counseling Competencies: Individual, Professional and Organizational Development.* Thousand Oaks, CA: Sage Publications.

Waters, J.L. (2002) 'Flexible families? "Astronaut" households and the experiences of lone mothers in Vancouver, British Columbia.' *Social and Cultural Geography 3*, 2, 117–134.

Whitfield, N. (2008) 'The impact of parent–child separation on Chinese Canadian immigrant families: An exploratory study.' Unpublished master's thesis. York University, Toronto, Ontario, Canada.

Whitfield, N. (2014) 'The return of satellite babies: Two studies exploring and responding to the needs of reunited immigrant families.' Unpublished doctoral dissertation. York University, Toronto, Ontario, Canada.

PART 4

Political and Legal Systems

CHAPTER 12

'Invisible Children'

How Attachment Theory and Evidenced-Based Procedures Can Bring to Light the Hidden Experience of Children at Risk from Their Parents

BEN GREY AND JEREMY GUNSON

Introduction

Child death enquiries over the last 50 years have questioned why the maltreatment of children that subsequently became fatal so often remained undetected. That is, why were those children's lives and experience rendered invisible to the professionals who worked with them? In the UK, the Serious Case Review of Daniel Pelka (Lock 2013), a 4-year-old murdered by his mother and her partner, highlighted the 'invisibility' of the child, and the failure to question the parental construction of the child's difficulties. These criticisms echoed those made a decade earlier, in the case of 8-year-old Victoria Climbié, murdered by her great-aunt and her partner in February 2000. Lord Laming (2003), who conducted the UK Government's 'Victoria Climbié Inquiry', puzzled at how Victoria could die 'abandoned, unheard, and unnoticed', despite significant professional involvement from a wide variety of agencies. The same criticisms emerge repeatedly from a long history of such investigations, suggesting the need to dig a little deeper, resisting the pressure to find someone to blame and looking beyond the conduct of individuals or services.

Attachment theory offers a lens to explain how children, parents and professionals may defensively distort and exclude information in response to danger. This chapter:

1. examines the operation of these defensive processes at three levels: the child, the parent/caregivers and the agency

2. demonstrates how understanding these processes can illuminate the experience of abused children that might otherwise remain hidden

3. informed by this perspective, offers practice suggestions.

The authors belong to a multi-agency working group in the UK, who collaborate in methods to assess attachment in supporting 'at risk' families. The group uses audio- and video-recorded procedures as part of their assessments. Using video analysis, the group can look at the minutiae of parent–child interaction and identify incongruities that reveal a mismatch between the child's overt presentation and her actual experience. These interactions, captured by technology, are highlighting how some children have developed a 'false positive' self at odds with their traumatised experience.

We can carefully use this analysis during an interview with the parent about their child. By helping a parent reflect on their parenting, we can bring to light a different understanding of their child's experience. We explore their 'script' or 'story' through which the child's experience is being filtered, distorted in extreme cases, and potentially missed by professionals. At the organisational level, we argue that reflecting on the way safety and threat in the professional contexts operate can be more closely examined. This may lead on to developing the kind of agency or hospital environment where the experience of maltreated children can be properly captured and truly 'heard'.

Informed by the tragic consequences for the children Daniel Pelka and Victoria Climbié (described above), we illustrate the (de-identified) example of 3-month-old baby Chloe and her mother Sally. Sally and Chloe's story is drawn from the work of the first author, who was employed by a charitable organisation that, alongside other projects supporting children, ran a residential unit to assess families where there were significant concerns. Sally was referred to the residential unit with her infant daughter Chloe. This meant that the mother–infant pair was living in a small flat (one of a set of nine comprising the residential unit and monitored by staff). Parent education and support groups were offered to Sally and the other residents.

The referral was due to concerns about Sally's parenting skills. All referrals to the unit came through the family courts, who in this case were simultaneously deciding on Chloe's long-term future. Sally's four older children had been removed from her care because of physical abuse, neglect and emotional harm. Sally was felt to be in a more stable situation than when she had parented her older children, and it was decided that her new circumstances warranted closer parent–child evaluation. In the same agency, separately located, one author led another team. This team examined attachment relationships in depth, to assist and support the work of different projects the agency was engaged in, including the residential unit where Chloe and Sally were living.

Whilst Chloe did not share the same level of risk as Victoria Climbié and Daniel Pelka, some of the same problems arose in this case. Unfortunately, this led to an unsatisfactory conclusion where grave concerns were identified yet were not fully addressed. However, this case demonstrates the lesson that it is possible to 'hear' the voice of the child and make her experience visible.

Invisible child – invisible risk: using attachment procedures to bring hidden patterns of relating to light
Defensive exclusion of information

John Bowlby described the process of 'defensive exclusion', where individuals exclude from conscious awareness the experiences that cause them to suffer (Bowlby 1982). To survive, all humans need their relationships; this leads them to being acutely responsive to threats within those relationships. From birth, infants make meaning from their interactions with their primary attachment figures and this 'shapes their ongoing engagement with the world' (Tronick & Beeghly 2011). We need to respond quickly to threat, so each one of us learns to attend more closely to what makes us safer (or feel safer) and ignore what is 'irrelevant'. Recent neuroscience suggests that this begins at a basic physiological level, with our body being attuned to signs of safety or danger in the environment, and managing our level of physiological arousal in response: 'up-regulating' or mobilising us to prepare for 'flight or fight'; shutting us down (a 'freeze' reaction); or when we perceive safety, maintaining a moderate state capable of social engagement, caregiving and intimacy (Porges 2017; Porges & Furman 2011).

Child attachment patterns and hidden risk

'Patterns of attachment' can be seen as the mental and behavioural strategies children and adults use to shape their life and relationships in response to threat (Ainsworth *et al.* 1978; Crittenden 2005). Evolutionary speaking, danger rather than safety is the dominant human condition (Crittenden 2016). From birth, children are active partners in their relationships. They are not simply recipients of what is done to them; they are co-creators in reciprocity with their attachment figures (Beebe *et al.* 2012). One of the key ways in which such patterns differ is how the child attends to and expresses negative affect (feelings such as anger, fear and desire for comfort). These feelings motivate self-protective responses (e.g. fighting off danger, running away or seeking comfort from others). These responses shape the relationships with the adults around the child, whether it is their sibling, parent or the professionals supporting their family.

Using attachment theory constructs, some children (seen has having an 'ambivalent', 'coercive', or 'Type C', attachment pattern) exaggerate their negative feelings and demands of others (Ainsworth *et al.* 1978; Crittenden 2016). They are especially afraid of invisibility when being overlooked by carers whose focus is elsewhere. As a result, the children do everything they can to get a response from those around them. However, even here the seemingly outrageous behaviour of these children can lead to their actual experience being discounted. Sometimes professionals become inured to ever-present and irresolvable problems these children present with, and in doing so become desensitised to the risk inherent in their relationships with their attachment figures. They may assume too readily that neither they, nor their parents, would ever do anything 'really serious', which may lead them to overlook the risks the child may be subject to.

We wish, however, to highlight the impact of attachment patterns labelled as 'avoidant', in extreme cases 'compulsive', or 'Type A' (Crittenden 2016). Children, with avoidant styles of attachment (and the adults they become) inhibit the expression of negative feelings. Children with these patterns of behaviours originally learnt them and had them reinforced as adaptive with the context of their family environments. They may have learnt that any overt expression of their emotional needs may lead to increased punishment, or withdrawal/abandonment by carers. Some children project a *false positive self* to please angry or withdrawn carers (Crittenden, Kozlowska &

Landini 2010; Farnfield 2014, 2016). These children engage in the care-taking of depressed, neglecting parents, as this is a survival response to prevent further abandonment or abuse. Being noticed by showing their anger or distress could provoke harsh/abusive responses by caregivers, or further neglect and withdrawal. These children need their true emotional experiences to be invisible. Being 'overlooked' is usually the safest path.

West African child Victoria Climbié was sent to live with her aunt in the UK by her parents in order to increase her life opportunities. Tragically, her aunt's boyfriend, Karl Manning, abused her, and together with her aunt was convicted of her murder. In his trial he admitted that at times he would hit Victoria with a bicycle chain. Chillingly, he said, 'You could beat her, and she wouldn't cry... She could take the beatings and the pain like anything' (Laming 2003).

Renowned, UK child psychotherapist and author Margaret Rustin analysed the tragedy of Victoria Climbié, arguing that we need to understand the states of mind of abused children, and those of the professionals who come into contact with them, 'in terms of defences against extreme mental pain' (Rustin 2005). For Victoria Climbié, the fear of abandonment, created in part by her displacement from her childhood parental home as well as subsequent frequent moves, was manipulated by her carers: 'This fundamental fear probably played a part in her frantic efforts to please [her great aunt] by her behaviour' (Rustin 2005).

An abused child may learn to project the kind of self that the parent needs from them. This might be the dutiful, servile, extra-obedient self – acquiescent as the extra-helpful 'little parent'. Children surviving in abusive households become self-sufficient and overly independent children. They also show other signs, such as being indiscriminately affectionate, or focussed on offering adults physical or emotional reassurance in a role-reversed relationship. These survival adaptations are frequently found in fatal or extreme child abuse, because they are commonly missed by professionals, leaving the child unprotected and allowing the abuse to continue unopposed. The same behaviour, designed to shut down and deflect abusive parental attention for the child, also serves to deflect potentially protective professional attention. Professionals are too often reassured by the child's adult-pleasing behaviour. For example, Victoria's childminder's adult son noted how 'Victoria had the most beautiful smile that lit up the room' (quoted by Laming 2003). In hospital, Nurse Sue Jennings observed Victoria 'twirling up and down the ward. She was a very friendly and happy child' (Laming, 2003).

All these observations occurred whilst Victoria was also receiving some of the worst child abuse imaginable, 'living and sleeping in a bath in an unheated bathroom, bound hand and foot inside a bin bag, lying in her own urine and faeces' (Laming, 2003). The critical point here is that these two extreme accounts of Victoria's behaviour are related to each other: Victoria's extreme dissociation from her own experience and her carefree presentation were a direct product of her ongoing brutal abuse.

Identifying attachment patterns

This of course raises the question of how the experience of children like Victoria can be made visible. Can the process by which frightened children like her learn to inhibit their pain be observed, and can professionals be taught to perceive it, as well as to question the child's 'happy' exterior?

Greater professional awareness of distorted and disturbed behavioural patterns for the non-verbal or muted child, alongside training in the subtle yet dangerous nature of these behaviours, would be a starting point. However, a range of assessment procedures to identify these patterns in children, together with formal training in their 'classification' or interpretation, already exists. For children the age of Victoria Climbié (8 years) and Daniel Pelka (4 years) there were child 'Story Stems' procedures, where the child is asked to complete attachment-related story beginnings using dolls or figures, which can offer a unique window into the inner experience of these children (Emde, Wolf & Oppenheim 2003; Farnfield 2016; Green, Stanley & Peters 2007; Hodges & Steele 2000). These researchers found that careful analysis of the child's discourse and behaviour in the task can give the child's distress, and, potentially, also their trauma, a 'voice'.

■ **Case example: Sally and Chloe** ■■■■■■■■■■■■■■■■■■■

Returning to Sally and her 3-month-old daughter Chloe, as Chloe was too young to put her experience into words a video-based assessment of parent–child interaction called the CARE-Index was used to gain an understanding of their relationship. The CARE-Index was developed by Patricia Crittenden initially under the tutelage of Mary Ainsworth, whose pioneering work first identified these kinds of disturbed attachment patterns. The CARE-Index has been widely researched, with over 40 publications attesting to its value in assessing both risk and strengths in parent–child interaction (Farnfield *et al.* 2010; Hautamäki 2014).

The CARE-Index uniquely provides indicators able to identify, from birth, the beginnings of a child's inhibition and development of the 'false self' described above. The CARE-Index assesses attachment relationships by seeing how the parent regulates the child's affect when engaged in a short (3-minute) free play interaction. In order for infants and young children to be able to play freely, the parent needs to help the child regulate their level of emotional arousal (internal states) to the point where the child is comfortable and alert. Playfulness and creative exploration are not possible in a state of high agitation or extreme low arousal (Porges 2017). The state of engaged attentiveness is only achieved when the child feels safe and unthreatened (i.e. when their attachment system is not activated by distress). However, the presence of a trained but unknown stranger filming the play can make both child and parent anxious. By observing how the dyad negotiates this experience, the child's pattern of attachment (or pre-attachment behaviour, in the case of young babies) usually becomes visible.

As part of our residential unit's standard process of assessment, in the second week of their stay, Sally and Chloe's 'free play' episode of the CARE-Index was filmed. That video was then analysed by a practitioner trained in the procedure. The following concerns were raised:

- When the film was reviewed carefully in slow motion, it shows Sally actually *twisting 3-month-old Chloe's arm* in a painful manner. Chloe makes no protest, and the chat between Sally and the staff member continues, suggesting that this action was not picked up by those observers present.

- After this point Chloe 'zoned out'. Although she must have been in pain, Chloe inhibited her response to such an extreme level that she shut down completely. She was observed to smile, but her eyes were shut, and she was not looking at her mother.

- Despite the mother offering stimulating play and using an apparently pleasant tone of voice, Sally appeared to use subtle coercion to press Chloe to perform for the camera. When Chloe could/would not give the response her mother desired, Sally became increasingly tense; her attempts to stimulate Chloe became agitated and unpleasant for her daughter.

Chloe's lack of protest suggests she had already begun to inhibit her natural pain reflex as well as her distress, even showing early signs of 'false positive affect'. She is seen on film as smiling when she is simultaneously frightened and in pain. These behaviours are commonly the early antecedents of a compulsive pattern of attachment (i.e. the development of a 'false self' to mask internal distress). For this mother and her daughter, unaccustomed to playing in the manner required of them, the direction for them to have free play introduced a problem for Chloe. Whilst Sally thought she knew what the observers wanted, Chloe did not. Chloe could not meet the expectations of her mother and was covertly punished for it. To survive the experience, Chloe already had developed the capacity to shut down her physical and emotional responses, so as not to invite further punishment. Although Sally's behaviour was distressing to observe, it is Chloe's adaptive impulse to a toxic relationship that was even more disturbing. It demonstrates a powerful and primitive defence response in a very young infant. As Porges' research has demonstrated (Porges 2017), the state of being in severe threat without the possibility of escape can activate the body's immobilisation system, slowing the heart rate and enabling stillness. Evolutionary, speaking, this is a 'death feigning' response, but in the context of her relationship with Sally, Chloe is ensuring that she is not offering her mother anything her mother might feel or interpret as a threat. As a result, Chloe has already learnt to inhibit severe pain, the most urgent of attachment signals.

Analysis of the CARE-Index enabled us to detect Chloe's actual pain, enabling her distress to be seen and given a 'voice' unheard by the adults with her. Without the ability to examine Chloe's responses carefully, the professionals around her misinterpreted Chloe's inhibition. They assumed they had evidence of a pleasurable (or at least safe) interaction from Chloe's occasional smiles to her mother's apparent social engagement. Chloe's terror and pain might have been forever missed, were the interaction not available for later video analysis.

The Meaning of the Child Interview:
Seeing the child behind the story

All living organisms interpret and make meaning from their environment, and those that are most successful, evolutionary speaking, do so in order to develop flexible and adaptable survival strategies in an ever-changing world (Crittenden & Landini 2015; Tronick and Beeghly 2011). The human brain learns to attribute significance to information in the environment, and to what carries the promise of safety or indicates danger. In most cases, our need to protect ourselves is instinctively extended to our offspring (George & Solomon 2008). However, parents who themselves have experienced significant danger can misread their environment, and either under- or over-represent danger for both themselves and their child. Hypervigilant to threat, they can also distort the meaning of a child's protest and come to view their child as a danger to them, and so respond to protect themselves *from their child*. All of this can distort the way in which parents perceive and give meaning to their child's experience. In their classic study of fatal child abuse, Reder and Duncan (1999) write:

> It was as though the children had acquired an undeclared script or blueprint for their life that submerged their personal identity or personal characteristics, and this meaning came to dominate the parent-child relationship... The children became 'actors' in someone else's play. (p.71)

When professionals distort or misinterpret signs, they too can be recruited into the disturbed parent's overriding 'story' of the child. For example, in the case of 4-year-old Daniel Pelka, professionals failed to challenge the 'script' of Daniel as a child with medical problems and see him instead as at risk of harm by parent. Daniel was the middle child of a family who came to the UK from Poland in 2005. He was found to be malnourished, had an acute subdural haematoma to the side of his head, and further evidence of deliberate neglect and physical abuse. However, his mother presented as a plausible and caring parent:

> Her manipulation, avoidance of contact with practitioners, deceit and actions...were not recognised for what they were, and her presenting image was too readily accepted... [Her] apparent good care of the other children...[gave] a false reassurance that Daniel's problems were not related to abuse. (Lock 2013)

Daniel's eating and scavenging for food were too readily assumed and treated as a medical issue, labelled as his '*obsession*', a problem intrinsic to Daniel. This was in stark contrast to the reality that starvation led him to scavenging, which was the result of his deprived environment and lack of care.

When professionals unquestioningly accept 'a story', it enables abusing parents to construct a 'blueprint' for how the child is perceived. The central question for professionals is to ensure that this does not lead them to overlook the child's true experience. We need to be vigilant as to how we find opportunities for the child to 're-emerge' and be discovered. We have used the Meaning of the Child (MotC) Interview (Grey & Farnfield 2017a, 2017b) as a means of making this process visible. This tool involves careful analysis of a semi-structured interview with the parent. Interviews are assessed by examining how parents talk about their child, describe their relationship with their child and think about their parenting. The MotC Interview was developed within and for clinical practice with families like Sally and Chloe. It is particularly sensitive to understanding different kinds of risk in parent–child relationships.

Critically, however, the focus of analysis is *the process* by which the parent interprets the child's experience, rather than simply the cognitive content of what the parent 'knows' about the child and parenting in general. The method of interview analysis draws upon the rich vein of research using the Adult Attachment Interview (AAI) developed by George Kaplan and Mary Main in 1985. Since then, 30 years of studies have established a link between the narrative coherence of the story being told about the individual's attachment relationships, and the adult's actual attachment security (Hesse, 2016).

The MotC Interview's process of analysis directs the attention of those trained in it to the sensory 'images' occurring in parents' descriptions of their experience. Images (of sight, sound, taste, smell and touch) are how the brain holds information as to the feelings associated with a particular event, in particular those associated with either safety or danger (Crittenden & Landini 2011, based on the work of Damasio 2003 and Schachter & Tulving, 1994). When embedded in speech, they give an indication of how the speaker feels about the child. Warm images, described in context, are evidence of a felt connection to a child. By contrast, evocative and powerful images of danger can evidence the parents' perception of the child as a threat, or failure to regulate themselves around the child. A lack of images where they might be expected can evidence the parents being 'shut down', and disconnected from both their own experience, and that of the child.

Similarly, close attention is paid to the mental states the parent ascribes to the child. The use of an interview transcript allows analysis of whether the manner in which the parent 'constructs' the inner world of the child is congruent with the context offered (i.e. makes psychological sense) and fits what the nature of the parents' language and images reveals about the parents' emotional state. It is also possible to assess the extent to which the parent is flexible and regulated enough to consider multiple possible interpretations of the child's behaviour, and so select the most life-enhancing one. Alternatively, parents may be seen as clinging doggedly to one particular understanding that serves their own psychological need, or be unable to consider the child's or their own internal states altogether.

The body of research into the mentalising ability of parents attests to the importance of being able to give credible meaning to the child's experience (and the experience of parenting), in order for the parent to stay emotionally regulated around the child, respond meaningfully to the child's signals of need, help the child manage and regulate their own affect, and repair ruptures in the parent–child relationship (Grey & Farnfield 2017a, 2017b; Grienenberger & Slade 2002; Slade 2005; Slade *et al.* 2005).

The lens through which the child is perceived and treated becomes the object of assessment and analysis, minimising the chances of the professional(s) uncritically adopting the parents' script, and interpreting the child's behaviour solely from within this framework, as occurred so tragically in the case of Daniel Pelka. Making this process visible using assessment procedures like the MotC Interview enables proper consideration of alternative perspectives; and the child's experience of the parent–child relationship can take centre stage.

▨ Sally and the MotC Interview

A couple of weeks after the CARE-Index was filmed, Sally participated in the MotC Interview. At this stage, unlike the CARE-Index, the MotC was only being piloted in the unit, but, anxious to prove herself, Sally engaged willingly. Afterwards, without reference to the earlier filming of the CARE-Index, her interview material was classified separately. However, both methods indicated similar risks for Chloe. Sally's narrative about Chloe and their relationship appeared to be driven by her need for validation and her conflict with others. Her discourse subtly, but powerfully, invited the listener to collude with Sally's perspective, or face Sally's rejection and disengagement. In this process, Chloe's experience of her mother, as someone who both fears her daughter's rejection, and needs Chloe to support and validate her mother, could be easily missed.

The evidence for this came from a pattern of covert hostility observed in the interview towards the child, interviewer, other parents and the residential unit. More specifically, this was characterised by:

- *Apparent cooperation:* Sally's superficial cooperation with the interview (and the residential unit more generally) was undermined by subtle complaints and mocking of others, as well as self-justifying comments.

- *Triangulation:* Sally's narrative style turned others either into allies who echoed her perspective, or enemies who were rejected or put down with hostility. She could not reflect upon other people's perspectives to challenge or widen her own. Sally's perceptions of Chloe were skewed by this process, limiting her ability to see Chloe in her own right, rather than as a vehicle to enable her indirectly to attack viewpoints she felt were a threat.

- *Incongruities between direct assertions and expressed affect:* Positive, generalised, statements about Chloe were undermined by hostile and belittling images, negative evocative language, and teasing humour. The images in Sally's transcript were extremely intense and almost always signified or contained a strong element of threat or desperate need, rather than comfortable intimacy.

- *Enmeshed thinking:* Sally's own needs and feelings were inappropriately 'read into' her baby's mind. Sally's understanding of her baby's experience was distorted by her own feelings of hostility towards, and rejection by, others.

- *Unresolved trauma:* Sally's own traumatic experience was irrationally 'mixed up' with how she perceived the internal life of her baby, for whom it was irrelevant.

Creating a secure base of interagency cooperation and exploration

Safety and threat in interagency work

In the Victoria Climbié Inquiry by Lord Laming (2003) into the circumstances surrounding her death, much attention is given to trying to make sense of how numerous agencies had contact with Victoria prior to her death; yet none of them were able to collaborate in a way that they could more accurately comprehend what was happening to Victoria. Without a deeper ability to understand what is going on within and between organisations, Lord Laming inevitably leaned towards blaming individuals and organisational cultures in ways that are unlikely to support lasting change, as evidenced by similar criticisms across later reports (for example, that into Daniel Pelka's death some ten years later). We suggest that the insights of attachment theory applied to a professional context might have assisted.

How threat is perceived, and thus responded to, will be both individually mediated and, for professionals, also heavily influenced by their workplaces. For example, what kind of reflective supervision (see Chapter 2), as distinct from line management or administrative supervision, is offered to those at the front line? How, if at all, does the organisation or agency manage its own inherent anxiety working with an understanding of human dangerousness? Rustin (2005) noted that professional 'malpractice' in Victoria Climbié's case was directly related to the disturbing impact of the situation they were trying to manage:

> Feelings of helplessness, of dependence and deference to authorities, of not knowing enough, of sticking to rules mindlessly like a terrorized child (indeed like Victoria herself…), of fear and of wanting to return to the 'normal' world as soon as possible predominate[d].

Emanuel (2002) noted how powerful dilemmas and associated anxiety surrounding disturbance in a child's relationships may be reflected in professional behaviour within the agencies supporting the family. She argues that without possessing a 'secure base' within the agency in which the worker is situated, the conflict between the child's needs and responding to the powerful needs of the birth parents can become intolerable, leading to lack of clarity and inaction.

There is a danger therefore, that without adequate reflective supervision that recognises the level of trauma that child protection workers encounter, defensive information processing may parallel the attachment style of the relationships under scrutiny, or at least become equally distorted in response. Agencies may develop cultures that reflect these same processes.

The case planning process may promote an ideal or exaggerated desire for a 'happy ever after' outcome, leading to overlooking overt and covert warning signals. This unrealistic dynamic may echo a vulnerable parent/caregiver's 'avoidant', or 'dismissing' or perverse attachment patterns. It also may lead to professionals becoming embroiled in conflict, where battles for hierarchy and dominance obscure focus on the child's experience (echoing ambivalent or dismissing patterns). As a result, complex power struggles, involving territorial disputes between professionals, services or agencies, may come to centre stage.

Conversely, strict adherence to policies and practices may also unwittingly obscure the child's experience. Sometimes these take on or reflect the characteristics of the trauma within the family, so that the boundaries between professional and client conflict and dysfunction are blurred. When this happens, the feelings of threat in both the family and the professional network are intensified. The ensuing confusion – assertions of who might be best qualified, or who is to blame – risks losing sight of the experience of the child amidst the duty of professional insecurity.

Blaming and scapegoating professionals creates conditions of increasing defensiveness. Just as children explore and discover when safe in the knowledge that they can return to a secure base, this is necessary for professionals too: we need to take some risks. We also need, at times, to be outside the relationship-oriented comfort zone so as not to be inducted and uncritically drawn into a parent's distorted narrative. Allowing ourselves to feel emotionally unsafe, yet supported enough in feeling this, might give us a clue as to how to reach the child's experience.

■ Sally, Chloe and the impact of organisational defensiveness ■

The work with Sally and Chloe was regrettably undermined by some of these very dynamics. While the attachment assessment procedures were carried out by a separate team working for the same agency, they were located and managed elsewhere. As a result, some residential workers resented and even felt threatened by this intrusion from a team perceived as 'outside experts'. The organisation's central management had recently made it known they wished to reform the residential unit, to better integrate the attachment-informed assessment with the day-to-day operation of the unit. However, in the short term, this led to the attachment assessment and work with Sally and Chloe being perceived as challenging the skills and status of their own residential workers.

Sally's pattern of covert hostility, following the form and rules of the residential unit, forming alliances with certain staff members, whilst defensively avoiding reflection on her parenting of Chloe, fed into this, exploiting pre-existing hierarchies and grievances within the residential unit itself. As a result, Sally and Chloe concluded their assessment and went home without our serious concerns being properly addressed. A report was provided to court that did allow the concerns about Chloe's experience to have a voice. However, the report was separate to the one prepared by the residential unit, and lacked the evidential power of a unified, coordinated, and coherent approach and narrative. As a result, Chloe's voice and experience was not truly heard by the family court decision makers.

Conclusion

We suggest that improved attention to how children, parents and organisations respond to any kind of threat can create opportunities where children's hidden, and obscured, experience can be more powerfully articulated. Victoria Climbié's tragic history illustrated how professionals were misled by her 'happy' exterior, a presentation which was actually needed due to her brutalised and terrorised experience. With greater use of procedures like Story Stems and the CARE-Index, and better training of professionals in these settings, we may prevent more damage to children's lives. Daniel Pelka's case showed that when professionals become inadvertently and uncritically recruited into a parent's construction, rather than being alert to concealed abusive circumstances, there can be tragic consequences. The use of tools like the MotC Interview can allow this unwitting process of recruitment to be questioned and the child's experience to re-emerge. The story of Sally and Chloe sadly illustrates how even good practice in this area can be undermined by issues of organisational threat and conflict, drowning out attempts to make the child's voice centre stage. We argue that it is only with sustained and thought-out attention to each and all of these issues that the 'hidden' lives of children in danger from their parents and caregivers can truly be made visible.

References

Ainsworth, M.D.S., Blehar, M.C., Waters, E. & Wall, S. (1978) *Patterns of Attachment: A Psychological Study of the Strange Situation*. Hillsdale, NJ: Lawrence Erlbaum.

Beebe, B., Lachmann, F., Markese, S. & Bahrick, L. (2012) 'On the origins of disorganized attachment and internal working models: Paper I. A dyadic systems approach.' *Psychoanalytic Dialogues 22*, 2, 253–272.

Bowlby, J. (1982) *Attachment and Loss: Volume 1: Attachment*. New York: Basic Books.

Crittenden, P.M. (2005) 'Using the CARE-Index for screening, intervention, and research.' *Bindungsorientierte Ansätze in Der Praxis Der Frühförderung 3*, (special issue 24), 99–106.

Crittenden, P., Kozlowska, K. & Landini, A. (2010) 'Assessing attachment in school-age children.' *Clinical Child Psychology and Psychiatry 15*, 2, 185–208.

Crittenden, P.M. (2016) *Raising Parents: Attachment, Representation, and Treatment* (2nd ed.). Abingdon: Routledge.

Crittenden, P.M. & Landini, A. (2011) *Assessing Adult Attachment: A Dynamic-Maturational Approach to Discourse Analysis*. New York: W.W. Norton & Company.

Crittenden, P.M, & Landini, A. (2015) 'Attachment relationships as semiotic scaffolding systems.' *Biosemiotics 8*, 2, 257–273.

Damasio, A. (2003) *Looking for Spinoza: Joy, Sorrow, and the Feeling Brain*. Orlando, FL: Harcourt.

Emanuel, L. (2002) 'Deprivation x3: The contribution of organisational dynamics to the "triple deprivation" of looked-after children.' *Journal of Child Psychotherapy 28*, 2, 163–179.

Emde, R.N., Wolf, D. & Oppenheim, D. (2003) *Revealing the Inner Worlds of Young Children: The MacArthur Story Stem Battery and Parent–Child Narratives*. New York: Oxford University Press.

Farnfield, S. (2014) 'Assessing attachment in the school years: The application of the Dynamic Maturational Model of Attachment to the coding of a child attachment interview with community and looked-after children.' *Clinical Child Psychology and Psychiatry 19*, 4, 516–534.

Farnfield, S., Hautamäki, A., Nørbech, P. & Sahhar, N. (2010) 'DMM assessments of attachment and adaptation: Procedures, validity and utility.' *Clinical Child Psychology and Psychiatry 15*, 3, 313–328.

Farnfield, S. (2016) 'The Child Attachment and Play Assessment (CAPA): Validation of a new approach to coding narrative stems with children ages 3–11 years.' *International Journal of Play Therapy 25*, 4, 217–229.

George, C. & Solomon, J. (2008) 'The Caregiving System: A Behavioral Systems Approach to Parenting.' In J. Cassidy & P. Shaver (Eds) *Handbook of Attachment: Theory, Research, and Clinical Applications* (2nd ed.). New York: Guilford Press.

Green, J., Stanley, C. & Peters, S. (2007) 'Disorganized attachment representation and atypical parenting in young school age children with externalizing disorder.' *Attachment and Human Development 9*, 3, 207–222.

Grey, B. & Farnfield, S. (2017a) 'The Meaning of the Child Interview: A new procedure for assessing and understanding parent–child relationships of "at-risk" families.' *Clinical Child Psychology and Psychiatry 22*, 2, 204–218.

Grey, B. & Farnfield, S. (2017b) 'The Meaning of the Child Interview (MotC) – the initial validation of a new procedure for assessing and understanding the parent–child relationships of "at risk" families.' *Journal of Children's Services, 12*, 1, 16–31.

Grienenberger, J. & Slade, A. (2002) 'Maternal reflective functioning, mother–infant affective communication, and infant attachment: Implications for psychodynamic treatment with children and families.' *Psychologist-Psychoanalyst 22*, 20–24.

Hautamäki, A. (2014) 'Mothers and Infants: Screening for Maternal Relationships With the CARE-Index.' In S. Farnfield & P. Holmes (Eds) *The Routledge Handbook of Attachment: Assessment*. London: Routledge.

Hesse, E. (2016). 'The Adult Attachment Interview: Protocol, Method of Analysis, and Empirical Studies: 1985–2015.' In J. Cassidy & P. Shaver (Eds) *Handbook of Attachment: Theory, Research, and Clinical Applications* (3rd ed.). New York: Guilford Press.

Hodges, J. & Steele, M. (2000) 'Effects of abuse on attachment representations: Narrative assessments of abused children.' *Journal of Child Psychotherapy 26*, 3, 433–455.

Laming, Lord (2003) *The Victoria Climbié Inquiry: Report of an Inquiry*. London: Department of Health.

Lock, R. (2013) *Serious case review re Daniel Pelka: born 15th July 2007 died 3rd March 2012* [full overview report]. Coventry: Coventry Safeguarding Children's Board.

Porges, S.W. (2017) *The Pocket Guide to the Polyvagal Theory: The Transformative Power of Feeling Safe*. New York: W.W. Norton & Company.

Porges, S.W. & Furman, S.A. (2011) 'The early development of the autonomic nervous system provides a neural platform for social behavior: A polyvagal perspective.' *Infant and Child Development 20*, 1, 106–118.

Reder, P. & Duncan, S. (1999) *Lost Innocents: A Follow-Up Study of Fatal Child Abuse*. London: Routledge.

Rustin, M. (2005) 'Conceptual analysis of critical moments in Victoria Climbié's life.' *Child and Family Social Work 10*, 1, 11–19.

Schachter, D.L. & Tulving, E. (1994) 'What Are the Memory Systems of 1994?' In D.L. Schachter & E. Tulving (Eds) *Memory Systems*. Cambridge, MA: MIT Press.

Slade, A. (2005) 'Parental reflective functioning: An introduction.' *Attachment and Human Development 7*, 3, 269–281.

Slade, A., Grienenberger, J., Bernbach, E., Levy, D. & Locker, A. (2005) 'Maternal reflective functioning, attachment, and the transmission gap: A preliminary study.' *Attachment & Human Devlopment 7*, 3, 283–298.

Tronick, E. & Beeghly, M. (2011) 'Infants' meaning-making and the development of mental health problems.' *American Psychologist 66*, 2, 107.

CHAPTER 13

Infants and Young Children Living Within High-Conflict Parental Disputes

'Keep Me Safe and Organise My Emotional World'

AN INTERVIEW WITH PROFESSOR JENNIFER McINTOSH BY SARAH J. JONES

Introduction

Infants and young children are most likely to be severely affected when their parents end up in high-conflict separations. Making more space to consider what agreements and plans might place the child at the centre of the 'decision-making' table is important for all of us who work with children. Fortunately, the previous language used, such as 'custody' (akin to being a possession or a prisoner), has been replaced by the notion of 'shared parenting'. When parents cannot find their own resolutions, legislative systems confer the task of mediating decisions to legal and allied representatives, or, in a minority of cases, to court determination. Regardless of the decision-making modality, these outcomes govern the infant and young child's emerging relational lives post-separation and divorce.

Professor Jennifer McIntosh is a specialist child psychologist and academic researcher, with decades of experience working within the arena of family law disputes. She has been a pioneer in challenging the family law system to think and act developmentally, and a fearless champion of children's rights in relation to custody and access disputes. Sarah Jones talked with Jennifer to ask what she has learnt from these infants and young children over her career.

Sarah: Jennifer, most of all we are interested in you offering your practice wisdom for those grappling with supporting young children whose parents are engaged in legal disputes. There are enormous questions for many of us in our daily practice, from child care, contact centres, women's refuges, community services, paediatric hospitals, etc. Commonly, because the conflict is so high, child professionals are, in my experience, seeing only one of the parents of a young child and usually not having any access at all to the other parent. They will hear a very negative view about the other parent and may lose the capacity to recognise that in order to support an infant optimally through family transitions, both sides of the parent system need to be thoughtfully considered. Decreeing there is a 'good' parent and then a 'bad' parent does not necessarily support an infant (acknowledging of course, in the context of any family violence, where one or both parents have been violent, there are heightened concerns).

So, in the light of this Jennifer, I have four questions to ask you. I would like to start with the broadest one of all: What do you consider are the most important practice principles for anyone directly involved in working with or supporting infants and young children under 5 and their parent/caregivers who are in legal disputes regarding their custody and access arrangements?

Jennifer: This is a really interesting question. Looking back on countless cases, I think one has to stay oriented to the raw nature of the love and passion that a parent has for their infant. We know that infants are designed to be compelling and to evoke in us the strongest of caregiving instincts; often given the ferocity that we often see in the legal battles between parents over infants and young children, I think it's too easy to judge parents or assume one or the other is operating from an ill motive. I find that, in working with these parents, if I can meet them in that space and harness that raw protective instinct to be with and protect their baby, then we disarm one of the major defences to begin with. I often want to remind professionals that I supervise, or the parents I work with, that I assume their love for their baby is like a turbine engine and their motivations to be with their baby are pure. All this energy is coming out of the power of the caregiving system. These urgent feelings are about survival. That is why they're so raw and that's why they're so enormous. From the outset this is very important to understand and to remember.

The second piece, then, is to understand how parents, unintentionally, create significant developmental conundrums for their babies in separation and divorce scenarios. Some parents have so little understanding of the developmental imperatives of these early years. They simply cannot fathom the extent to which, through their separation, they are confounding the developmental tasks of infancy. What I typically see happen, Sarah, is a competition for time with the baby, where the amount of time with the baby becomes a prize. In pursuing that battle and sometimes getting lawyers to champion that battle, they create this horrid developmental conundrum for the baby, whose raw instincts are trying to speak at the same time. If those instincts could be verbalised, they would say, 'Keep me safe and organise my emotional world.'

So, the first principles professionals need to be addressing are the developmental needs of the younger child. The developmental and relational framework is absolutely imperative in any work that we do with families and separating families with children under 5. Over 5 and into the teens, the comprehension, of course, of the emotional world and where these things come to land in the intrapsychic space is also important. Yet, it is the 'developmental architecture' that's being threatened in these scenarios for the infant and the pre-schooler. We know that this early maturational stage of neural development means infants are more vulnerable than the school-age child, and this is what makes this work uniquely important. When I see cases being run in courts, with disregard of these developmental foundations, I get very concerned indeed.

So where are we up to? I've spoken about: 1) the raw true honourable caregiving instincts of each parent; and 2) their desire to be with their baby. The next principle of practice would be: 3) to attend to the challenges for parents of working together. I would want to see how those three things could be harnessed together into an effective intervention with the parents. Some of the language that I use with parents, I guess, is flagrantly motivational. It's used in order to inspire them to understand their crucial role as attachment figures – especially what a privilege that is. I outline how they are the necessary equipment for the baby's growing emotional world. I try and help them understand how coordinated that equipment has to be. I outline with them and for them how, in a sense, they are architects of their baby's early emotional life.

So, in my work, with the principle of working together, in the earliest possible moments of parental separation – even parental conflict without separation – I think there's a teaching space in there with parents which is therapeutic. If I can help them come to know that their contributions and commitment to the needs of the child in this early developmental phase are of the utmost importance, they have a better chance of continuing to prioritise the baby's physical and emotional developmental needs within any negotiations occurring about the baby's care. This shared perspective needs to become the goal of mediating parenting disputes – way above winning the battle.

Sarah: And when you say the 'teaching space' for the parent, it's to be able to inspire them to think about the baby, not the prize, nor fighting for equity in time keeping?

Jennifer: I'll often say to parents, 'We know so much more about babies' development than our parents did.' We have been through the decade of the brain and we know what an extraordinary amount of brain development and the emerging emotional world is dependent on experience, dependent on caregiving qualities. This is exciting and that's daunting at the same time. Fortunately, babies don't need perfection and they thrive on rupture and repair, so we can get that to work for us in a sense; but I think it's about, for me, the teaching space. So, this is what I tried to do with my online parent education program called Young Children in Divorce and Separation (YCIDS for short[1]). The aim was to create a teaching space to convey these early foundations in 'ordinary' *Women's Weekly* language and to get parents excited about how irreplaceable they were in the unfolding of the baby's emotional world.

I sometimes speak about how the attachment relationship really needs to function like a four-wheel-drive. It's a relationship that gets the baby around every corner and crevice of their emotional life – the good, the bad, the ugly and the scary. The ease with which a parent can

---

1   YCIDS is an 80-minute online program for parents and also for family law professionals, to help them understand and re-focus on the needs of very young children within separation disputes. It has five short chapters, and a helpful set of questions for parents to answer about the context of their own separation. There can be no rules or laws about caring for very young children after separation, but there are some important developmental principles for parents to follow. YCIDS shows you what these are. YCIDS is available at www.childrenbeyonddispute.com.

take the baby through those emotional trips – day in, day out; moment in, moment out – matters.

The other metaphor that seems to make sense is that parents, separated or not, are co-pilots of their baby's emotional life, social and emotional development. The co-piloting is a powerful metaphor. For a majority of parents who choose to separate, or in fact were never together as parents, their relationship failed in the very, very early days or never began. This makes it much harder, without any co-parenting history behind them, to form something good enough in the relationship that can endure and grow over so many years to come. We also know there is an important minority of parents who can't, won't, and indeed shouldn't co-parent, because they or their relationship is unsafe. Then the co-piloting metaphor is not only irrelevant but may be dangerous. We must consider the full spectrum of co-parenting.

Sarah: My second question is related to wanting to ensure there is recognition in this book, as to how we support all kinds of families. What have you noticed are some of the issues for LGBTQIA[2] couples or gay and lesbian shared parenting arrangements when there are break-ups? How do workers navigate this for the infants and children?

Jennifer: I just can't see it as different in any way, so I'm racking my brains now, Sarah. Following 33 years of work, I have seen very few gay or lesbian couples in a separation with a baby. I think they are so invested in, and planful about, having a baby together that their parenting relationship may last longer. In my longitudinal sample of 169 families, six were gay or lesbian parents; and while that isn't a large enough sample to make any valid comments about, I will say that we used to wonder about what these families could teach others, because they were so well-functioning in their separation.

So, your question sort of surprises me at one level because the sex or sexual orientation of the caregiver makes no difference to the infant. The infant doesn't have a gender bias. The infant has a bias for warm receptive care. They have no awareness of the gender or sexual identity of the person holding them. The only thing they care about, frankly, is whether they're being nurtured in a predictable, attuned and devoted manner.

---

2 LGBTQIA is commonly defined as lesbian, gay, bisexual, transgender, queer/ questioning, intersex and asexual.

Sarah: Can you comment on any issues you have dealt with?

Jennifer: Well, some of the far more complex cases I have seen are battles between a donor and a lesbian couple, when the donor father realises that he wants a relationship with a baby, but that a role for him wasn't anticipated or negotiated in the first place. Building a relationship with the child was not the expectation, and these battles can become epic.

Sarah: A chapter in this book (Chapter 17) deals with donor-conceived infants from assisted reproductive technology. I would be interested in you commenting, even speculating, on what you think might contribute to the epic nature of these conflicts; for example, when gay couples separate are there implications for the sperm donor father and a donor-conceived child? We will be seeing more of these as our society changes and as the very higher rate of single women who now move to motherhood via ART (Artificial Reproduction Treatments).

Jennifer: As I mentioned, I have worked with several family law cases in which the lesbian couple separated when the child was in their kindergarten or primary school years, and the donor father issued a contest over parenting time. On reflection, I think what got activated in the donor father was the idea of becoming a meaningful part of a caregiving system, as the original unit of care came undone. One can't anticipate what caregiving instincts really feel like until the baby is on the way or becoming some sort of reality. I can understand the way in which these donor arrangements can begin sincerely with a desire to assist, and some dispassionate feelings about one's own role with a potential baby, so conversations such as 'Yes, we're good friends, and we can manage this, no problem. I have no interest in having a child of my own, but let me help you to have one.' John Bowlby hypothesised that the caregiving system, like the attachment system, is innate and biologically driven. I've come to believe this even more these days, where I may not have believed it quite as strongly earlier in my career. When the caregiving system becomes activated in the donor and this was not anticipated, nor planned for from the beginning, the activation of that system in the male can feel like a threat or unwanted challenge to the emotional world around the child, co-constructed by the women partners. It creates an adult/parent triad where she/he didn't want one. I think that is threatening and potentially destabilising for some parents.

So, these battles, then, are epic because the child is in a three-way challenge. Everybody wants time with the child – the donor father, the two split lesbian parents – and a battle for ascendency over who's the primary mother and these sorts of things. I have to say these are right up there with the highest conflict cases I've ever seen.

Sarah: The legal position for donors and recipient parents accessing donors to assist in the Artificial Reproduction Treatments to create a child differs from country to country. Our own state does not require these parties to have legal support and legal contracts. How do you work with some of these challenges?

Jennifer: I try to help parents, and professionals for that matter, to think about an important distinction. What we want all decision makers to have regard for is the psychological utility for the child of (a) contact and (b) the relationship. For the baby, we also have high regard for the developmental utility of the time spent with other carers. Sometimes it's a case of getting people to slow down on contesting for time with the baby, and to go at the developmental pace of the infant. For example, a donor father in this case might be encouraged to first build something of a visiting uncle role rather than jumping straight to the active father role that he wants.

I find the evidence quite compelling that we can inadvertently create developmental conundrums for infants by fragmenting their early care. The baby is in need of a solid rhythm and a predictable pattern of care with at least one person; that's not to the exclusion of all others. The idea of 'fragmenting an infant's early care' sounds judgemental because you've got to remember you've got three people who love this baby and would probably give their life for the baby. But fragmentation does happen when so many adults want to be very active in the infant's care, although of course there is no intent to harm. I think that's where some of the narratives have become skewed about parent intentionality.

Sarah: The third question relates to an even more complicated issue that arises in practice. There are two parts to this question: How have you managed cases where one parent accuses the other of sexual interference during the Family Court processes? Do you think the child gets lost in such spaces?

Jennifer: This is indeed very, very tricky territory and always requires specialist input and careful assessment. Sadly, I have seen many of these cases, too. I think one needs to have regard for the cases in which it is true that sexual interference did occur. When the child is verbal – say at 3 years or more – it becomes very important to spend time with the child and to look carefully at the child's experience, in what they can show us through their play and interactions about their authentic, lived experience. In other cases, following a thorough assessment, it becomes very clear that there has been no sexual interference, and it is more evident that the accusation represents an unprocessed fear for one parent.

I try to find ways to support this parent, to explore these feelings, and at the same time to affirm that it is always a parent's role to ensure the safety of their child. For a parent to raise concerns in a dubious context isn't a bad thing.

It's important to look and look again, and ensure that as we look, we do not fail to see this child and their experience, rather than see what we may want to see. When the allegations are not substantiated, I need to find the right scaffold with the accusing, fearful parent to help them to begin to think about that very issue. What else could they do with the fear or hatred toward the other parent which they projected outward with such force and conviction that it indeed came to feel like a certain truth about the other parent? This again is complex work that requires specialist input, respect and care.

We know that sometimes the impetus for these allegations comes from intergenerational trauma. Sometimes it comes from humiliation and hatred. For me, the greater therapeutic success – if that's the right word – is to help this accusing parent to see how a small part of them may see a confirmed allegation as a form of proof that the other parent's behaviour is indeed 'despicable', and that person should be exiled from the child's life. In cases of unsubstantiated claims, I then try speak to that part of the parent's mind which definitely does *not* want it to be true. And ultimately, at the end of the day, the part of the parent that is *relieved it isn't true* may ascend.

Sarah: Final question, Jennifer: How would you approach a Court order which requires a 2- or 3-year-old to start seeing the child's other parent after a lengthy absence of having no contact?

Jennifer: I supervise many contact services around Australia and this type of order is routine. The first thing that I always encourage the contact centre to do is to assess the viability of such an order. The problem, of course, is that the 1-, 2- or 3-year-old can't say 'no' in the way that the 8-, 9-, 10-year-olds can and do; so refusals of contact, as we call them in the trade, don't happen in the pre-school years because the baby doesn't actually say, 'No, I don't want this,' and workers are generally not trained to recognise the signs the baby tries to give of their acute discomfort. The baby, toddler, or pre-schooler doesn't say 'no' and doesn't protest *in the way that many professionals are accustomed to recognising.*

So, I think that's an important piece of the work, because sometimes in these reunification cases the older child will bring transparently to the fore their anxiety, their fear, their worry. Whether it comes from them or in interaction with their residential carer, they'll bring it. The infant is silenced in this system. I train, teach and support people to look and look again at the signs that the infant will bring of their discomfort.

I can vividly remember a case of a Court-determined reunification for a 9-month-old. Having had DNA testing to establish that he was the biological parent, the father wanted an active and ongoing relationship to begin straight away. There had been quite horrible circumstances of violence against the mother and yet the Court ordered the contact service to facilitate the father to have regular contact with this young baby. And, of course, something of the mother's anxiety was in the baby and the strange circumstance the baby found themselves in, being in a contact centre, without their mother, as, due to an Intervention Order, she couldn't be there. The Court's reasoning was he hadn't harmed the baby, he'd 'only' harmed the mother, and therefore it was fine for him to see the baby. These cases are so very hard to work with, when the system gives scant thought to the experience of the infant in the middle of it all.

In all our work, we need to hone our observational skills; this is the key. We need to use them when looking at the baby's or toddler's communications. We need to create informed ideas as to the meaning of their behaviours. We might be the one person in the system who refuses to say the child was simply 'naughty'. Putting all these pieces together and sorting them out is critical.

In this case, the 9-month-old baby was not ambulatory. Together with the case-worker, I observed her with her father during a

90-minute visit. In our debriefing afterwards, we were comparing our observations. The worker said, 'Well, that went well. The baby didn't cry.' I commented gently, 'I wonder what we might make of the fact that the baby gripped her bottle for 90 minutes so hard that her fingers turned white?' I also wondered with the worker, 'What did you make of it when the mother walked in the door after the father had left, and the baby popped like an overfull balloon with this anguished cry?' We then speculated together that we would rightly ascribe some level of stress and tension to the baby. This baby, who might initially be viewed as unprotesting and therefore 'fine', was communicating considerable distress.

The beautiful thing about working with the under-3s in these complex cases is that they don't blame, and they don't judge. They don't attribute wrong to a parent and so we can honestly say to the visiting parent, 'The baby isn't thinking that you are getting this wrong, or this is somehow your fault that they're uncomfortable. And your baby most certainly has not read the Court report! But your baby will signal when they're uncomfortable and that's what we look for and respond to with care and reassurance. It's kind of an honour and a privilege if the baby feels safe enough to signal to you, and we need to encourage them to do that rather than discourage it.'

Sarah: What I'm hearing, which is different, I think, from a lot of other practitioners, is that you share your framework more transparently. You seem to come from a strong place of offering a supportive yet also educative narrative, one that you then share with the parent/s.

Jennifer: And do you know, this is in contrast to infant mental health training. I think it reflects 25 years in the family law trenches where things move fast. For those of us in the trenches, we haven't got a lot of time to work; we've got to get some core messages across and you've got to try to prevent some damage quickly. The apparent luxury of the wondering and reflection that we would prefer to do at a parents pace, to me, I have never felt that works terribly well in the family law field.

Sarah: This seems to be an important take-home message to practitioners and workers in this area: It might be useful to be more transparent with the narrative you are sharing with the parents – what you are seeing, what you're looking for and what it means. I think that's a really important contrast between an infant mental health perspective or intervention and perhaps a more legal-focused intervention. Yet at the same time I feel there are some very considerable advantages in the translation of that into infant work and infant mental health practice. So yes, we may collectively (or not) have time for the pace of the family, but often they're not convinced we can be helpful and they're not necessarily going to stay in treatment. However, some explanatory schema that is pertinent and germane to the infant in the room I think is one of the big things we can learn from you; the translation of science, research and the decade of the brain into a story that makes sense for distressed infants we are seeing and their parents who are wanting the best for them.

Jennifer: In the scheme of my work, which is often only a 1-hour conversation that I have with parents, I go pretty hard at it and yes it can be decidedly educative in tone. It is a teaching space, but one in which I'm trying to nurture motivation, and trying to cut through hatred and animosity. I'm trying to reach the good enough parent within the litigant to make an alliance for the baby. Sometimes – many, many times – I can get there by motivating them to see their unique role in the baby's development and how inadvertently through the way in which the legal battle is being fought, they're at risk of creating some damage for their baby. After that, we can afford to ponder and wonder and notice and observe together; but we can't do that unless they're with me, and unless they come back.

Some of Professor Jennifer McIntosh's landmark papers

McIntosh, J.E., Pruett. M. & Kelly, J.B. (2014) 'Parental separation and overnight care of young children, part II: Putting theory into practice.' *Family Court Review 52*, 2, 257–263. Retrieved 00/00/00 from https://doi.org/10.1111/fcre.12088

McIntosh, J.E., Smyth, B. & Kelaher, M. (2013) 'Overnight care patterns following parental separation: Associations with emotion regulation in infants and young children.' *Journal of Family Studies 19*, 3, 224–239.

McIntosh, J.E. & Tan, E.S. (2017) 'Young children in divorce and separation: Pilot study of a mediation based parent education program.' *Family Court Review 55*, 3, 329–344.

Pruett. M., McIntosh, J.E. & Kelly, J.B. (2014) 'Parental separation and overnight care of young children, part I: Consensus through Theoretical and Empirical Integration.' *Family Court Review 52*, 2, 241–256.

Sadowski, C. & McIntosh, J.E. (2015) 'On laughter and loss: Children's reports of parenting behaviors that enable security in shared-time living arrangements.' *Childhood 23*, 1, 69–86.

CHAPTER 14

Playing Behind the Barbed-Wire Fence

Asylum-Seeking Infants and Their Parents

CHRISTINE HILL

Introduction

This chapter gives voice to asylum-seeking infants in detention. The perverse nature of their treatment by Australian authorities is described, and a review of the literature highlights the invisibility of refugee infants world-wide. I explain my rationale for establishing a baby playgroup in a detention centre, describe some of the obstacles and discuss the challenges for health professionals working as volunteers in complex settings. Several case studies illustrate the impact of detention on the infant's experience and the difficulty of bearing witness to this experience. The conclusion offers some thoughts on managing task and role in such situations.

Background

Children now account for more than half of the 24.5 million people around the world who are seeking refuge (UNHCR 2018). The Australian response to this humanitarian crisis is unique.[1] Despite the fact that the act of seeking asylum is a human right under international law, the Australian government classifies asylum-seekers who enter the country by boat as Illegal Maritime Arrivals (IMAs). The military-managed 'Operation Sovereign Borders' is the product of a determined 'Stop the boats!' political campaign, (News Limited 2012) which claims

---

1   See Refugee Council of Australia (2017) for a full description.

to discourage people smugglers and to prevent drownings at sea. The *modus operandi* is to detain IMAs indefinitely and to forcibly turn back boatloads of asylum-seekers found in Australian waters. People arriving in Australia after 19 July 2013 are detained offshore, on the islands of Manus or Nauru, where they are beyond the protection of Australian law.

As an Australian citizen, I was unconvinced that the end justified the means (the mandatory, indefinite detention of innocent people seemed like a high price to pay for border protection). As a perinatal psychotherapist I was particularly concerned for the infants. I discovered that, while government policy stated that children were not held in detention centres, the reality proved otherwise. It appeared that if a detention facility was called a 'Transit Centre', it could indeed detain infants and children and their parents for long periods, apparently without contravening official policy.

After making a number of enquiries through my personal and professional networks, I was introduced to Brigid Arthur, who co-ordinates the Brigidine Asylum Seekers Project, an advocacy and support group. In early 2014 she invited me to join her weekly visits to a Melbourne detention centre. At that time, detainees, as they were called, were permitted to meet us in the Visitors' Centre – a large, guarded and double-locked space between reception and the detention centre proper. Visitors were required to leave phones, money and anything sharp in the lockers provided. We had to specify who we were visiting, provide our personal details, including proof of identity, and sign in and out. The rules would change from time to time without warning, and on one occasion, and for no particular reason, toys for babies were banned.

Once inside, it was chaos. There were perhaps a hundred men, women and children of many different nationalities, all talking at once. Babies in prams lay silently beside mothers with blank faces while the older children ran wild. Families greeted Brigid warmly as she patiently listened to concerns and noted requests. People approached me too, quite randomly; they were shy and embarrassed as they asked if I could provide them with legal advice, waterproof shoes, a rain jacket for a 3-year-old, a pair of men's trousers, and fruit for the children. I felt overwhelmed but I needed to think: Apart from good will and material goods, was there something particular that I could offer?

During my visits I noticed that some of the babies and their mothers avoided each other's gaze. I wondered if, with a little help, they could find some joy in discovering themselves and each other. Was it possible to make a space for infant–parent play in this deprived and depriving environment? Encouraged by Winnicott (1971), who observed that 'to arrange for children to be able to play is itself psychotherapy' (p.50), I decided to try.

Literature review
Incidence of mental health problems

The field of Infant Mental Health is concerned with the social and emotional health of infants (0–3 years) and their care-givers. It recognizes that infancy is a particularly vulnerable period in a child's life and therefore requires special attention from health professionals, ethicists, educators, and law- and policy-makers. An interdisciplinary field, it is 'rooted in the understanding that developmental outcomes emerge from infant characteristics, caregiver-infant relationships, and the environmental contexts within which infant-parent relationships take place' (Fitzgerald & Barton 2000, p.1).

The fact that infants are rarely mentioned in the available literature on immigration detention highlights the invisibility of our most vulnerable asylum-seekers. In Australia, this may be partly explained by a detention regime that appears unable to treat people humanely.[2] A Kafkaesque system holds detainees in limbo indefinitely, makes access difficult for mental health professionals, and leaves them powerless to act upon their assessments. Treatment options are limited when the expert finding is that detention itself is the main contributing factor to a negative mental health assessment (Steel *et al.* 2004). For the infants, it is often only when a physical problem requires a hospital admission that their mental health can be addressed. In some cases, hospital staff, respecting their duty of care, refuse to discharge infants back into detention (Doherty 2016a; Hatch, Smith & Ireland 2015).

Another reason for infant invisibility is The Australian Border Force Act (ABF), which makes it an offence, punishable by up to 2 years in jail, for a person to 'make record of or disclose protected information' (ABF 2015). In this environment of fear, the truth about the health and well-being of people of all ages in detention becomes a casualty;

2   A list of children's experiences in detention, collated by Steel and colleagues (2004), makes for chilling reading.

informed public dialogue is silenced. For nearly 18 months the Act effectively prevented health professionals from providing appropriate, timely referrals for detainees, and from openly sharing their experience and findings with colleagues. It was not until October 2016, after a group of health professionals proposed a High Court challenge, that the Australian Government amended the Act to exempt a range of health workers from its secrecy and disclosure provisions (Doherty 2016b).

While we have limited data on the mental health of infants (aged 0–3) in immigration detention, there is well-established evidence that the mental health of older children is seriously compromised (Fazel & Stein 2002; Mares & Jureidini 2004; Newman & Steel 2008; Robjant, Hassan & Katona 2009). A psychiatric assessment of 10 families, comprising 14 adults and 20 children (aged 3–19), who had been held in a remote Australian detention centre for more than 2 years, described 26 psychiatric disorders among the adults and 52 among the children, noting that 'every adult was diagnosed with a major depressive disorder and the majority (12, 86 per cent) also were diagnosed with PTSD… All but one child received a diagnosis of major depressive disorder and half were diagnosed with PTSD' (Steel *et al.* 2004).

When retrospective comparisons found that 'the adults had a threefold and the children a tenfold increase in psychiatric disorder subsequent to detention' (Steel *et al.* 2004), Steel and colleagues warned policy-makers of the dangers of prolonged detention. Their warning went unheeded.

In April 2004 the Australian Human Rights and Equal Opportunity Commission (HREOC) published its report from the National Inquiry into Children in Immigration Detention. The report opened with this quotation from the United Nations Convention on the Rights of the Child, article 37(b):

> No child shall be deprived of his or her liberty unlawfully or arbitrarily. The arrest, detention or imprisonment of a child shall be in conformity with the law and shall be used only as a measure of last resort and for the shortest appropriate period of time. (HREOC 2004)

The Inquiry found that, on 1 October 2003, just 30 percent of the 121 child detainees had been detained for less than 3 months; 57 percent had been detained for more than 1 year, 51 percent for over 2 years, and 7 percent for more than 3 years. The longest a child had ever been in immigration detention as at 1 January 2004, was 5 years, 5 months, and 20 days (HREOC 2004).

Ten years later, another Australian Human Rights Commission (2014) National Inquiry into Children in Immigration Detention found that these children had been forgotten. The Inquiry heard that, at the end of March 2014, there were 153 children under 2 years of age held in detention, and by September 2014 the average length of detention for children and parents was 1 year and 2 months.

From January 2013 to March 2014 there were 128 babies born to mothers in detention. A Freedom of Information request revealed that each birth was recorded on an incident form, categorized as a 'minor' incident, and given a number (Australian Government DIBP 2014). It is not clear if this number is used as ongoing identification of the now stateless infant who, by some strange logic, is deemed to have entered the country illegally. Parents bitterly complained that guards replaced fathers as the person accompanying mothers to hospital for the birth of their babies, and on at least two occasions, mothers were separated from their newborns as punishment for protesting against the policy of sending babies and their families to Nauru (personal communication).

Post-natal depression

A literature review, conducted across ten databases, to examine the rates of post-natal depression (PND) among refugee, asylum-seeker and immigrant women, found that PND 'may affect up to 42% of migrant women, compared to around 10–15% of native-born women' (Collins, Zimmerman & Howard 2011). The impact of parents' depression on infants in the normal population has been well documented (Brazelton, Koslowski & Main 1974; Cohn & Tronick 1983; Field 2010; Murray 1992). Less is known about PND and the infant–parent dynamic in immigration detention; a literature search failed to find any publication on this topic. However, a Netherlands community-based study (van Ee *et al.* 2016) of post-traumatic stress disorder (PTSD) examined 'a highly traumatized sample of 68 asylum seekers and refugees and their children (18–42 months) [and found] that parental symptoms of PTSD are directly related to children's insecure attachment and disorganized attachment'.

Interventions

Slobodin and de Jong (2014) conducted a critical review of research findings on a wide range of interventions that had been designed especially for traumatized asylum-seekers and refugees. The efficacy of the intervention was determined by quantitative assessment; and while the majority of studies reported positive outcomes, others were limited in their scope. The reviewers noted that 'there is a dearth of evidence-based data that would confirm the applicability of systemic family intervention' to refugees and asylum-seekers; they concluded that there were insufficient guidelines available for researchers and clinicians wanting to tailor interventions for these groups. Despite the breadth of this review, interventions specifically for infants did not feature.

Similar omissions occur in *A Practical Guide to Therapeutic Work With Asylum Seekers and Refugees* (Jalonen & Cilia La Corte 2018). Here, one chapter is devoted to separated asylum-seeking children, but the particular needs of infants are not addressed.

A report for the World Health Organization (Priebe, Giacco & El-Nagib 2016) reviewed the evidence on mental health care for refugees and asylum-seekers in Europe. The report does not mention infants specifically but refers to the Inter-Agency Standing Committee (IASC)[3] Guidelines on Mental Health and Psychosocial Support in Emergency Settings, where the needs of children aged 0–8 years are considered. These guidelines are very clear: Play is a priority. Managers are explicitly instructed to 'rapidly organize safe spaces where children can play…[and] support parents and community members to better support and care for their children' (IASC 2010). However, the mental health of infants, including the importance of enabling a psychological space for infant communication and play, is not taken up here.

Immigration detention in Australia could well be described as an 'emergency setting' for families, but attention to mental health and psychosocial support, especially for infants and children, is inexplicably absent. In their assessment of ten consecutive referrals to a remote Immigration Reception and Processing Centre, Mares and Jureidini (2004) noted that parents of children under 5 years of age complained that their children 'didn't know how to play'. More than 10 years later, my own observations of infants and young children in a Melbourne

---

3   The IASC comprises representatives from both UN and non-UN humanitarian organizations.

detention centre (Hill 2016) suggest that there is no psychological space for play in the Australian detention system.

Play and Infant Observation

Play starts at birth, if not before; it is how a baby communicates with her mother, father and others. Behavioural research (Bullowa 1979; Condon & Sander 1974; Malloch & Trevarthen 2010; Stern 1985) describes the infant as a sociable being who is eager for new experiences. Neuroscience shows how quickly and early synaptic connections are made in the infant brain, and, together with attachment research, demonstrates how these connections depend on the quality and quantity of the infant's interactions with others (Bick *et al.* 2017; Schore 2015;). Play between infant and mother marks the beginning of the infant's creative life:

> We find either that individuals live creatively and feel that life is worth living or else that they cannot live creatively and are doubtful about the value of living. This variable in human beings is directly related to the quality and quantity of environmental provision at the beginning or in the early phases of each baby's living experience. (Winnicott 1971, p.71)

Infant-led play, a feature of 'Watch, Wait, and Wonder' (Cohen, Lojkasek & Muir 2006), is now a widely implemented psychotherapeutic intervention that aims to help the parent and infant 'discover for themselves a new way of relating' (Cohen *et al.* 2006). The infant is the focus of the therapy, and the parent is invited to support the infant's play by being attentive but not intrusive, and by reflecting on the infant's experience with the help of a therapist.

Infant Observation was originally developed by the child psychoanalyst Esther Bick (1987) as a training method. Concerned with the developing inner world of the infant, this disciplined observation technique pays close attention to infant–parent interactions (play), and has been shown to have a transformative effect on the infant–parent relationship (Rustin 2006; Thomson-Salo 2014). In this way it can behave like a therapeutic intervention:

> The observer by visiting regularly and reliably, and through her consistent interest in the baby and its mother (and sometimes

sibs) seems often to sustain mother's attention to her infant. She may also provide [*sic*] some additional temporal structure in a situation where boundaries may be lacking, where a mother may feel engulfed by her infant's needs, and/or her own. (Rustin 2006)

Infant Observation and infant-led play informed the baby playgroup I will now describe.

The playgroup

I requested and was granted permission from the Department of Immigration and Border Protection (DIBP) to facilitate a playgroup for infants and their parents in detention. Two colleagues joined me: A Maternal and Child Health Nurse, and a psychologist, both experienced Infant Mental Health clinicians. Inexplicably, despite thorough and repeated security screening, detention centre staff treated us with a mixture of disdain and suspicion. Our genuine efforts to engage them were ignored. Feeling helpless and stuck gave us a very real sense of the detainees' experience, but we persisted.

Knowing that early infant experience has long-lasting effects, and hoping that the play space would facilitate some positive early experiences, we decided that the group would be offered to infants aged less than 12 months. The task we set ourselves was to use our Infant Observation skills with a very gentle 'Wait, Watch, and Wonder' (Cohen *et al.* 2006) approach to encourage play – to wait for the infant to lead, to help the mother recognize and enjoy her infant's efforts, and to join the infant when invited. While acknowledging the therapeutic potential of play, and having our professional ethics inform the work, our role did not include providing therapy or advice. And so, every Monday morning, for 18 months, we brought from our homes and gardens swathes of coloured material, sweet-smelling flowers, infant-friendly fruit and simple toys to create a beautiful and welcoming space. Then we waited, ready to play.

Guidelines for intervening

The emotional fragility of the infants and mothers required great sensitivity and care; positive interactions were celebrated. Our focus was the babies' play – often our only shared language. Parents were encouraged to observe their babies, to allow space for and marvel at their curiosity and skill, to admire their attempts to master a task, and to share the enjoyment of their successes.

Referrals to outside services were impossible in this environment. We made numerous attempts to communicate with the detention centre health staff, but our emails and messages went unanswered. We were left to carry considerable anxiety about the mental health of some babies and parents. Regular group supervision[4] with an infant psychiatrist helped us accept the reality of this impossible situation, but sometimes we found ourselves struggling to stay in role.

There was a high degree of uncertainty at every level. The centre's administration repeatedly lost our paperwork, causing long delays and confusion. Making a space for play needed to be held firmly in our minds as, despite official assurances, there was no guarantee that the physical space would actually be available to us. Security staff often used the room for their tea/lunch breaks, for meetings, or to watch television; it was as if we did not exist. No one seemed to know how long families would be detained, and the families themselves did not understand how or why people were suddenly moved into the community or sent to Nauru. Government policy itself was changeable, and both its own departments and asylum-seeker advocates had trouble keeping up. The only constant from one week to the next was our presence.

As the mothers and babies came to know us as benign and reliable, they became more relaxed in our presence and made good use of the play space. It was not so much that we made them 'feel special', as described by volunteer health workers in the UK (Balaam *et al.* 2016), but that we recognized them as normal human beings. Nevertheless, as the months passed, parents became more depressed and, disturbingly, their babies were less able to play. Infants born in detention marked their first birthday in detention. Parents, babies and we three volunteers struggled together against despair. How long could we go on?

Most guards knew only the names and faces of men in the families; it seemed that the mothers and infants were invisible, known only by their allocated numbers. Frequent staff changes made it impossible

---

4   Supervision with an experienced professional in the field provides a confidential space to process one's feelings about the work, to reflect on the work and to justify one's interventions.

for us to establish a working relationship with any of the guards and so other visitors became our only reliable source of information about the presence or absence of babies in the centre. Because we had no way of knowing who would come to playgroup, if they would or could come, and if they would or could come again, we could work only in the moment.

The following fragments of non-identifying case studies offer a small window into the playgroup. The scenes are taken from the confidential observation notes I wrote following the group each week as I tried to make sense of what I was seeing and experiencing.

■ Case study 1

The baby, about 3 months old, lay motionless in her pram. Her mother looked at us warily. We invited her to lay baby on the floor, assuring her that the rug was safe and clean. Mother found a baby blanket in the pram and laid the baby on her back on the blanket on the rug. The baby looked about. Mother picked up a rattle and shook it. Her baby looked at the rattle. Mother noticed this and shook it again. Baby's arms and legs moved excitedly, her eyes focused on her mother and the rattle. Mother laughed and baby vocalized.

■ Case study 2

The father brought his baby girl to playgroup because his wife was too ill. After being told that they will be sent back to Nauru, she has attempted suicide, twice. Beautifully dressed and neatly wrapped, the baby lay very still in her pram. When father placed her on the mat I spoke to her gently. She responded readily with a smile and moved her arms to the soft sounds coming from the toy music-box. The next week she was tense, with arms straight by her sides, and hands clenched into fists; her face was pale and expressionless; her eyes dull. Father told us he does not sleep but watches his wife all night to make sure she does not self-harm. Now the sole carer for his baby daughter, he is physically and emotionally exhausted. My colleague turned the lever on the music-box and baby moved her head towards the sound. We smiled hopefully at this but father, not registering his baby's interest in the music, talked bitterly of his desperate situation. We talked of play and passed him a brightly coloured, soft toy to tempt his baby daughter. He held it above her, half-heartedly, and while she was able to look at it, she made no attempt to reach for it. The following week, the father politely apologized that he could no longer come to playgroup because he must watch his wife. We had to accept that we could do no more, but the baby who had no one to play with stayed in our minds and now lives on this page.

Case study 3

The little girl was nearly 4 years old but looked half that age. She was tiny, anxious and vigilant. Her mother looked worn out and complained that her daughter refused to eat; as if to prove it, she offered the girl a strawberry from the bowl on the low table. This was met with an emphatic 'No!'

The playgroup had been created for babies who were not yet walking, but we quickly realized that we needed to be flexible; the original boundaries we had set were unhelpful. Nevertheless, the psychologically safe environment we were creating also had to be physically safe. When two very bouncy 6-year-old boys wanted to join their baby siblings, we were able to persuade them to play outside so they could still see their mothers through the large window but not disrupt the babies' play. At other times we needed to be firm and very clear, particularly with detention centre staff, that we were not providing childcare. In this case, the desperate anxiety of the little girl, in the presence of a mother who did not know what to do, could not be ignored. They had come to us for help. The next week I brought from home a miniature doll's house, positioning it a safe distance from the babies on the floor. The tiny girl soon discovered it, loving its tiny people in tiny rooms with tiny furniture. Each week she would make straight for it, letting out high-pitched squeals when she found her favourite pieces. She was especially attached to a tiny cabinet with doors that opened and closed, and she cried inconsolably when it was time to leave. Her mother wanted us to hide the cabinet so that her daughter would not be distressed. My colleague suggested that the cabinet might represent all that the girl had lost but did as mother requested. The little girl explored the rest of the doll's house and became very engaged with two dolls she called 'Mummy and Daddy'; she put them to bed and carefully tucked them in.

After the playgroup session the three of us wondered together about the cabinet: Would it help the little girl if we allowed her to take it with her, as a sort of transitional object to hold her together from one week to the next? Or was it more helpful to keep it safe for her so that she could rediscover it over and over, and build within herself a sense of certainty and reliability? The problem was that we never knew from one week to the next if families would be transferred; sudden and forced removals of families to Nauru were not uncommon. We made sure the cabinet was there for her each week, but when she put it down to play with something else, as she gradually came to do quite happily, the mother would always hide it. Over the following weeks, after playgroup, and in supervision, we had robust discussions about the little girl's versus the mother's needs, and how we might possibly offer the reliability so desperately required. Then one day, without warning, the little girl popped a strawberry in her mouth, then another, and clutching her little cabinet, she looked around at everyone and smiled.

▇ Case study 4 ▇

Very occasionally we were joined by an elegant woman with a beautiful but expressionless face, rather like a Byzantine Madonna. Her baby never left the pram but sat up and looked at us with a face so vacant that I felt quite desperate, my mind flooded with pictures of emotionally deprived Romanian orphans. Gathering myself, I offered her a brightly coloured ball. She grasped it eagerly, almost hungrily. When it slipped from her fingers to the floor she howled mournfully. This made her mother annoyed. I invited her onto the mat to explore and play, but mother refused, saying that if her daughter started playing and enjoying herself she would be upset when she had to leave. I found myself almost begging, on behalf of the baby, to let her play, but mother was resolute: baby stayed in the pram. We later learned something of the history of the trauma this mother had experienced and how that left little room for joy. More recently, we heard that the family is now in a community detention setting where the work continues towards enabling mother to allow her little girl to have her own experience.

Role and task

We had certainly under-estimated the complexity of the task of managing a playgroup in such a difficult setting. A complete lack of meaningful institutional support and our volunteer status made this a playgroup like no other. Tensions soon developed between us. At first it seemed that perhaps our task and role had not been clearly enough defined and accepted by all three of us. Boundaries were constantly re-negotiated as we attempted to respond to need. Mostly this was managed thoughtfully, as with the little girl and the doll's house, but on occasions, when we felt particularly helpless, we could not think clearly and tended to defensively retreat into our respective clinical roles. For example, when a mother expressed concern about her baby's physical development, my colleagues commenced a physical examination; one colleague's frustration with an inattentive mother led her to pick the baby up and make him face his mother, resulting in an angry response from both; one day I found myself manically re-arranging furnishings and play-things; and on another occasion a happily playing baby felt so intruded upon by my too-intense watching that she physically pushed me away!

We became aware of other pressures: tensions felt by the poorly trained security staff, clearly on edge, and perhaps feeling vulnerable; political tensions in the community and the media about accepting or rejecting asylum-seekers; and racial tensions amongst the detainees themselves. Uncertainty was unsettling and contagious, prompting rigid thinking and rigid behaviour from politicians, policy-makers, policy-enforcers and policy-victims, all the way down the line. We too risked being inflexible. As Bion (1962) reminds us, clinging to a fixed psychoanalytic position does not always promote development; we needed to use psychoanalytic concepts as 'guiding metaphors' (Woodcock 2000), not life-rafts. Regular professional supervision gave us a safe forum to explore tensions, to help us stay in role and on task, and to not drown.

The vicarious effects of uncertainty and helplessness on health professionals who are employed to provide mental health assessment and treatment for families in Australian immigration detention have been extensively described in a report by Mares and Jureidini (2004). Their own Kafkaesque experience prompts them to go so far as to question the ethics of attempting to provide mental health care to people who are held against their will in a system that only serves to perpetuate their mental illness.

Learnings and recommendations

When the function of immigration detention is to build uncertainty and destroy hope (as is the case in Australia), therapeutic work is obstructed and becomes painfully difficult. This work requires more than good intentions. It demands a deep understanding of relationships from a psychodynamic perspective and a strong, supportive, supervised space for reflection. It requires one to show respect and goodwill, to be open to exploring difficulties, and to be committed to holding the space. Rigid rules of engagement are unhelpful and likely to be defensive.

Boundaries are constantly challenged, re-assessed and re-formed. Ethically, the work requires us to regularly think and question: What is the task here and now? And who is doing what for whom?

As mental health professionals volunteering in a highly unusual playgroup setting, we came to understand that, essentially, the task is to be kind – to babies and parents, to detention centre staff and to each other. We learned that perhaps the best we can do when there is so much uncertainty is to reliably show our humanity, to play our authentic selves in a space we create and share; in this way we can allow a space of hope for infants even, or perhaps especially, when there appears to be none.

Acknowledgements

I warmly thank Brigid Arthur for her helpful introductions, Michele Meehan and Kerry Judd for their kind support, and Dr. Julie Stone for her thoughtful supervision. Thanks also to the Victorian branch of the Australian Association for Infant Mental Health whose philanthropy fund generously provided playgroup items. Most importantly, I wish to acknowledge the babies and their families who came to play.

References

ABF (2015) *Australian Border Force Bill (2015)*, as passed by both Houses, The Parliament of the Commonwealth of Australia, House of Representatives. Retrieved 22/01/19 from http://parlinfo.aph.gov.au/parlInfo/download/legislation/bills/r5408_aspassed/toc_pdf/15016b01.pdf;file Type=application%2Fpdf.

Australian Government DIBP (2014) *FOI Disclosure Logs*. Retrieved 05/02/19 from https://archive.homeaffairs.gov.au/AccessandAccountability/Documents/FOI/FA131200509.pdf.

Australian Human Rights Commission (2014) 'Findings and recommendations.' *The Forgotten Children: National Inquiry into Children in Immigration Detention*. Retrieved 05/02.19 from www.humanrights.gov.au/publications/forgotten-children-national-inquiry-children-immigration-detention-2014/2-findings-and.

Balaam, M. Cl., Kingdon, C., Thomson, G., Finlayson, K., & Downe, S. (2016) '"We make them feel special": The experiences of voluntary sector workers supporting asylum seeking and refugee women during pregnancy and early motherhood.' *Midwifery 34*, 133–40. Retrieved 22/01/19 from www.sciencedirect.com/science/article/pii/S0266613815003411.

Bick, E. (1987) 'Notes on Infant Observation in Psycho-analytic Training.' In *Collected Papers of Martha Harris and Esther Bick*. Perthshire: Clunie Press. (Original work published 1964).

Bick, J., Fox, N., Zeanah, C. & Nelson, C.A. (2017) 'Early deprivation, atypical brain development, and internalizing symptoms in late childhood.' *Neuroscience 342*, 140–153. Retrieved 22/01/19 from www.sciencedirect.com/science/article/pii/S0306452215008453.

Bion, W.R. (1962) *Learning From Experience*. New York: Jason Aronson.

Brazelton, T.B., Koslowski, B. & Main, M. (1974) 'The Origins of Reciprocity: The Early Mother-Infant Interaction'. In M. Lewis and L.A. Rosenblum (Eds) *The Effect of the Infant on Its Caregiver*. New York: Wiley-Interscience.

Bullowa, M. (Ed.) (1979) *Before Speech: The Beginnings of Human Communication*. London: Cambridge University Press.

Cohen, N.J., Lojkasek, M. & Muir, E. (2006) 'Watch, Wait, and Wonder: An infant-led approach to infant-parent psychotherapy.' *The Signal 14*, 2, 1–4.

Cohn, J.E. and Tronick, E.Z. (1983) 'Three-month-old infants' reaction to simulated maternal depression.' *Child Development 54*, 185–193.

Collins, C.H., Zimmerman, C. & Howard, L.M. (2011) 'Refugee, asylum seeker, immigrant women and postnatal depression: Rates and risk factors.' *Archives of Women's Mental Health 14*, 1, 3–11. Retrieved 20/01/19 from https://link.springer.com/article/10.1007/s00737-010-0198-7.

Condon, W.S. & Sander, L.S. (1974) 'Neonate movement is synchronised with adult speech: Interactional participation and language acquisition.' *Science 183*, 99–101.

Doherty, B. (2016a) 'Doctors refuse to discharge "Baby Asha" because of fears for safety on Nauru.' *The Guardian,* 12 February, 2016. Retrieved 22/01/19 from www.theguardian.com/australia-news/2016/feb/12/doctors-refuse-to-discharge-baby-asha-because-of-fears-for-safety-on-nauru.

Doherty, B (2016b) 'Doctors freed to speak about Australia's detention regime after U-turn.' *The Guardian,* 20 October, 2016. Retrieved 22/01/19 from www.theguardian.com/australia-news/2016/oct/20/doctors-freed-to-speak-about-australias-detention-regime-after-u-turn.

Fazel, M. & Stein, A. (2002) 'The mental health of refugee children.' *Archives of Disease in Childhood 87*, 5, 366–370. Retrieved 22/01/19 from www.ncbi.nlm.nih.gov/pubmed/12390902.

Field, T. (2010) 'Postpartum depression effects on early interactions, parenting, and safety practices: A review.' *Infant Behavior and Development 33*, 1, 1–6. Retrieved 22/01/19 from www.sciencedirect.com.ezproxy.lib.swin.edu.au/science/article/pii/S0163638309000976.

Fitzgerald, H.E. & Barton, L.R. (2000) 'History of Infant Mental Health: Origins and Emergence of an Interdisciplinary Field.' In Joy D. Osofsky & Hiram E. Fitzgerald (Eds) *WAIMH Handbook of Infant Mental Health (Vol. 1): Perspectives on Infant Mental Health* (1st ed.).Hoboken, NJ: John Wiley & Sons. Retrieved 22/01/19 from www.researchgate.net/publication/232709421_History_of_infant_mental_health_Origins_and_emergence_of_an_interdisciplinary_field.

Hatch, P., Smith, B. & Ireland, J. (2015) 'Royal Children's Hospital refused to discharge mother and child to detention.' *The Age*, 11 October, 2015. Retrieved 22/01/19 from www.theage.com.au/victoria/royal-childrens-hospital-refused-to-discharge-mother-and-child-to-detention-20151011-gk6exf.html.

Hill, C. (2016) 'Playing in the reality of detention.' *Socioanalysis 18*, 89–91.

HREOC (2004) *A Last Resort? National Inquiry Into Children in Immigration Detention*. Sydney: Human Rights and Equal Opportunity Commission. Retrieved 22/01/19 from www.humanrights.gov.au/sites/default/files/document/publication/alr_complete.pdf.

IASC (2010) *Mental Health and Psychosocial Support in Humanitarian Emergencies: What should Protection Programme Managers Know?* Geneva: Inter-Agency Standing Committee (IASC) Global Protection Cluster Working Group and IASC Reference Group for Mental Health and Psychosocial Support in Emergency Settings. Retrieved 22/01/19 from https://interagencystandingcommittee.org/iasc.

Jalonen, A. & Cilia la Corte, P. (2018) *A Practical Guide to Therapeutic Work with Asylum Seekers and Refugees*. London: Jessica Kingsley Publishers.

Malloch, S. and Trevarthen, C. (2010) *Communicative Musicality: Exploring the Basis of Human Companionship.* Oxford: Oxford University Press.

Mares, S. & Jureidini, J. (2004) 'Psychiatric assessment of children and families in immigration detention – clinical, administrative, and ethical issues.' *Australian and New Zealand Journal of Public Health 28*, 520–526.

Murray, L. (1992) 'The impact of postnatal depression on infant development.' *Journal of Child Psychology and Psychiatry 33*, 3, 543–561.

Newman, L.K. & Steel, Z. (2008) 'The child asylum seeker: Psychological and developmental impact of immigration detention.' *Child and Adolescent Psychiatric Clinics of North America 17*, 3, 665–683. Retrieved 22/01/19 from www.ncbi.nlm.nih.gov/pubmed/18558318.

News Limited (2012) 'Abbott vows to turn back asylum boats.' *Herald Sun*, 21 January 2012. Retrieved 27/01/19 from http://link.galegroup.com/apps/doc/A277736400/STND?u=slv&sid=STND&xid=bd5c606e.

Priebe, S., Giacco, D. & El-Nagib, R. (2016) 'Public health aspects of mental health among migrants and refugees: A review of the evidence on mental health care for refugees, asylum seekers and irregular migrants in the WHO European Region.' *Health Evidence Network Synthesis Report 47.* Copenhagen: WHO Regional Office for Europe. Retrieved 22/01/19 at www.ncbi.nlm.nih.gov/books/NBK391045.

Refugee Council of Australia (2017) *Recent Changes in Australian Refugee Policy.* Retrieved 05/02/19 from www.refugeecouncil.org.au/publications/recent-changes-australian-refugee-policy.

Robjant, K., Hassan, R. & Katona, C. (2009) 'Mental health implications of detaining asylum seekers: Systematic review.' *British Journal of Psychiatry 194*, 4, 306–312. Retrieved 22/01/19 from http://bjp.rcpsych.org/content/194/4/306.

Rustin, M. (2006) 'Infant observation research: What have we learned so far?' *Infant Observation 9*, 1, 35–52. Retrieved 22/01/19 from http://roar.uel.ac.uk/305.

Schore, A. N. (2015) *Affect Regulation and the Origin of the Self: The Neurobiology of Emotional Development.* New York: Routledge.

Slobodin, O. & de Jong, J.T. (2014) 'Mental health interventions for traumatised asylum seekers and refugees: What do we know about their efficacy?' *International Journal of Social Psychiatry 61*, 1, 17–26. Retrieved 22/01/19 from www.ncbi.nlm.nih.gov/pubmed/24869847.

Steel, Z., Momartin, S., Bateman, C., Hafshejani, A. *et al.* (2004) 'Psychiatric status of asylum seeker families held for a protracted period in a remote detention centre in Australia.' *Australian and New Zealand Journal of Public Health 28*, 527–536.

Stern, D.N. (1985) *The Interpersonal World of the Infant. A View from Psychoanalysis and Developmental Psychology.* New York: Basic Books.

Thomson-Salo, F. (Ed.) (2014) *Infant Observation: Creating Transformative Relationships.* London: Karnac.

UNHCR (2018) *Figures at a Glance.* Retrieved 16/9/18 from http://www.unhcr.org/figures-at-a-glance.html.

van Ee, E., Kleber, R.J., Jongmans, M.J., Mooren, T.T.M. & Out, D. (2016) 'Parental PTSD, adverse parenting and child attachment in a refugee sample.' *Attachment & Human Development 18*, 3, 273–291.

Winnicott, D.W. (1971) *Playing and Reality.* London: Routledge.

Woodcock, J. (2000) *Refugee Children and Their Families: Theoretical and Clinical Perspective.* London: Whurr Publishers Limited. Retrieved 22/01/19 from http://citeseerx.ist.psu.edu/viewdoc/download?doi=10.1.1.463.2553&rep=rep1&type=pdf.

PART 5

Mental Health, Community Nursing and Medical Systems

CHAPTER 15

Infants With Cancer

The Oncology Unit as Their Second Home

MARIA McCARTHY AND HELEN SHOEMARK

Introduction

With many paediatric cancer diagnoses occurring in the first years of life, infants and young families are disproportionately impacted by childhood cancer. Infants undergoing oncology (cancer) treatments can spend weeks to months of their first two years in hospital. The oncology ward frequently becomes a 'second home' to young families, who, in addition to their infant with cancer, may also be caring for younger or older siblings. Caring for these sick infants therefore extends beyond treatment of the disease to embrace emotional and developmental impacts, and requires the expertise of the multidisciplinary oncology healthcare team.

A diagnosis of cancer in infancy is devastating and has traditionally been associated with a very poor prognosis. Fortunately, changes in treatment protocols have resulted in significantly improved survival rates over the past decade. In addition, growing numbers of infants with complex, non-malignant immunological conditions (e.g. bone marrow failure, immunodeficiency) are being treated with traditional oncology treatments such as bone marrow transplantation. These changes have led to an increased focus in oncology upon the infant, their illness experience, and the quality of their attachments and family life.

Area of practice

During the newborn period and early months of life, cancer treatment vastly alters the sensory, psychological and social/emotional world of the infant and their family. In this highly complex medical environment, the treatment team must understand and address the needs arising from an infant's exposure to noxious medical procedures and treatment side effects. In addition, there is heightened emotional stress for the parent/attachment figures and impingements on the infant–parent attachment relationship. In this context, the ecological system of the family may be intact and simultaneously under threat. Alternatively, families may enter the medical system with pre-existing, multiple psychosocial risk factors that may challenge their capacity to endure in this highly stressful setting. Doctors, nurses and allied health staff work together to ensure that the infant's experience is recognised and their evolving relationship with their family is maintained and strengthened. This includes privileging the parents' capacity to retain a nurturing and protective role.

In this chapter, we aim to outline the typical hospital experience for these infants. A case example is provided which exemplifies the possibilities of supportive infant and family interventions. We hope that this chapter will be helpful to clinicians seeking to adopt an infant-sensitive lens to their work with medically unwell young children. We also hope that readers will gain a greater insight into the infants' experience, and what their family members may have endured. These children will commonly go on to be seen in the community by maternal and child health nurses, general practitioners, paediatricians, and staff in childcare centres and schools. We propose that if community professionals know more about the infant's cancer experience, it may also enable them to help make sense of such early severe and profound interruptions in the lives of these families.

■ Baby Oscar

Oscar was a much-wanted baby of Lydia and Paul and conceived through assisted reproductive technology treatment, as was his older brother Henry. Oscar required care in the neonatal nursery for the first five days of life and Lydia was unable to hold him for two days. At 3 months of age, Oscar was admitted to hospital with a fever. This was the first of several admissions over a period of months, including two admissions to a paediatric intensive care unit. At 9 months Oscar was diagnosed with congenital neutropenia, a genetic disorder of the bone marrow, and, at 12 months of age, he was hospitalised to undergo a bone marrow transplant.

Most healthy 12-month-old infants, in well-functioning families, would typically experience a caregiving environment committed to providing settling, enjoyable and playful experiences with available attachment figures providing consistent routines. In contrast, Oscar faced many potential perils to his physical and psychological wellbeing. Bone marrow transplant is a particularly complex medical intervention which requires intensive drug therapies, has high morbidity and mortality risks and requires weeks to months of hospitalisation. This physical confinement results in prolonged social isolation and anxious and exhausted parents. Further, on a daily basis, Oscar was required to interact with numerous healthcare professionals, resulting in constant disruptions to usual infant routines. All of these factors contributed to what could have been a potentially traumatic environment for little Oscar and his family.

Trauma, illness and treatment

Infants undergoing oncology care undergo multiple invasive treatments. These include central nervous system-directed chemotherapies and procedures such as lumbar punctures, accessing of infusaports and intravenous lines, and insertion of nasogastric tubes. These treatments are distressing for both infants and their parents/caregivers. For the infants, they can result in numerous unpleasant physical side effects such as infections, nausea and significant pain. Assessing infant pain is complex and there is often concern that pain is under-recognised and under-treated in these patients (Stevens 2007). Additionally, there is the potential for damaging psychological and developmental impacts which may further disrupt and impact the infant's relationships with their primary attachment figures as well as impair cognitive and motor skill development (Adamson, *et al.* 2011; Anderson & Kunin-Batson 2009; Green *et al.* 2013).

Infants receiving oncology treatments are therefore, by necessity, subject to a large magnitude of stresses, both physical and emotional, for prolonged periods. Despite a robust literature describing the traumatic impacts of childhood cancer, relatively little research has been specifically directed to understanding these impacts for infants and their families (Graf, Bergstraesse & Landolt 2013; Kazak & Baxt 2007). Research has demonstrated, however, that infants exposed to 'toxic' stress (excessive or consistently high stress levels), can experience disruption to developing brain circuitry and other regulatory systems, creating a lasting impact on their physiology, behaviour and health (Garner *et al.* 2012; American Academy of Pediatrics 2012; Shonkoff, Boyce & McEwan 2009). For medically compromised newborns, toxic stress can be precipitated by any paediatric hospitalisation, and particularly so in the absence of a parent and other buffering supports (Sanders & Hall 2018; Shah *et al.* 2016). Although there is not currently direct research examining toxic stress and infant cancer, it is reasonable to extrapolate these findings to the experience of infants who undergo oncology treatments.

Situational medical trauma is evident in many descriptions parents give of their experiences of their infants' treatment and hospitalisations (Jones 2007). Parents frequently report re-experiencing the moment they learnt of their child's diagnosis and re-live unpleasant memories associated with their child's treatment (Kazak & Baxt 2007). Additionally, parent's anxieties are heightened around whether they are doing a 'good enough job' of caring for their baby. This can influence and also restrict the ability for the parent(s) and infant to discover a sense of ease or reciprocity in their still-evolving relationship. First-time parents may be particularly vulnerable in this regard, with little or no reference points to appraise the nature and quality of the relationship.

Even with the best possible care, infants and families will experience at least some aspects of their illness or treatment as traumatic. A trauma-informed approach to care is necessary to guide professionals in creating a safe and containing environment for families, identifying the need to build trusting partnerships with infants and their families, and ensuring assiduous attention to preventing unnecessary experiences of pain, distress or separation. This requires the highest standards of care, a strong commitment to reflective practice (Weatherston, Weigand & Weigand 2010) (see also Chapter 2 on reflective supervision) and flexibility to ensure opportunities for infants and families to express their emotional responses to their experiences.

▓ Oscar's adaptation to illness ▓

Reflecting on his precarious first days and recurrent illnesses, Lydia described Oscar as a 'mellow, happy-go-lucky' baby. Despite experiencing numerous hospitalisations, Lydia reported that Oscar showed minimal distress when being treated by his doctors and nurses. She noted that the hospital staff were always keen to interact with Oscar, and Lydia thought that perhaps they were 'drawn to his easy-going personality'. During the transplant phase of his treatment, Oscar would be required to endure far more intensive medical treatment than he had previously experienced. Lydia reported that the 'gentleness' of the nursing and medical staff were particularly important in reducing any distress associated with Oscar's medical procedures. She also identified the importance of her role in supporting Oscar. In particular, Lydia had always been allowed to hold Oscar in a comfortable position (e.g. on her knee, or hugging hold) during treatments or as he was given general anaesthetics, so that he always fell asleep in her arms prior to operating room procedures. This approach was utilised for any medical procedures during transplant, and Lydia and Paul were encouraged to advocate for this in instances where staff were not known to, or familiar with, Oscar and his parents' knowledge of how to comfort him. It was noted that Oscar responded well to diversion strategies; for example, he used a favourite squeezy ball, which he like to hold while his dressings were changed. Play therapy and music therapy staff engaged with him and Lydia, and discovered additional sensory diversion techniques of singing, music and picture books that helped him during procedures.

The first steps in building a treatment plan for Oscar and his family required the multidisciplinary oncology team to assess and reflect on how to support the primacy of Oscar's attachment needs within his caregiving system. Oscar's previous capacities of resilience in the context of many medical procedures, consideration of his experiences with previous hospitalisations, and his parents' strengths and vulnerabilities were critical factors in creating an infant-centred psychosocial care plan.

Managing procedural pain and distress

Pain control is always crucial, but even more so when young infants are not able to explain, locate or even protest in a way that identifies the level or location of pain. In addition to pharmacological help, such as sucrose (which suppresses the experience of pain), oncology nurses, procedural pain clinicians, play and music therapists can help with behavioural interventions that can reduce infant pain and distress, and provide coaching to parents on optimal procedural techniques. These include the physical containment of swaddling very young infants, or positioning the older infant or toddler on a parent's lap in a hugging hold, and sensory diversion techniques such as blowing bubbles, colourful toys or noise makers, singing and music or sensory toys (Wilson-Smith 2011). An encouraging and calm presence and interactive style, including positive language and soothing intonation of the voice from parents and oncology staff is crucial (Jones 2007; Rennick *et al.* 2018). Importantly, observing the infant's cues and their individual response to medical procedures will enable staff and parents to identify, anticipate and implement more effective pain management strategies (Harris 2005). As Sanders and Hall (2018) stated, 'parents should be central in the prevention, assessment and management of their babies' pain and stress'.

The everyday experience for the hospitalised infant

For infants and parents in oncology, treatment requires days, weeks or months of being confined to a hospital ward or room. In the bone marrow transplant unit the infant is confined to their single room for the duration of their stay, with only parents and two other 'support' visitors allowed during this period. One parent is allowed to stay with the infant overnight. Siblings are not allowed to visit and must rely on telephone calls and video interactions with their parent and infant sibling. The infant may be monitored on a screen at the nursing hub, allowing staff to see the baby at all times. A typical day will commence with early morning nursing monitoring and the medical team rounds where as many as 6–8 healthcare professionals will discuss the infant's status. Due to infection risk, anyone entering the patient's room is required to wear a gown and face mask which obscures facial expressions. For the newborn infant, facial expression, body tone and reading one's own sympathetic responses make important contributions to communication (Reddy & Trevarthen 2004; Rustin 2014; Stern 1974). Multiple 'visits' from both familiar and unfamiliar people continue throughout the day, from doctors, nurses, allied health staff, kitchen staff and cleaners, and frequent nursing checks occur overnight. The infant typically has several intravenous lines attached from their body to a monitoring device on a pole that irregularly emits loud beeps that require nursing staff to enter the room to reset the equipment. Numerous other non-contingent noises, including overhead loudspeakers, sirens and alarms occur throughout the day and night. If the infant is to undergo a general anaesthetic for a procedure, they may be required to fast (i.e. not eat) for many hours prior to surgery. Infants who become precariously unwell may be transferred to the intensive care unit for critical medical care.

Families in a restricted hospital environment are confined to a singular focus: their infant's day. The daily experience is a blend of mundane predictability, simmering anxiety and a concerted attempt to retain some control over the world 'outside their door'. There is a lot of waiting, wondering and thinking. Parenting in this environment is highly complex and each parent brings their own personality, life experience and social context to this experience. Some parents seem to function on 'autopilot', others cannot manage their emotions and create great disruptions, others find the experience overwhelming and suffer greatly yet in silence, and others become fierce advocates for their infants. We also know these differing emotional responses and coping mechanisms are not mutually exclusive. As a result, these infants may live each day within the influence of a dysregulated, anxious or traumatised parent, and, as such, a less than optimal situation for their healthy development.

Infant-centred hospital care

Despite significant illness and the vastly altered environment, infants can also have periods of being well, in which they need to play and experience joy and fun. The older infant has already developed an expectation of daily life and continues to be mobile and vocal; and the demanding busyness is unrelenting – the toddler continues to be a toddler! Without the opportunity for usual, incidental and regular interactions with others, most parents try to consciously and actively create ordinary experiences for their infant and themselves. Parents often experience the hospital programme, which shapes and restricts their days, as unrelenting. At their disposal, they have only what is already in the room, and are at constant risk of feeling unable to provide adequately at a crucial time in their infant's neurological development. They are reliant on someone from that permitted group of staff actually arriving at their door to bring interactive experiences such as music, play and art. While a play therapist may regularly arrive with new items for play, the older infant or toddler tires quickly of these, and the parent must find the mental and physical energy to construct creativity, vitality and initiative. When provided with resources and opportunities for play and activity, parents and infants are often tenacious in their willingness to maximise any such prospect. This appetite for novelty and activity is commonly evident, regardless of the parent's current vulnerability, as the delivery of new activities and resources gives parents respite from their unrelenting presence in their child's room.

While opportunities for 'normal' activities may be sparse, the intrusiveness of medical treatments and monitoring is not. Consequently, providing opportunity for predictability and routines in the hospitalised infant's day can be particularly challenging. For parents, this can be experienced as a loss of control and a source of great frustration. The importance of preserving sleep is fundamental to the wellbeing of the infant (and parent!). Usual and daily infant routines are often profoundly disrupted, particularly during the night when the infant's sleep will often be disturbed. Nurses play a key supportive role in this arena, encouraging parents to adopt an eat-play-sleep routine with their infant whenever possible, using signs on the door to indicate an infant is sleeping, and tailoring their interactions to the infant's degree of wakefulness. Incidental interactions in the middle of the night are to be avoided, and careful consideration of the need and timing of medical interventions, minimising random noise and dimming lights during 'quiet time', can significantly reduce unnecessary disruption to the infant's daily hospital experience, creating a settled sensory experience.

The crying infant can present particular challenges to carers. While crying is an appropriate expressive communication in healthy infants, it can also be a sign of pain in the medically unwell infant. For nurses, and parents, there can be an impulse to 'fix' things, often due to a concern about pain, and they may do this by providing analgesia or because of a lack of time in a busy ward, thus avoiding engaging in soothing behavioural strategies. Developing skills in interpreting infant cues is crucial and best achieved with parents and nurses working closely together. A referral to an allied health or infant mental health clinician is helpful when an infant's distress or attachment difficulties are alarming. The task is to encourage parents and staff to find space in their minds and their days to observe, listen and reflect on what the infant is communicating. An exhausted infant and parent need to feel emotionally and psychologically validated and also supported to find different ways of understanding what each might be feeling and trialling different comfort strategies.

Infant-centred psychosocial teams

Play is recognised as a crucial part of the development of a secure attachment. Experiences in which the parent–infant pair share exploration, novelty and pleasant surprises are essential in the development of their relationship together, but parents may worry about the risk of upsetting their baby and therefore may keep their interactions muted. Play, art and music therapists draw on the infant's desire for playful companionship and musicality to engage them in an array of creative experiences which promote age-appropriate development. For brief episodes of time, this creates a sense of normality, in which fun and joy emerge to balance the medicalisation of daily life (Shoemark *et al.* 2018). Additionally, physiotherapy or occupational therapy can provide assessment and tailored interventions when development is impinged on by both the illness and treatment.

Many of the medical tests require that infants fast (go without food). This is stressful for the newborn, particularly under 6 weeks old, and for the breastfeeding mother as medical interventions can interfere with establishing breastfeeding routines and also impact a mother's milk supply. Fasting for the older infant can be confusing and distressing when they cannot understand why a mother would refuse them nourishment. Dieticians consider any child under the age of 2 as a high-risk patient due to the risks of withdrawing access to nutrition and hindering successful feeding routines. Dieticians note that feeding an infant is often a fragile new developmental skill and a process that is easily compromised, creating a punishing cycle of stress for parents.

▧ Oscar at 12 months

At 12 months Oscar impressed everyone as a smiling, happy-looking baby with a shock of dark hair and a curious, busy nature. Fortunately, Oscar had also had times of being well, during which he reached his milestones. Lydia recalled Oscar's normal development: he began to sit up at 7 months and was commando crawling and pulling himself to stand at 12 months. Lydia reported he was 'into everything' and enjoyed interactive play. Oscar could take turns in play, babbled frequently and had a few single words: 'mum', 'dad' and 'hi'. Lydia was worried that the impending bone marrow transplant could change Oscar's personality.

Oscar presented as enjoying a strong and secure attachment with his parents which enabled him to withstand the multiple medical challenges he faced. He continued to cope well, even during periods of being very sick. However, during transplant, Oscar stopped using the single words he had developed. Some developmental and emotional regression is typical during periods of prolonged hospitalisation and may be related to how unwell the infant is, the baby's loss of sense of agency over their environment, and/or increasing dependence on parents and staff to meet daily needs. Conversely, when feeling relatively well, Oscar continued to be interactive and playful. Daily visits from the music therapist were a highlight for both Oscar and Lydia. Lydia would sing good morning to Oscar and this routine continued after they returned home. Singing and enjoying music together helped Lydia and Oscar to maintain a healthy, mutually satisfying interaction, with Oscar building his expressive communicative skills even without words.

Parent–infant attachment

The ordeal of cancer treatment threatens to affect the infant's experience of their parents as primary attachment figures. At times, parents may be unable to protect them from a fearful context and experiences of pain. Clinicians need to take every opportunity to remediate this threat by supporting opportunities for parent and infant to grow their capacity to interpret and ascribe congruent and compassionate meaning to behaviours and interactions.

Despite best efforts, hospitalisation results in at least some degree of parental separation as multiple hospital staff literally step between parent and infant to conduct physical examinations and medical procedures. As a result of the disruption to their 'secure base', the hospitalised infant may appropriately protest, requiring a careful emotionally-modulated approach to avoid greater infant distress or despair. For those infants who are greatly distressed by being left alone, the solo parent must plan even ordinary events, like showering, or washing clothes. The partnership with nurses is key as they attend to the infant, allowing the parent those moments away.

■ Oscar's attachment

An indication of Lydia's capacity for reflection and concern for her son's emotional life was evident when she questioned whether the bone marrow transplant would change Oscar's personality. Oscar's resilience and his healthy capacity to protest were demonstrated when one of his parents was not present with him. On one occasion, when Lydia attempted to leave his hospital room to get some dinner, Oscar pulled out his medical lines. In this protest, Oscar showed emotional strength and determination, whereas other more compromised infants may simply give up and withdraw. Oscar was one part of a strong dyadic relationship in which he had learnt that protest was useful and responded to when his sense of security and safety was threatened. Lydia and Paul provided a consistent parental response. For example, they would 'tag team' with 'five-minute handovers' when Paul arrived in the evenings to stay overnight to ensure Oscar was not left alone and to enable Lydia to go home to see Henry. If one parent was unwell or unavailable, the other remained 24 hours a day. Lydia reported that in order for Oscar to see she was still present, she knew she had to leave the bathroom door open.

Parent experience and their wellbeing

Parents of hospitalised infants feel stress, strain, separation, depression, despair, disappointment, ambivalence and lack of control over their situation, as well as vacillation between hope and hopelessness (Obeidat, Bond & Callister 2009). Research has consistently identified that parents of children with cancer experience elevated rates of acute and post-traumatic stress symptoms (PTSS) (Kazak & Baxt 2007; McCarthy *et al.* 2012; Vernon *et al.* 2017). Importantly, we know that parents' own trauma histories are related to their psychological adjustment (Price *et al.* 2016). Elevated rates of PTSS, depression and anxiety symptoms have been linked to poorer mental health outcomes for parents and less optimal parent–infant relationships (Cho, Holditch-Davis & Miles 2008; Muller-Nix *et al.* 2004). Infants, as part of an attachment system, will be influenced by the parents' emotional state, thus the availability of parent support and counselling in this context is critical.

When siblings, grandparents, and extended family and friends are restricted due to infection risks, parents may experience the loss of their familial support structure at a critical time in the life of the family. Across the hospital admission, staff look for the cues that indicate a significant change in the parents' resilience and coping abilities. Key events such as the loss of a partner's presence on the ward due to work commitments, signs of emerging PTSS or significant developmental change in the infant (e.g. separation anxiety) should trigger psychosocial referrals. However, access to hospital psychosocial services is not always timely and may be constrained due to limited resources, creating further risk for those overwhelmed families.

▦ Oscars' parents, Lydia and Paul

Lydia told us that, as a child, she suffered from anxiety and depression. She recalled that this commenced around the age of 12 and was associated with her own mother's serious illness. Lydia continued to take anti-depressants over many years and used many strategies to assist her psychological health – these included daily exercise (walking), cleaning/organising, and ensuring she got out of the house with the children each day. Importantly, Lydia was aware that these strategies would not be available to her during Oscar's transplant and she was keen to receive her own psychological support. Lydia described herself as a relaxed parent. She and Paul maintained strong routines with both their children. Paul was less known to hospital staff but, like Lydia, presented as a warm and loving parent. Despite being anxious about Oscar's transplant, he expressed confidence in the medical team and was optimistic the transplant would be a success. Paul had arranged to have six weeks off work to help care for Oscar, and to stay overnight so Lydia could return home to Oscar's brother Henry. The family were well supported by extended family members who were particularly available to care for Henry.

When a social work or mental health referral is made, these services are often provided to the parents, and primarily to the mother of the infant. A mother's concerns can be quite practical (e.g. 'not knowing if I can pick him up'), and the referrals from nurses to infant mental health or social work services can be quite simple (e.g. 'Mum is a bit down'), through to more formal assessment of risks to parental mental health. Treatment for more substantial PTSS, depression and mental health issues is key in preventing longer-term psychological sequalae for these parents and their infants (Kazak & Baxt 2007), and cognitive behavioural strategies, mindfulness and supportive counselling are approaches used in helping parents to manage the powerful thoughts and feelings associated with the uncertainty of their child's health and future (Kazak 2005). In a few cases, experiences of contingent interaction may be offered directly to the infant of parents who are emotionally unavailable, and close collaboration across the team ensures the infant engages in regular interaction with familiar people.

▓ Lydia and Paul's experience ▓▓▓▓▓▓▓▓▓▓▓▓▓▓▓▓

Lydia reported feeling 'claustrophobic' in the hospital room. She initially experienced considerable distress during the first days of Oscar's admission. She was particularly anxious about the prospect of the prolonged admission and enforced social isolation. As soon as was feasible, the nursing staff moved Oscar to a more light-filled room with a garden view, which Lydia found more calming. Throughout the transplant, Lydia was encouraged to engage in her own pre-admission creative outlets such as decorating Oscar's room and various craft activities that reflected her own professional skills as a designer. Over the course of Oscar's treatment Lydia responded positively to regular therapy sessions with a mental health worker. Paul was also seen intermittently and this also enabled both parents to appraise the emotional adjustment of their two children as the family adapted to life on the oncology ward for such an unpredictable time period. Oscar experienced many medical setbacks during his transplant, and parent counselling and support during these periods increased.

Lydia and Paul demonstrated quite different coping styles. Lydia seemed very organised, and took responsibility over the long periods of hospitalisation and home-based care. She kept a daily journal and used her professional skills to create a photographic record of Oscar's hospitalisation. Although he regularly stayed at the hospital with Oscar, Paul preferred not to know too many details of Oscar's treatment. When they eventually went home, Lydia chose to chart on a calendar all Oscar's medications/treatments, which she utilised to actively involve Paul in Oscar's medical care.

Practice approach/principles

Just as it takes a village to raise a child, it takes a team to care for an infant in oncology. By demonstrating an interest in the infant as a baby rather than as just a patient, clinicians can support a parent's focus on shared experiences (mutual regulation) in which parent and infant experience are attuned to one another and the adults recognise the infant as a social partner in an evolving relationship (Jones 2007). For the mental health worker/social worker, supporting this infant–parent partnership is a delicate balance between sharing an interest in the baby's development and at the same time being available to support the parent in distress.

Young babies need psychologically available, authentic connections wherever they are, but crucially when they are sick and frightened.

The staff work to help create and support the attachment system. This in turn is key in sustaining parental self-efficacy and their own sense that they can protect, promote and enhance the life of their infant. Equally, capturing the self-agency of the infant – for example, when Oscar would protest at his parent's departure during medical procedures – recognises that the infant has their own separate emotional responses and experiences. The infant is just as entitled to be heard, thought about and responded to in a congruent and supportive manner. This provides the infant with important relational and socio-emotional experiences which validate what their developing internal states are telling them about how to organise their emotional responses to big and often overwhelmingly painful and distressing events. Oscar asked for help and sought comfort from his parents, and at his tender age he experienced ongoing trust in his caregiving world.

In modern medicine, parents are rightly regarded as central members of their child's team. Current models of paediatric care call on parents to be active partners in delivering aspects of their infant's medical care which were previously the province of professionals (e.g. delivering medications, nasogastric tube feeding, physical therapy and supporting their child during painful procedures). These actions reduce the number of new people the infant has to learn to trust for their care. However, it also distorts the normal parent–child relationship as the parents administer treatments which may be unpleasant or painful despite any protest from their infant. Importantly, access to partnerships with those who 'know babies', such as maternal infant nurses and allied health clinicians, provides moments of normal experience in which parents learn about their own capacity to parent, ask the questions that most parents ask and are allowed to retain a little of the expected trajectory as they celebrate those unimpinged aspects of their baby's ongoing development. Creating opportunities to build connections with other parents of infants is also sustaining, even if it is within the hospital world.

Continuity of care beyond the hospital is also critical for families as they continue ongoing responsibility for the infant's care. It may only be following the end of treatment that the developmental impacts upon the infant or the psychological sequalae for parents can be addressed. Further, many of these infants will require years of medical surveillance, and the threat of relapse remains a major fear for parents. Community-based workers, such as allied health clinicians, maternal infant nurses and early childhood educators, may be particularly helpful in providing interventions for these infants and families or in helping the infant's transition back to engaging in 'normal' early childhood activities.

◼ Oscar post-transplant

Once home, Lydia and Paul began the process of re-establishing their family life. Oscar rapidly settled into a usual pattern of home life. Once he was medically well enough, he demonstrated no troubling anxiety when he separated from Lydia and Paul, and was cared for by his grandparents or extended family. Lydia and Paul explained that they experienced numerous aspects of Oscar's illness and treatment as traumatic and were referred to an external family therapist to work through the impact this had on their couple and family relationships. They found a short number of sessions were very helpful. Oscar has continued to remain well and increasingly is engaging in preschool activities.

Conclusion

The literature and research into the impacts of trauma in the life of an infant does not tend to include the experience of cancer or oncological treatment. The threat to the infant's life at the cellular level is accompanied by the harshness of medical treatment which threatens the parental role as protector and nurturer. This is rarely simple, and usually complex, with the cycle of threats and progress often repeated before there is a hope of resolution. Families, in all their forms, seek to provide the best loving and supportive context that they can while the practitioners around them simultaneously cure the cellular insult caused by the disease, minimise the consequences of that treatment and sustain the infant and family's opportunities for emotional and relational growth, development and happiness.

Acknowledgements

We are deeply grateful to 'Oscar's' family for allowing us to share their experiences.

Our sincere thanks to the families and staff of the Royal Children's Hospital Children's Cancer Centre, whose extraordinary efforts shape the life of each baby every day.

References

Adamson, P.C., Bagatell, R., Balis, F.M. & Blaney, S.M. (2011) 'General Principles of Chemotherapy.' In P.A. Pizzo & D.G. Poplack (Eds) *Principles and Practice of Pediatric Oncology.* Philadelphia: Lippincott Willians & Wilkins.

American Academy of Pediatrics (2012) 'Policy statement: Early childhood diversity, toxic stress, and the role of the pediatrician: Translating developmental science into lifelong health.' *Pediatrics 129,* 1, e224–e231.

Anderson, F.S. & Kunin-Batson, A.S. (2009) 'Neurocognitve late effects of chemotherapy in children: The past 10 years of research on brain structure and function.' *Pediatric Blood and Cancer 52,* 159–164.

Cho, J., Holditch-Davis, D. & Miles, M.S. (2008) 'Effects of maternal depressive symptoms and infant gender on the interactions between mothers and their medically at-risk infants.' *Journal of Obstetrics, Gynecology and Neonatal Nursing 37,* 1, 58–70.

Garner, A.S., Shonkoff, J.P., Siegel, B.S., Dobbins, M.I., Earls, M.F. & McGuinn, L. (2012) 'Early childhood adversity, toxic stress, and the role of the pediatrician: Translating developmental science into lifelong health.' *Pediatrics 129,* 1, e224–e231.

Graf, A.E.B., Bergstraesse, E. & Landolt, M.A. (2013) 'Posttraumatic stress in infants and preschoolers with cancer.' *Psycho-Oncology 22,* 1543–1548.

Green, J.L., Knight, S.J., McCarthy, M.C. & DeLuca, C.R. (2013) 'Motor functioning during and following treatment with chemotherapy for pediatric acute lymphoblastic leukemia.' *Pediatric Blood and Cancer 60,* 1261–1266.

Harris, J. (2005). Critcally ill babies in hospital – considering the experience of mothers. *Infant Observation 8,* 3, 247–258.

Jones, S. (2007) 'The baby as subject: The hospitalised infant and the family therapist.' *Australian and New Zealand Journal of Family Health 2,* 3, 146–154.

Kazak, A.E. (2005) 'Evidence-based interventions for survivors of childhood cancer and their families.' *Journal of Pediatric Psychology 30,* 1, 29–39.

Kazak, A.E. & Baxt, C. (2007) 'Families of infants and young children with cancer: A post-traumatic stress framework.' *Pediatric Blood and Cancer 49,* 7 (suppl.), 1109–1113.

McCarthy, M.C., Ashley, D.M., Lee, K.J. & Anderson, V.A. (2012) 'Predictors of acute and posttraumatic stress symptoms in parents following their child's cancer diagnosis.' *Journal of Traumatic Stress 25,* 5, 558–566.

Muller-Nix, C., Forcada-Guex, M., Peirrehumbert, B., Jaunin, L., Borghini, A. & Ansermet, F. (2004) 'Prematurity, maternal stress and mother–child interactions.' *Early Human Development 79,* 2, 145–158.

Obeidat, H.M., Bond, E.A. & Callister, L.C. (2009) 'The parental experience of having an infant in the newborn intensive care unit.' *Journal of Perinatal Education 18,* 3, 23–29.

Price, J., Kassam-Adams, N., Alderfer, M.A., Christfferson, J. & Kazak, A.E. (2016) 'Systematic review: A reevaluation and update of the integrative (trajectory) model of pediatric medical traumatic stress.' *Journal of Pediatric Psychology 41,* 1, 86–97.

Reddy, V. & Trevarthen, C. (2004) 'What we learn about babies from engaging their emotions.' *Zero to Three 24,* 3, 9–15.

Rennick, J.E., Stremler, R., Horwood, L., Aita, M., *et al.* (2018) 'A pilot randomized controlled trial of an intervention to promote psychological well-being in critically ill children: Soothing through touch, reading, and music.' *Pediatric Critical Care Medicine 19,* 7, e358–e366.

Rustin, M. (2014) 'The relevance of infant observation for early intervention: Containment in theory and practice.' *Infant Observation 17,* 2, 97–114.

Sanders, M.R. & Hall, S.L. (2018) 'Trauma-informed care in the newborn intensive care unit: Promoting safety, security and connectedness.' *Journal of Perinatology 38,* 3–10.

Shah, A., Jerardi, K., Auger, K. & Beck, A. (2016) 'Is hospitalization a toxic stress?' *Pediatrics 387,* 1–3.

Shoemark, H., Rimmer, J., Bower, J., Tucquet, B. *et al.* (2018) 'A conceptual framework: The musical self as a unique pathway to outcomes in the acute pediatric health setting.' *Journal of Music Therapy 55,* 1, 1–26.

Shonkoff, J.P., Boyce, W.T. & McEwan, B.S. (2009) 'Neuroscience, molecular biology, and the childhood roots of health disparities.' *JAMA 301,* 21, 2252–2259.

Stern, D.N. (1974) 'Mother and Infant at Play: The Dyadic Interaction Involving the Facial, Vocal and Gaze Behaviours.' In M. Lewis & L. Rosenblum (Eds) *The Effect of the Infant on Its Caregivers.* New York: John Wiley and Sons.

Stevens, B. (2007) 'Pain assessment and management in infants with cancer.' *Pediatric Blood and Cancer 49,* 7 (suppl.) 1097–1091.

Vernon, L., Eyles, D., Bretherton, L. & McCarthy, M. (2017) 'Infancy and pediatric cancer: An exploratory study of parent psychologcial distress.' *Psycho-Oncology 26,* 3, 361–368.

Weatherston, D., Weigand, R.F. & Weigand, B. (2010) 'Reflective supervision: Supporting reflection as a cornerstone for competency.' *Zero to Three 31,* 2, 22–30.

Wilson-Smith, E.M. (2011) 'Procedural pain managment in neonates, infants and children.' *Reviews in Pain 5,* 3, 4–12.

Addendum

A MOTHER'S PERSPECTIVE

Oscar's mother Lydia (the pseudonym used in this chapter) was invited to read Maria McCarthy and Helen Shoemark's chapter on infants with cancer and share her perspective with others of her experience as a mother of a child with a serious illness requiring hospitalisation. She was interviewed by co-author Maria McCarthy and this is what she had to share.

Maria: Having read the chapter, is there any advice that you would give to parents who are staying in hospital with a young baby with a serious illness?

Lydia: My biggest piece of advice is just to go with your gut, because you know your baby the best and as much as people are trying to tell you things, that this is how they should be reacting, you are the one who is with them 24/7. You need to just go with what you're feeling and what you think your baby is feeling.

Maria: Do you think that would be in terms of talking to the medical team or the nursing staff about what you, as his mother, think is going on?

Lydia: I found that the first few times that we went in I was just relying completely on other people like doctors and nurses. Then I was getting frustrated because I wasn't getting answers. After that I put my foot down and went, 'Right, no. This is my baby. This is what I think is going on. Let's talk about it. Let's see what we can do to make him feel better and make him feel safe as opposed to just going with what they would do on a normal day.' When it came to procedures and things, it's sort of like 'No, this works better for him – let's do this for him.'

Maria: I can hear you really advocating for him. Is there anything you wish you'd known or been told before you actually came in, particularly I guess for the bone marrow transplant?

Lydia: Well I'm the type of person who wants to know everything, but my husband is the type of person who doesn't want to know anything, so that's always the hard balance. How much information can you give people before going into a transplant?

Maria: How does Oscar describe his experience? Does he have any words, or does he talk about it at all?

Lydia: We do talk about it because of all the photos we took during this time. Yes, and we've got books and things; and the other day his father was reading a book to him about being in hospital and Oscar asked his dad why he had his nose tube. He says that he remembered it though I had never heard him say that before. That conversation was only a few days ago. On the calendar I've got his transplant anniversary and when he's got an appointment at the hospital, and his brother always asks why he was in hospital. I say you know because he was sick when he was a baby, and now he's better but we have to still watch him.

Maria: And does his brother often ask you questions? Does he ever talk about it or bring it up?

Lydia: No, he seems to not really remember. He remembers the fun stuff, like how we stayed at the hotel in the hospital for Christmas. He thinks that that was great, and he would ask for a long time when we are going back. Yeah, so, the memories that…his brother recalls, they are the fun things.

Maria: Do you think he remembers any of the difficult things, or does he ever talk about the separation of not having you around?

Lydia: No, because he had one of us – either me or his father – at least one of us with him every day.

Maria: How often do you look at the photographs?

Lydia: It is just random. I don't really look at them that often.

Maria: When the anniversary comes up, do you talk about it then or do you just have it in your diary or on your calendar just as a reminder?

Lydia: I like to sort of think of it as like another birthday kind of thing. I think it's a good thing, I think? It is like he's got his real birthday but then he's got his transplant birthday, so I always take a really nice photo of him. Yes, just to remember that day.

Maria: Would there be any advice that you would give health professionals working with infants and families and given your experience?

Lydia: It would probably be to speak in layman's terms, because there were a lot of medical terms that were always thrown around. For us as parents, that was all new to us, so we sort of didn't know – it took a long, long time to figure out what they were talking about.

Maria: In terms of the emotional care or psychosocial care of Oscar being a baby, for someone so very young, is there anything, any advice you would give the staff, having been through your experience?

Lydia: I think it's a particular experience having a young baby in hospital – I remember all of the interruptions. We had to be disrupted during those nights (for medical reasons) and I was sort of thinking about it the other day – just what could have been done differently? I don't know why I was thinking about it. I was thinking about the cleaner, as they were my number one issue and they would come in and not know what had happened throughout the night. Then they would make a whole lot of noise. Maybe there would be a system that they could change. They would just sort of barge in and say, 'We got to clean.'

Maria: Thank you so very much (for giving consent to write about Oscar and your reflections).

CHAPTER 16

High-Risk Infant Mental Health Outreach

Creating a Professional Community of Caregivers Using a Collaborative Mental Health and Nursing Approach

PAUL ROBERTSON, AMITY MCSWAN AND LOUISE DOCKERY

Background

Infants cannot verbalise their distress, hurts and traumas as older children and adults do. As practitioners, we need to be present to what infants are showing us about their experiences. To flourish they need parents and a caregiving community to be attuned to their needs, including those concerned with their mental health. However, traditional Child and Adolescent Mental Health Services (CAMHS) have not always recognised the mental health needs of infants. Some community-based child health services, such as Maternal Child Health Nurse (MCHN) services, have long recognised the need for greater infant mental health services, or at least socio-emotional support services, but found linking to such services challenging. The clinical services system must seek different solutions for infants and very young children if they are to provide effective care.

This chapter illustrates the development of an important infant mental health collaboration between CAMHS and a local MCHN service in the Australian state of Victoria. It focuses on infants and their families where the infant's physical, emotional and social development is disturbed or at high risk of adverse outcomes.

In Victoria, the MCHN service is state-funded and universally accessible. It provides a health, wellbeing and developmental support service for all families with children aged from birth to school age. Historically, few children under 5 years of age were seen by CAMHS. However, the last decade or more has seen changes with the development of evidence-based infant mental health services within CAMHS, with an emphasis on meeting the needs of infants with, or at high risk of developing, severe and complex mental health problems. In order to reach our community's most vulnerable infants, an interagency collaboration with a community-wide program such as the MCHN service made immense sense.

This chapter describes a pilot clinical program developed as a partnership between MCHN and CAMHS. We begin by outlining what CAMHS and the MCHN service do. We then discuss how our two services worked together, what we learnt from one another, our achievements and some of the challenges we faced. A brief summary of guiding key concepts within the infant mental health literature is included. To illustrate our work, a case example of John, aged 30 months, and his family helps demonstrate how we have collaborated to engage and work with an infant at high risk. We hope this description will be helpful to others hoping to build such collaborations so as to support vulnerable infants and their caregivers.

Practice context of the MCHN service and CAMHS in the local community
Maternal Child Health Nurses

Victoria's MCHN service sees nearly all the newborn infants from birth to 4 years. Following a baby's birth, each local MCHN service across the state of Victoria is notified by the maternity hospital. After arriving home with their baby, the MCHN is usually the first professional new parents meet in their transition to parenting. The Universal MCHN model provides for ten scheduled appointments (Education and Training Victoria 2018), whereby the child's development is reviewed and supported. For high-risk families, further and extended visits are available. MCHNs have completed a four-year degree in General Nursing and Midwifery, plus an additional one-year postgraduate qualification in Maternal and Child Health Nursing. In addition, they usually have substantial prior hospital and community nursing experience.

MCHNs work to engage the full diversity of families across cultures, socioeconomic circumstances and levels of disadvantage, as well as other marginalised families such as LGBTQIA[1] parents. Their work includes supporting infants who face complex issues around medical, environmental, social and relational risk factors. In recognition of the very high needs of some infants and their families, a second tier of MCHN was established in 1999 called the Enhanced MCHN (EMCHN) service (see Education and Training Victoria's *Enhanced Maternal and Child Health Program Guidelines 2018*). The EMCHN service receives referrals for infants and their families who present with multiple risks and adversities; for example, infants with delayed development; troubled infant–parent relationships; parents with severe mental illness and those with unresolved psychological trauma impinging on parental caregiving capacities. Referrals to the EMCHN service also include families where recent child protection involvement has been required, those with a history of child protection involvement with previous children, or because of challenges resulting from the parent's own experiences as former child protection clients.

EMCHNs work alongside the Universal MCHNs. They are experienced in home-based care and undertake a more substantial assessment of the infant and family's developmental and socio-emotional context. Alongside providing support, advice and direct intervention, they often coordinate a broad interagency system of care, including general practitioners, paediatricians, early childhood services, child protection, family support services and family violence services, as well as others. The long history of the provision of infant care provided by Victoria's Baby Health Centres, the first of which was established in 1917, has ensured that generations of families have been visited by MCHNs. This has cemented their status as trustworthy, important and accepted infant experts who are often allowed into family homes where other professionals are not (Crockett 2000). This longstanding community trust in, and respect for, their role – even amongst newly arrived migrants and asylum seekers – makes this profession central and enormously important to the professional provision of care to infants.

However, this profession has faced enormous obstacles in having infants and their families, especially those with, or at high risk of, infant mental health problems, accepted for treatment into

---

1   LGBTQIA is commonly defined as lesbian, gay, bisexual, transgender, queer/questioning, intersex and asexual.

clinic-based CAMHS. This had been due to long waiting lists, rigid exclusion criteria, a lack of trust in mental health services and a disbelief that infants can have mental health challenges. Additionally, cumbersome telephone-based triage models and clinic-centered practices in CAMHS have been an impediment for families. Families have found the referral processes difficult and inaccessible or have felt that the infant and themselves as carers have been stigmatised. For parents who themselves have had previous mental health and/or child protection involvement, engaging with services for their infant can be frightening. CAMHS clinics are not always geographically accessible to families who live in outer suburbs or rural areas. This is compounded by a perception that it is hard to be accepted into CAMHS, and, if accepted, the system is not always flexible in managing the chaos or difficulties facing those families who are experiencing multiple risks and disadvantages. The combination of these challenges in providing mental health care for high-risk infants led us to recognise the need to create a different approach.

Child and Adolescent Mental Health

CAMHS has traditionally provided developmental-focused, family-centered mental health assessment and intervention for children aged 5–18 years, using a diversity of therapeutic approaches including cognitive behavioural, psychodynamic, family therapy, parental interventions and pharmacological treatments. Whilst CAMHS mental health care is largely anchored in the young person's family and relational world, infant mental health is entirely relationally focused. Whilst infants might be diagnosed with particular disorders, how these disorders are understood to have emerged is through assessing their primary relational environment, their social connections, their developmental stage and biology (Zero to Three 2016). Interventions with infants, by necessity, are focused on their relationship with parents and carers.

The recognition of infant mental health as a distinct area of practice began in the late 1960s (Harman 2003; Zeanah 2019). Today, infant mental health, including the scientific understanding of early brain development, has profoundly elevated the knowledge base and respect for the mental capacities of infants. There is too much research, literature, intervention programs and ideas pertaining to infant mental health to list here; however, our work is based on what we consider to be some foundational perspectives that guide our work:

- the psychodynamic tradition of child development and psychodynamic psychotherapy, in particular, that derived from Donald Winnicott (1960)

- Attachment Theory (Ainsworth *et al.* 1978; Bowlby 1969; George 2014; Main 1995) and the role of attachment relationships in shaping psychosocial development (Bernier, Carlson & Whipple 2010; Hinshaw and Joubert 2014; Music 2016; Newman 2012)

- psychodynamically informed evidence-based Child–Parent Psychotherapy (Lieberman & Van Horn 2008)

- the impact of psychological trauma, both current and historical, on early development, attachment relationships and its intergenerational nature (Fraiberg, Adelson & Shapiro 1975; Lieberman 2007; Lieberman *et al.* 2011)

- the impact of systemic and contextual disadvantage on family functioning and child development (Clark, Bond & Hecker 2007; Emmen *et al.* 2013; Morris *et al.* 2007)

- sociopolitical views of family from a feminist and gender lens (Goldner *et al.* 1990; Luepnitz 1988) and recognition of the impact of family violence on children's outcomes (Lieberman & Van Horn 2005)

- Infant Observation (Bick 1986; Rustin 2009; Waddell 2013)

- Watch, Wait, Wonder (Cohen 2006; Cohen *et al.* 1999)

- Ed Tronick's (2007) concepts of match, mismatch and repair in infant–parent relationships

- Reflective Supervision (O'Rourke 2011; Tomlin, Weatherston & Pavkov 2014) – the foundation upon which all the concepts and approaches are held and integrated into our clinical practice (see Chapter 2).

Used in symphony, these key theoretical components underpin how we make sense of the work we do and provide integration of thinking and doing in the clinical space.

A collaborative practice approach: what we decided to do differently

What might be a better way to engage difficult-to-engage families? A pilot program between the MCHN service and CAMHS was established, with a weekly meeting between the CAMHS clinician and the EMCHN held in our MCHN service centre. The families discussed were chosen by the EMCHN. Following this meeting, the EMCHN and the CAMHS clinician provided a joint family consultation for an infant and their family in the family home. This joint family consultation built on the already established relationship the EMCHN had with the family and the existing EMCHN's assessment of the infant and family.

This one-off collaborative approach between the EMCHN service and CAMHS became a central piece of our work. For some families this joint family meeting led to further intervention by the EMCHN service, enriched by a greater infant mental health understanding. For others it facilitated broader interventions by the care system; for example, introducing family violence services or enabling effective child protection involvement. For some families it opened up the possibility of ongoing mental health assessment and interventions such as child–parent psychotherapy. Direct, ongoing mental health intervention was not always possible or considered as most appropriate; for example, when the immediate need was for safety from violence in the family. Broadly, the joint consultation gave the EMCHN a more focused infant mental health perspective to support her work or that of other services; it also helped her to advocate for the infant and work on the challenges that arose for the family in their efforts to care for their infant.

What we learnt and how we understood the work

Child–Parent Psychotherapy considers concepts of engagement with families through different points of entry (Lieberman & Van Horn 2008) and framed our thinking. We recognised at least three ways of working with an infant and their parents within the consultation. Whilst any particular visit might include some or all woven together, we describe them separately to outline our thinking.

The first was directly relating to the infant as a person in their own right and not experiencing them only as the 'described baby' that emerges from the parent's mind, reflecting the parent's internal representations. We know that really relating to and knowing the infant requires us to find a way to engage them directly (Thomson-Salo 2014). We need to discover the infant's emotional and relational capabilities and to do so in the presence of their parents. We found that a playful interest in the infant's communications, emotional exchanges and behaviours, alongside sensitive and non-judgemental comments directed to the infant, were particularly effective. We respected the infant's inner emotional world and worked hard to find a way to reach infants, even when they were withdrawn and hard to understand or relate to. The parent's experience (Cohen 2006) of this relational interchange between their infant and the worker can offer the parent a new way to notice and consider their infant's emotional world, and their infant's drive for a relationship with them. In itself, this dialogue with the infant often brought the parent into a higher-level engagement not only with their infant but also with the EMCHN and mental health clinician.

The second approach was working with relationships in the present moment in the room. We observe, think and work with the infant–parent relationship as a relationship in real time, and right there in front of us. We aim to be alive to the back-and-forth, interactional exchanges between the infant and their parent. For example, in one consultation a baby cried. We experienced this as the baby signalling a need for comfort. We observed her mother respond with fear and trepidation to her baby's communication. This, in turn, further frightened the baby, and increased further her distress and need for her mother. It escalated into a crescendo of distress for the dyad. We observed interactional exchanges mismatching in real time but also caught moments where this infant was matched by her mother in a synchronous way (Tronick 2007). We sometimes actively intervened by overting parents' capacity to manage their own strong emotions, and then exploring how they could support their infant to manage feelings of distress. Additionally, we were alive to other relationships in the here and now, such as the co-parenting relationship, between parents and grandparents and between the parents and the EMCHN and clinician. All these relationships were observed, thought about and worked with in the here and now of the consultation and helped to bring to the parent a greater understanding of their infant and how important they were to the infant.

A third aspect was working with the parent's own internal experiences – how they perceived their infant as well as their perception of themselves as parent to this infant. 'Maternal representations'

(Benoit *et al.* 1997; Madigan *et al.* 2015; Vreeswijk, Maas & van Bakel 2012) refers, in part, to how a parent perceives their infant based on their own past experiences of how they were parented, or how they imagine their infant could or should be, rather than discovering the real baby in the present. The parental representational world is expressed in how parents describe their infant and themselves as parents. We listened carefully to how the mother and father described their experiences of being parents to this child. This might be harsh, critical and self-deprecating; or sometimes it was laced with powerlessness and ineffectualness in being able to help or protect their infant; or sometimes it was a struggle for some parents to find words, as this was just too painful and difficult to think about. Yet we also worked with the parents' wish to be a good parent and belief they could be good parents (Lieberman 2007).

Regardless of what we noticed, the EMCHN and clinician's empathy for the parent(s) position was one of our most potent tools. Empathically holding in mind the common challenges of parenting, along with the burden of trauma and losses – both personal and intergenerational – and the extraordinary here-and-now challenges of disadvantage facing many of these families, was central to our work. This involved supporting parents to move beyond current burdens and explore new ways of being a parent, and new ways of being with their infant. For example, a young father struggled to cuddle his new baby daughter, as he felt he was a danger to her; he was frightened he might be violent like his own father and grandfather had been. Through empathically holding both the burden of his past trauma and recognition of his love and concern for his daughter, something new emerged which allowed him to respond to his daughter with safety, love and tenderness.

Irrespective of where we started with the family, we knew that if we were lively players in a relationship with the infant and parents, it made a difference. We aimed for every encounter to be therapeutic. We tried to plant the seed that ongoing engagement would be both welcomed and helpful. The experience of being warmly held in mind, noticed and supported was crucial to engagement. We needed to go beyond a language-based, rational explanation of the need for mental health treatment into something more enlivened in the immediate relationship experience between the family and ourselves.

Working with the barriers we encountered

We saw infants emotionally disengaged or withdrawn, or alternately hyper-vigilant and over-reactive. We saw older toddlers and pre-schoolers with internalised models of traumatic relationships that were repeatedly enacted in the consultation. The parent's experience of the helping relationships offered by the EMCHN and mental health clinician was often experienced through the lens of unacknowledged past trauma from abusive and rejecting relationships with their own caregivers. Parents sometimes struggled to trust the care we offered, felt suspicious of our intention or felt unworthy of care. They were sometimes rejecting, attacking or angry towards our involvement.

Though unable to explore every one of the theoretical underpinnings of our work, we believe an understanding of relational dynamics between clients and professionals is essential (Gabbard 2004). This is particularly so when relationships are infused with, and distorted by, unresolved parental past trauma. The parent's unacknowledged and unresolved trauma impacts or transfers onto the worker's emotional state and capacity to think and so influences the clinical relationship between worker and parent. Reflective practice through supervision helps the worker understand or be aware of the influence of unresolved trauma in a family's story. It is an essential part of the model (see Chapter 2 to read more about the role of Reflective Supervision). For clinicians and EMCHNs it was provided within our respective services. The joint meeting between the EMCHN and clinician in the MCHN service centre also provided a reflective space. Supported by reflective practice, we worked to be thoughtful about our relationship with the family, to understand our experience of the infant and to think more deeply about what was unspoken for the parent(s). This was in order to develop and offer them back something different and to deepen their understanding. Reflective practices also enabled our work to go beyond the work with the family and included reflecting on the relationship between the professionals and between components of the wider service system.

A case example: John and his family

At 30 months John and his mother, Mandy, lived in a small rented apartment and he was her only child. Mandy did not have a partner, and her mother lived a couple of hours away and was some support. John attended childcare three days each week. John's parents separated when he was 18 months old. There was a history of family violence, as well as relationship and financial difficulties. John stayed with his father, Michael, every second weekend from Saturday morning to Sunday afternoon. His father lived with a new partner and their 1-year-old baby boy, whom John spent time with on his visits. These arrangements were by voluntary agreement between the parents, but nevertheless Mandy felt worried about Michael's impact on John and feared John was becoming aggressive like his father. She received no financial support for John's care. Mandy had experienced both physical and emotional abuse from Michael during their relationship, which left her feeling not 'good enough' and somehow deserving of the abuse.

The EMCHN had only met John three times as the family were new to the area. She was concerned about Mandy's mental health, John's aggression and his difficulty following instructions and the family environment. The EMCHN brought her concerns about John to the meeting with the CAMHS clinician along with the hope that an infant mental health perspective would assist. In the consultation they reflected on John's behaviour and underlying emotional distress and troubled relationship with his mother. A joint visit by the EMCHN and clinician to John and Mandy's home was arranged.

The EMCHN had previously witnessed John's distress, expressed by hitting and kicking his mother and breaking things at home. When his wishes were frustrated, he raged angrily at Mandy, saying he hated her. Mandy said no matter how upset he was, he never cried. John was very interested in, bordering on obsessed with, some particular toys: animal caricatures and martial arts warriors called Ninja Turtles. His play was repetitive and full of aggression and fighting. His vocabulary was limited for his age and he was hard to understand. John was often upset and negative about himself. Going to bed at night was an exhausting process due to his distress and the conflicts that arose with Mandy. She found it difficult to recognise his anxiety around bedtime, rather seeing him as 'naughty'. For 6 months, childcare staff had complained to Mandy about John's aggression towards other children and she feared they would ask her to remove him.

John's physical development was good and he was meeting normal milestones. While having good motor coordination, he struggled to remain focused during play and activities, and rapidly became boisterous and disorganised, shifting from one thing to another. The EMCHN had observed poor impulse control and low frustration tolerance. Although John's eye contact with the EMCHN was poor, he clearly remembered her following her first visit. Perhaps he remembered that she was interested in his world and that she was able to help his mother feel better. Maybe when she visited, it felt like something was different.

During the EMCHN's second visit Mandy had commented: 'I am such a bad mum.' Mandy alternated between self-criticism and anger with John. She felt his behaviours were deliberate so as to upset her. Mandy wondered aloud to the EMCHN about what she was doing wrong and what she did to deserve such treatment. She could see a likeness in John to his father and this scared her. Mandy told her story of their early beginnings as a family, her ambivalence about having a baby and how it had been marred by Michael's violence towards her. She also spoke of the difficulties around parental separation 18 months before and the ongoing difficulties in the post-separation relationship. Parent-focused interventions, advice and a paediatric referral by the EMCHN around helping Mandy with John's behaviour had been helpful, but not enough; John's behaviours were not getting better. Mandy remained overwhelmed by the negative emotions between herself and her little boy and they remained in a cycle of escalating relational, emotional and behavioural difficulties.

On the day the EMCHN and clinician jointly visited, they were met at the door by Mandy, who took them to sit at the kitchen table. The three adults sat at the table whilst John played beside the table. He chose to play with some toy dinosaurs and was making loud dinosaur noises whilst moving in quick succession from one adult to the other. He was pleased the EMCHN and clinician reciprocated his interest in them, approaching each with curiosity and showing them his dinosaurs. He was busy, active and demanding of adult attention and seemed increasingly excited at having visitors. Within a few minutes he began standing on a child's chair, which was unstable, and he was at risk of falling backwards while trying to climb onto the kitchen bench. His risky behaviour was driven by an excitement that was beginning to overwhelm him. However, it also functioned to maintain connection with the adults around him. Mandy commented that John was always doing dangerous things and pleaded with him to stop, but to no avail. She felt controlled by John and ineffectual to bring change or safety. The clinician was left feeling anxious that John would hurt himself and found herself drawn to intervene with John's behaviour. The EMCHN had experienced this dilemma on previous visits.

The clinician got up from the table and invited John to play, both hoping to create a shift in his risky behaviour but also wanting to understand John's inner world. She commented on his dinosaurs, asking questions about what they were called and engaging in a playful dinosaur fight. The game shifted to two dinosaurs 'talking' through the clinician about John being big, strong and unable to be hurt. John became less frantic and more focused, with a look of interest on his face. Using the dinosaurs, the clinician began to play 'peek a boo', and John laughed and relaxed. The clinician interrupted this back-and-forth play and tried to divide her attention between Mandy and John as Mandy seemed to urgently want to talk to the clinician. The clinician felt torn between the needs of the child and the mother, as they both talked at once. With the disruption of the clinician's attention, John immediately escalated his behaviour. His mother instantly asked him to stop. John angrily lifted up the child's chair and smashed it on the floor and screamed 'I hate you' at his mother. Mandy responded by crying: 'This is what it is like every day.'

After John threw the chair, the clinician got down on the floor with him and spoke calmly about how he must be feeling very angry. The clinician, using what had just happened in the 'here and now' and what was known from the EMCHN's existing assessment, responded to John's feelings of anger and fear. She spoke directly to John about these feelings and his frustration when not listened to and when having fun stops. John became calmer and his angry face softened. The clinician focused on holding the engagement with John, recognising his sensitivity to relationship ruptures and yearning to have his emotional world understood.

In parallel, the EMCHN moved to help Mandy manage her arousal, reflecting on what was happening in John's emotional world and acknowledging her need for someone to witness how hard things were for her. The EMCHN moved her chair and herself closer to Mandy and spoke about how the clinician was trying to understand John's feelings and help him with his behaviour by doing this. She did not comment directly on Mandy's feelings but recognised that both mother and son were having similar difficult feelings and that in talking aloud about John's feelings the clinician was also, in some ways, talking about Mandy's feelings. She worked to create a space for John and the clinician separate to the mother's distress in the consultation. With Mandy's own feelings more contained, it created a capacity for Mandy to observe John in interaction with the clinician and become aware of his emotional world and capacity to respond to help in talking about how he felt.

Seeing John in interaction with the clinician shifted something for Mandy and allowed her to be more able to trust both the EMCHN and clinician and be optimistic about getting help. As the visit progressed, Mandy spoke of her difficulties in parenting John and her ambivalent feelings towards him. The clinician and EMCHN's interest in, and empathy for, Mandy's parenting experience and the struggle she had to see herself as a good mother was important. The clinician and EMCHN worked to hold and normalise these difficult feelings, helping Mandy to tolerate and be with her distressing experiences of parenting. Mandy spoke of her fears for John and herself in regard to John's ongoing visits with Michael, and of her confusion about how John liked seeing his father but was aggressive when he returned. She still feared Michael's capacity for violence. Her own family-of-origin experiences were yet to be explored, although she alluded to difficulties.

Fifteen minutes or so later, the atmosphere felt easier. Powerful feelings in both John and Mandy had been acknowledged. But what might happen next? Powerful feelings were getting in the way of their relationship and no doubt would surface again. An infant mental health perspective helped the workers to understand John's behaviour as coming from his internal emotional distress which could not be sufficiently held or assuaged in his relationship with his mother. He needed a different response from Mandy to help him with managing his emotions and experiences. This might open the door to his finding different responses to his feeling states. Ongoing mental health care for John and Mandy provided by the clinician through the CAMHS clinic was arranged. This mental health intervention was to parallel the ongoing work provided by the EMCHN.

Ongoing positive engagement with Mandy was crucial if an alliance was to be built with CAMHS and the provision of ongoing mental health treatment. The ongoing collaboration between the mental health clinician and EMCHN supported this engagement. An assessment for a possible Autistic Spectrum Disorder (ASD) was recommended; and despite Mandy's fears of what such a diagnosis might mean, it was welcomed. This specialist assessment did not confirm an ASD and a transgenerational formulation around trauma associated with family violence was the shared understanding of John's difficulties and directed interventions to follow. Mental health intervention using child–parent psychotherapy, including child-focused parent therapy, was the mainstay of mental health intervention. It was flagged that Michael might participate in the intervention, though through separate sessions, as he was an important attachment figure. Though anxious, Mandy agreed and the clinician telephoned Michael to invite him to be part of the process.

At times Mandy's distress, triggered by memories and experiences explored within the treatment, became overwhelming and she wished to flee. The working together of the EMCHN and clinician and the therapeutic relationship that was built helped to hold Mandy's distress and supported her through the treatment. As treatment progressed, Mandy became better at tolerating as well as making sense of her own distress and became more reflective about John's behaviours and less frightened by his need for a more attuned relationship with her. She began to notice subtle, positive changes in their interactions which increased Mandy's confidence and commitment to change. In time there were improvements for John and Mandy. Apart from telephone contact, Michael never engaged with the treatment. In these conversations Michael, while clearly expressing positive feelings for John, did not accept John had problems or needed help.

Conclusion

Through creating a strong collaborative clinical partnership between a CAMHS and MCHN service we were able to provide a much-needed infant mental health intervention for John and his mother, as we were doing for other families. This project demonstrates a better way forward in delivering infant mental health care to infants with, or at high risk of, mental health difficulties. Such a collaborative clinical model between services is now being implemented more widely. There are also, however, some cautions!

We need to not forget those infants and their families who do not get seen. Are their mental health needs met through the Universal MCHN service or by other professionals who have contact with infants within the wider service system? Within this MCHN service, Universal MCHNs collaborate with migrant and refugee services to support the needs of culturally diverse families. Universal MCHNs work with same-sex parenting couples, father-led families and LGBTQIA+ parents to support their infants. While the aspiration of this specific project was to meet the needs of those infants most in need, we hold a broader, more aspirational goal to bring an infant mental health perspective to all infants and their families in need in our community. Reflecting on the future role of CAMHS in delivering mental health care for all children and adolescents with severe mental health difficulties, there is a need to ensure that infants are seen as core clients whose needs are recognised and that equity of access is provided. Whatever this might look like, it will be in collaboration with our community partners, such as the MCHN services, to create effective multiagency professional care systems for infants and all children.

Acknowledgements

Thanks to Eastern Health CYMHS and Maroondah City Council MCHN service and in particular, Maureen O'Brien, Senior Social

Worker at Eastern Health CYMHS, and Vicki Middleton, Senior MCHN at Maroondah City Council for assisting in the preparation of the chapter.

Thanks to Professor Jennifer McIntosh, Deakin University Centre for Social and Early Emotional Development, for editorial comments on the chapter and assistance with references.

References

Ainsworth, M.D.S., Blehar, M.C., Waters, E. & Wall, S. (1978) *Patterns of Attachment: A Psychological Study of the Stage Situation.* Oxford London: Lawerence Erlbaum.

Benoit, D., Zeanah, C.H., Parker, K.C.H., Nicholson, E. & Coolbear, J. (1997) '"Working model of the child interview": Infant clinical status related to maternal perceptions.' *Infant Mental Health Journal 18*, 1, 107–121.

Bernier, A., Carlson, S.M. & Whipple, N. (2010) 'From external regulation to self regulation: Early parenting precursors of young children's executive functioning'. *Child Development 81*, 1, 326–339.

Bick, E. (1986) 'Further considerations on the function of the skin in early object relations.' *British Journal of Psychotherapy 2*, 4, 292–299.

Bowlby, J. (1969). *Attachment and Loss: Vol. 1. Attachment.* New York: Basic Books.

Clark, M.S., Bond, M.J. & Hecker, J.R. (2007) 'Environmental stress, psychological stress and allostatic load.' *Psychology, Health & Medicine 12*, 1, 18–30.

Cohen, N.J. (2006) 'Watch, wait, and wonder: An infant-led approach to infant-parent psychotherapy.' *The Signal 14*, 2, 1–4.

Cohen, N.J., Muir, E., Lojkasek, M., Muir, R. *et al.* (1999) 'Watch, wait, and wonder: Testing the effectiveness of a new approach to mother-infant psychotherapy.' *Infant Mental Health Journal 20*, 4, 429–451.

Crockett, C. (2000) *Save the Babies: The Victorian Baby Health Centres' Association and the Queen Elizabeth Centre.* Victoria: Australian Scholarly Publishing.

Education and Training Victoria (2018) *Enhanced Maternal and Child Health Program Guidelines.* Retrieved 22/01/19 from www.education.vic.gov.au/Documents/childhood/professionals/health/enhancedmchprogguidelines.pdf.

Emmen, R.A., Malda, M., Mesman, J., van Ijzendoorn, M.H., Prevoo, M.J. & Yeniad, N. (2013) 'Socioeconomic status and parenting in ethnic minority families: Testing a minority family stress model.' *Journal of Family Psychology 27*, 6, 896–904.

Fraiberg, S., Adelson, E. & Shapiro, V. (1975) 'Ghosts in the nursery.' *Journal of the American, Academy of Child Psychiatry 14*, 3, 387–421.

Gabbard, G. (2004) *Long-Term Psychodynamic Psychotherapy: A Basic Text.* Washington, D.C.: American Psychiatric Publishing.

George, C. (2014) 'Attachment Theory: Implications for Young Children and Their Parents.' In K. Brandt, B.D. Perry, S. Seligman & E. Tronick (Eds) *Infant Mental Health: Core Concepts and Clinical Practice.* Washington, D.C.: American Psychiatric Publishing.

Goldner, V., Penn, P., Sheinberg, M. & Walker, G. (1990) 'Love and violence: Gender paradoxes in volatile attachments.' *Family Process 29*, 4, 343–364.

Harman, R.J. (2003) 'Thirty years in infant mental health.' *Zero to Three 24*, 1, 22–28.

Hinshaw, S.P. & Joubert, C.L. (2014) 'Developmental Psychopathology: Core Principles and Implications for Child Mental Health.' In K. Brandt, B.D. Perry, S. Seligman & E. Tronick (Eds) *Infant Mental Health: Core Concepts and Clinical Practice.* Washington, D.C.: American Psychiatric Publishing.

Lieberman, A. (2007) 'Ghosts and angels: Intergenerational patterns in the transmission and treatment of the traumatic sequelae of domestic violence.' *Infant Mental Health Journal 28*, 4, 422–439.

Lieberman, A. & Van Horn, P. (2005) *Don't Hit My Mommy: A Manual for Child–Parent Psychotherapy With Young Witnesses of Family Violence.* Washington, D.C.: Zero to Three.

Lieberman A., Chu A., Van Horn P. & Harris W.W. (2011) 'Trauma in early childhood: Empirical evidence and clinical implications.' *Development and Psychopathology 23*, 397–410.

Lieberman, A. & Van Horn P. (2008) *Psychotherapy with Infants and Young Children: Repairing the Effects of Stress and Trauma on Early Attachment.* New York: The Guilford Press.

Luepnitz, D.A. (1988) *The Family Interpreted: Feminist Theory in Clinical Practice.* New York: Basic Books.

Madigan, S., Hawkins, E., Plamondon, A., Moran, G. & Benoit, D. (2015) 'Maternal representations and infant attachment: An examination of the prototype hypothesis.' *Infant Mental Health Journal 36*, 5, 459–468.

Main, M. (1995) 'Recent Studies in Attachment.' In S. Goldberg, R. Muir & J. Kerr (Eds) *Attachment Theory: Social, Developmental, and Clinical Perspectives.* Hillsdale, NJ: Analytic Press.

Morris, A.S., Silk, J.S., Steinberg, L., Myers, S.S. & Robinson, L.R. (2007) 'The role of the family context in the development of emotion regulation.' *Social Development 16*, 2, 361–388.

Music, G. (2016) *Nurturing Natures: Attachment and Children's Emotional, Sociocultural and Brain Development.* London: Psychological Press.

Newman, L. (2012) 'Infant Development and Developmental Risk.' In L. Newman & S. Mares (Eds) *Contemporary Approaches to Infant and Child Mental Health.* Melbourne: IP Communication.

O'Rourke, P. (2011). 'The significance of reflective supervision for infant mental health work.' *Infant Mental Health Journal 32*, 2, 165–173.

Rustin, M. (2009). 'Esther Bick's legacy of infant observation at the Tavistock – some reflections 60 years on.' *Infant Observation, 12*, 1, 29–41.

Thomson-Salo, F. (2014) 'Engaging with the Baby as a Person: Early Intervention with Parents and Infant.' In C. Paul. & F. Thompson-Salo (Eds) *The Baby as Subject.* Melbourne: Karnac.

Tomlin, A.M., Weatherston, D.J. & Pavkov, T. (2014) 'Critical components of reflective supervision: Responses from expert supervisors in the field.' *Infant Mental Health Journal 35*, 1, 70–80.

Tronick, E.Z. (2007) *The Neurobehavioral and Social-Emotional Development of Infants and Children.* New York: W.W. Norton & Company.

Vreeswijk, C.M.J.M., Maas, A.J.B.M. & van Bakel, H.J.A. (2012) 'Parental representations: A systematic review of the working model of the child interview.' *InfantMental Health Journal 33*, 3, 314–328.

Waddell, M. (2013) 'Infant observation in Britain: A Tavistock approach.' *Infant Observation 16*, 1, 4–22.

Winnicott, D.W. (1960) 'The theory of the parent–infant relationship.' *International Journal of Psychoanalysis 41*, 585–595.

Zeanah Jr, C.H. (2019) *Handbook of Infant Mental Health* (4th ed.). New York: The Guilford Press.

Zero to Three. (2016) *Diagnostic Classification of Mental Health and Developmental Disorders of Infancy and Early Childhood (DC: 0–5).* Washington, D.C.: Zero to Three.

The ART of finding Authentic Discourses for Parents About and With Their Donor-Conceived Children

SARAH J. JONES

Introduction

Everyone has a right to know who they are and how they came to be. Infant mental health literature tells us that that this 'knowing' grows from relationships – the intersubjective space between two people – and stories shared. But what if one's being was generated from advancements in science, not the birds and the bees? The birth of a child no longer requires sexual intercourse. In the fertility domain, rapid change has recently arrived on the wings of scientific discoveries and legislative transformation. With the availability of Assisted Reproductive Treatments (ART), hitherto unimaginable treatment options are now available for people with either biological infertility, social infertility or both. In Australia, legislative change has meant that babies can now be born into families with single parents, parents who are same sex, transgender or intersex, married or unmarried. In the United Kingdom and the United States and Canada, for example, we now see and celebrate children born into families with much greater diversity, using a revolution of discoveries in reproduction techniques. The focus of this chapter is the need for child-centered thinking in the field of ART and how to support parents reflecting on and allowing for their infant's unique birth story to be narrated, over time, and with age-appropriate stories.

Whilst the domain of fertility practice and theorizing is vast, I wish to explore this area from an infant mental health perspective. My own professional background is Child and Family Social Work, training in Family Therapy in London, and Couple Psychotherapy in Melbourne. For 15 years, I worked in Melbourne's Royal Children's Hospital, joining their pioneering infant mental health group. Then I made a move into own private psychotherapy and supervision practice. When a large infertility clinic invited me to provide reflective supervision to their staff, it became a privilege and a challenge how to keep the 'infant to be' central in our thinking. Many who work in this field observe how the infant, in large medical systems, is at risk at times of being obscured by the difficulties experienced by the adults, leaving the consequences for the early developing infant–parent relationship under-examined. During the 5 years of providing group reflective supervision, I began to explore, with an infant mental health lens, the enormously diverse ART literature.

This chapter contains two sections.

The first section outlines 'child welfare' and 'child rights to identity' in the context of the Victorian (Australia) UN Convention on the rights of the child (1989). I then use an infant mental health perspective to explore concepts relating to 'parental states of mind' and their importance in shaping the emerging mind of their infant. Worldwide developments and debates relating to advancements in ART are then briefly described. I conclude by reviewing the literature on parents' narratives regarding their child's donor conceptions, the difficulties experienced by parents around disclosure, and lessons which can be applied from adoption research.

The second section provides (composite and de-identified) examples of work undertaken with parents and their struggles with an infant's conception story for their children.

Section 1: Victorian legislation: welfare as paramount and rights to identity

The State of Victoria within Australia was the first in the world to regulate the provision of infertility treatments, with the Infertility (Medical Procedures) Act, No. 10163, in 1984. It is germane to the goals of this chapter that I note the guiding principle of the Act, which states that *"the welfare and interests of persons born or to be born as a result of treatment procedures are paramount"*. This principle remains unchanged in the following Assisted Reproductive Treatment Act, No. 76, of 2008.

The infant as a person with rights

The United Nations International Children's Emergency Fund 'Convention on the Rights of the Child' (1989) considered that the child has rights to identity and for assistance with this to be provided. Article 8 states:

> States Parties undertake to respect the right of the child to preserve his or her identity, including nationality, name and family relations as recognized by law without unlawful interference. Where a child is illegally deprived of some or all of the elements of his or her identity, States Parties shall provide appropriate assistance and protection, with a view to re-establishing speedily his or her identity.

There is, therefore, an obligation for those directly and indirectly involved in ART to consider the identity needs of future children, however complex this might seem.

The importance of infant mental health within the ART field

More than 30 years ago, these landmark principles enshrined children's needs and rights. Despite this, there remain no established evidence-based or clinically informed 'industry' standards of practice which articulate how to hold the child's welfare as paramount, although many have worked hard to offer some guidance (Blyth and Cameron 1998; de Lacey, Peterson & McMillan 2015).

My motivation in writing a theoretical as well as practice-based chapter about ART is to offer a way in which those in this and related fields can make "paramount" the "interests of the persons born" from treatments, and examine how we as practitioners can "respect the right of the child to preserve his or her identity".

The 2008 Victorian Assisted Reproductive Treatment Act allowed treatment provisions for single women and same-sex couples, as well as for the provision of altruistic surrogacy (i.e. surrogacy without intention of profit). It ushered in a law to support those previously discriminated against. With almost unrestricted access to infertility services, the patient population seeking ART inevitably changed.

The Victorian Assisted Reproductive Treatment Authority annual report of 2017 noted that single women continued to be the largest proportion of women treated with *donor sperm* (53 percent), followed by women in same-sex relationships (34 percent) and heterosexual relationships (13 percent). Twenty-five percent of all patients were women over 40 years of age (Victorian Assisted Reproductive Treatment Authority 2017).

With such huge changes over the last 10 years, there is an urgency to consider how parents and professionals can attend to the child's identity needs. To leave a child's future personhood as only a theoretical and legal ideal means we avoid the issues, only to place a greater burden on donor-conceived children in the future to address them.

An infant mental health lens tells us that alone, there is "no such thing as a baby", as the infant is fully dependent on their caregiving system (Winnicott 1960); babies grow their identity in and through relationships. Compelling evidence from psychoanalytic and attachment research informs us that a child's emergence of a self is contingent upon, and will be influenced by, the "mind" of their parent or parents/primary attachment figures (Fonagy, Luyten & Strathearn 2011; Fonagy & Target 1997).

Through their concept of "state of mind", George and Solomon (1996) have demonstrated that the way in which caregivers comprehend their own early childhood caregiving experiences implicitly shapes what they expect from other, subsequent relationships. This corresponds with what Bowlby (1980) described, which was explored in more detail by Holmes "Bowlby's key concept...is that of the individual's internal working models" (Holmes 1993, p.78). This has implications for their child's quality of relationship with their significant attachment figures – their attachment status (Salter-Ainsworth & Bowlby 1991; Zeannah *et al.* 1994). Fonagy and Target (1997) proposed the notion of "reflective functioning" to describe "the developmental acquisition that permits a child to respond not only to other people's behaviour, but his conception of their beliefs, feelings, hopes, pretense, plans and so on". Further, from earliest infancy, the baby's growing conception of the internal state of the other, informs her view of herself.

Slade (2005) applies these constructs to exploring and explaining how a mother's capability to manage her own emotions, as well as organize her thoughts and feelings about her own early relationship history, is linked to her capacity to regulate, sort out and sensitively relate to her own child's needs for comfort and closeness. What this means is that the child's capacity for sorting out her own feelings, her "states of mind", is in the earliest period directly dependent on the parent's reflective function capacity. The child learns to "self-organize" – gain a sense of their own feelings, emotions and beliefs via the mind of the attachment caregiver.

A caregiver's own "internal working model", their capacity for "reflective function", and "state of mind" are key in influencing a healthy development of the infant or child's emergent sense of self. In the light of this, significant difficult or traumatic life experiences, left unresolved and unexamined for parents or caregivers, may complicate the parent's attachment relationship with their infant and in turn the infant or child's sense of self (Lieberman *et al.* 2005). For example, "insecure attachment may be seen as the infant's identification with the caregiver's defensive behaviour" (Fonagy & Target 1997).

These constructs offer us a way of thinking about how the diversity of methods of conceiving may leave parents profoundly affected. We have enough knowledge and research to now understand how the parent's state of mind is an important construct which helps explain the transgenerational transmission of attachment. If an infant's parent remains troubled by their medical or social infertility, and the impact of invasive treatments feels unresolved in such a way that it leads to concealing salient truths from a child, it is possible that this may impinge on the infant's earliest attachment experiences. Where a parent's own mind is preoccupied with ambivalent feelings associated with their infant's birth story, something of that ambivalence may be transferred.

Worldwide developments and debates

When considering this phenomenon globally, we find that in the need to meet the desires of prospective parents, ART services all over the world establish, adapt and develop. Infertility clinics exist both in developed and developing countries, and babies are born via a multitude of service systems which might be regulated or unregulated, state or public, legal or illegal. Culley and colleagues (2013) have coined the evocative term "fertility tourism" for those engaged in cross-border reproductive treatment, where a parent might travel to another country for fertility treatment which is illegal or too expensive to obtain in their home country. As a result, some babies may have multiple "siblings" they never meet; they may have been told they are the one and only child and yet also may have, but never know about, "biological siblings", or "donor-related siblings". Many children, born to what is known as the "commissioning parent(s)", may have been conceived via gamete (egg or sperm) donation in an overseas country. Babies can be conceived via egg and/or sperm donation, or an embryo transfer, in clinics for both local and overseas applicants. For the latter, often once a women's pregnancy has been confirmed, she may immediately return to her home country. Some prospective parents commission an overseas surrogate who carries a child, with or without the commissioning mother's or father's own gametes, (i.e. a sperm or egg that unites with another cell to form a new organism). For surrogacy arrangements, the child is often born in that country/state and then brought back to the commissioning parent's home country/ state. Deonandan (2015) notes that women producing babies for others as surrogates is a worldwide phenomenon, such that in 2009 Canada hosted the First International Forum on Cross-Border Reproductive Care (Nygren *et al.* 2010).

Following international condemnation regarding high-profile baby scandals, Mexico, Thailand, Nepal and India have all recently introducing legislation to restrict foreign nationals from "fertility tourism" that risks exploiting their own citizens. Australian academics Cuthbert and Fronek (2014) caution that "commercial surrogacy is usefully framed as the latest shift in a highly dynamic market for accessing children for the purposes of family formation" (p.55).

A global (and lucrative) market in fertility services, combined with the more recent liberalization of laws both banning and supporting the acquisition of previously inconceivable treatment methods, requires more nuanced research on the impact on identity from the donor-conceived person's perspective.

Creating coherent narratives regarding child donor conceptions

Kirkman (2003) raises the complex nature of family stories in her exceptionally rich research with 55 recipients (parents who used donor sperm, egg or embryos) and 12 offspring. Interviewing a group of participants from across the world, she explored different family narratives about donor-assisted conceptions where children were told, had not yet been told or were in part told their birth stories. She found parents whose children were born as a result of donor-assisted conception "manage the construction of their children's narrative identity along a continuum, from omitting any mention of third-party involvement, to inclusion of the donor in the story from birth". One of her conclusions was that "amongst those parents are those who have difficulty because *they* have not yet incorporated donor conception within their own narrative identity in a satisfactory way" (Kirkman 2003). The task that Kirkman describes for parents of donor-conceived offspring is that there needs to be the creation of what she calls "a narrative identity" that is authentic and supports the children's emotional and psychological development. The ideas from Fonagy and Target's (1997) work offer us a way to consider the difficulties the parents of donor-conceived children may experience in being able to "mentalize" (i.e. reflect upon an experience and create a coherent account of the emotional impact of that experience). Slade's (2005) work helps explain that if the parent has not been able to organize her thoughts and feelings about her own history this may impair her ability to self-regulate, and to sort out her own memories and meanings in such a way that she is able to relate to her own child's needs for a narrative about her conception that makes sense. This can then obscure her appreciation of, or ability to, empathically appraise her child's need for disclosure as a result.

Others have explored how non-disclosure for children finds its way into the emotional life of these families. Becker, Butler and Nachtigall (2005) introduce the term "resemblance talk" to explain how the common ritual amongst families commenting about who a child looks like can become vexed for parents of donor-conceived children: "Resemblance talk was not only ubiquitous, unavoidable, and uncontrollable, but it also had the capacity to exacerbate ongoing uncertainties about their disclosure decision (or lack of one)."

Actively avoided and unspoken things of significance (such as the identity of the donor) can prohibit the honest discussion about what truly is this child's genesis. For some couples and individuals, any disclosure might become fused with shameful feelings about failure in procreation, or, in the case of some women, a complete absence of any sexual life prior to presenting at an ART clinic. The consequences of such non-disclosures may create complex layers of relational misunderstandings and incongruencies.

Difficulties experienced by parents around disclosure

It is perhaps surprising to learn that ART researchers report that most donor-conceived offspring remain uninformed of their genetic history (Kirkman 2003; Lycett *et al.* 2004). Daniels and Taylor (1993) report that secrecy in sperm donor insemination heterosexual families may be to protect the infertile male partner from the stigma of male infertility. They state: "More openness in donor insemination would be advantageous to all of those involved. Couples, professionals, and policymakers are therefore urged to re-examine their views about the need for maintaining secrecy in the area." Readings and colleagues (2011) discuss how when there are partner differences in reasons for, or the extent of, the secrecy, this often creates a prohibition on telling. Landau (1998) proposes that "parents may define a particular secret as protective, but the child upon its disclosure may regard it as intentional concealment".

Nordqvist and Smart's (2014) excellent book, *Relative Strangers: Relative Strangers, Family Life, Genes and Donor Conception*, is based on in-depth interviews and explores the lived reality of donor-conception families. They observed that when the parent concealed the information about a child's donor history, they found "the absent presence of the donor thus lingered on in a perpetually unsatisfactory way which meant that the (sperm) donation gave rise to feelings among the parents that they could never resolve" (p.109).

These authors propose "paradoxically, thinking about the unknown donor produces the ongoing presence of the donor in the life of the donor conceived family" (p.109). Their work drew on ideas developed by Konrad (2005), who described the donor as the ghost, whose presence was felt through an active form of not knowing. In exploring how the presence of the donor remained in the mother's mind, they noted a process of concealment. They termed this phenomenon the "absent presence" (Nordqvist & Smart 2014, p.107), believing that children sensed the silences in stories; we could think about this as the donor being a ghost-like and invisible but still detected presence. However, Nordqvist and Smart (2014) suggest that, as with adoption procedures some years ago, there is "not yet a widely accepted social narrative (for donor conceived children) for translating the idea of openness into practice" (p.88).

The application of adoption literature in appreciating the ART experience

Initially, the links between the research literature on adopted children and children conceived via ART might seem confusing. However, we now know the implications of the past practice of withholding information when placing children for adoption and the subsequent findings about negative consequences resulting from such secrecy.

McGee, Brakman and Gurmankin (2001) argue that "privacy concerns…are outweighed by the negative consequences of holding… family secrets and by the child's right to, and medical need for, information about his/her origin". There is a convincing reason to support children's knowledge of their donor's genetic history given the expansion of genome science, and advances of personalized medicine; however, the implications for exploring these further are outside the scope of this chapter.

British adoption researcher Feast (2003), in her paper "Using and not losing the messages from the adoption experiences for donor-assisted conceptions", makes a compelling comparison on how alike their child/adult experience is: "They often related the same feelings and desires about the need to complete their full family and genetic history in order to achieve a fuller sense of identity." She draws out the comparisons, saying: "It is generally (now) accepted that adoption needs to be a child centered service in which underlying principles of openness and honesty are embraced. However, the same does not appear to be the case for donor conceived people."

SECTION 2: challenges faced by parents and examples with practice principles

Health professionals working with children and families will not necessarily know if a child has had an ART conception. We will meet many parents who are comfortable in providing a sensitive and open way of telling the "how we became a family" story. Other parents may find the disclosure too complex, and they may not have felt sufficiently supported or even want to begin to formulate their own unique family story. In my therapeutic work and supervision consultations, I have found that parents may have complex understandings regarding their feelings and associated meanings about their child's conception.

Samantha

A professional single woman of 45 years, Samantha came to see me after a psychiatric admission. She seemed to minimize the experience of having had a psychotic episode after her twins were born. Samantha told me that she felt enraptured that she had had her now 1-year-old twins by ART. She presented as having minimized any impact of her long and very secret years of receiving ART treatments. Following a year and a half of psychotherapy, she came one day to tell me, unexpectedly, that this was the last session. When we worked hard in that session to discover what underpinned her fixed decision, she was finally able to identify how she felt offended that I raised any notions exploring her thoughts about telling her children how they were conceived. Samantha also felt that I had not supported her in her anger about the legal requirements relating to registering the children's donor conception on their birth certificate (a legal obligation in Victoria).

Samantha's distress at finding the legal obligations would override her desire for concealment did cause a dilemma. Whilst with her, I found myself thinking about her current need for secrecy for her and her little twins, and the impact of that secrecy should it have remained fixed. Could she and I not tolerate different feelings being explored?

Helping a parent create coherence in their own internal narrative about their child's genesis may facilitate them finding words to help make sense of this genesis for their child. Samantha found me raising this as persecutory. Enquiries of this nature are offered in the spirit of helping parents to allow themselves to get to know their real baby, and how to be present with them; not the idealized version of what having a child would be like and that they may have held onto for so long. This example with Samantha illustrates how delicate this work is and leaves open for reflection what I might or could have done differently. I was endeavouring to explore her "state of mind" and her capacity for reflective functioning regarding the needs of her two little infants. I was aware of my feelings for the emerging two infants' capacity for their own sense of self, their own history and the development of their own independent states of mind.

The next case example comes from supervision offered to a nurse parent–infant practitioner, in her supervision sessions.

■ Dianna

Dianna, one of my supervisees, was seeing a series of single mothers who culturally identified as having Asian backgrounds, and who conceived their infants via ART; sometimes donor sperm, sometimes donor embryos were used. These mothers were also bringing up their children a long way from their own extended families. My colleague discussed how she met with a new mother, whom I shall call "M", and her young baby, for a first session. The mother spoke in whispers, revealing that there was "no father". In a subsequent meeting, M said, in front of her 6-month-old, that she had conceived via donor sperm fertility treatment. Dianna asked what she thought she might tell her son. M seemed somewhat offended and declared: "Nothing!" With the help of Dianna, she was then able to explain that she felt embarrassed that she was not able to find a good husband. She told Dianna that her parents wanted her to return to them, but she wanted to live her own life. Dianna, taking an infant perspective, gently explored what all this might mean for her new little baby; that her wish to live her own life could also include helping her son know about his own life and his mother's strong wish for him, and also her wish for him to grow up to be a good man.

Months later, Dianna met again with this mother and little boy, and amongst other things, enquired as to M's current thoughts about what her son might need or want to know in years to come. M said she had thought some more and now felt it was important to honestly inform her son. Dianna responded: "Would you like it if we practise this together? He is still young, but I can help you start to try to find a little story today."

M's declaration about "having no father" for her son appeared to have been linked to her embarrassed feelings about the absence of a father/husband. This in turn was potentially leading to under-examined consequences, including withholding the conception story from her infant. The mother wanted "nothing said". Dianna gently explored what it could mean for the little boy, if M remained fixed in her own internal world, with her maternal shame.

We need to recognize what might precipitate such dilemmas and be able to hold these in our minds when with parents to see the implications for their infant. Galhardo and colleagues (2011) emphasized the shame some parents associated with assisted conceptions. They highlighted "the importance of emotional regulation processes such as internal and external shame, and self-judgment…[and] suggest that these issues should be addressed in a therapeutic context". If this can be openly worked with, a mother has a much better chance of offering her child a more developed meaning of her drive for motherhood and offering her baby a more coherent narrative to support their attachment relationship.

The following example came from a conference seminar where I presented on infants and ART. In the discussion, an experienced maternal and child health nurse offered a reflection:

■ Sheila

"I have worked with many women whose babies have been born via ART. It has never once occurred to me to ask them what they have told their children, or how they feel about the conception. I never thought to ask how they have made sense amongst all the tough times of those stories for their children. I now think this is very strange of me."

We might understand this "form of not knowing" as similar to some parents' views. Our own internalized cultural norms are being challenged by such significant social changes. Sheila asked: "How could I not have thought about this?" The more we can think and reflect, the more we can "mentalize" and think about what governs our own minds.

When I was running a support group for single mothers, one parent declared the following experience.

■ Jane

"I have just found out my son has 26 siblings – all overseas, thank goodness. I don't want him to meet any of them. How can I protect him? How can he comprehend that there are 26 siblings when he is, and forever will be, an only child? I don't have enough money to go and finance another one."

This child is an "only child" and yet has blood siblings. This mother reported how a health care professional, had "normalized" her concerns. However, she told the group: "There is nothing 'normal' about my child's sibling situation." This mother needed help to think through what this information meant for her, and how she might reconcile her desire to "protect" her child whilst at the same time prepare her child for such information. It is complex for anyone to consider how one might feel about being a single child, with a "ghostly" group of secret blood-related half siblings.

Together with this mother I speculated if this might touch on fears of not being "good enough" to provide a "real sibling" and feelings of inadequacy or perhaps even shame. Maybe she was aware that both these ideas seemed to dominate their relationship (i.e. these ideas and fears of her toddler son having "both too many, and at the same time too little and as such missing out"). We must not underestimate what an attuned challenge from a professional might achieve in just one honest and supportive encounter.

Older children, young people and adults conceived through ART can go to extraordinary attempts to seek out their conception stories. The Internet has made this task even more tantalizing, and easier to search for and sometimes find the missing parts of a childhood story. Being able across the course of time to support her child's "knowing" legitimates being allowed to "make up his/her own mind" on the meaning of donor relatedness.

Guide to professional practice

In considering the infant's perspective, we can change the way we take an initial family history. This work has led me to advocate for infant–parent professionals being curious about a child's "genesis stories", and that this becomes part of our initial enquiries with families. This approach suggests that we are open to hearing that babies come from diverse conceptions. Asking about the "genesis story" allows us to explore with parents and offer them support for finding a way to develop a coherent narrative for the child about who they are and how they came to be. We can do this in the following ways:

- Help create a family narrative that places the infant, not the parent, at the centre; for example, "In what ways and how did you become a family?" is an open enquiry, allowing for diversity.

- When we meet an infant, we need to be open to gaps in their conception story which might alert us to concealed parts of their conception story.

- The use of the word "donor" becomes useful. A donor is someone who gives a gift, a donation. There is a "someone", a person who has helped individuals become mothers and become fathers, and who has enabled each individual child to be conceived. "What we know about your donor" is used by fertility counsellors, in contrast to "the other mother/the nice man who helped".

- Increase clients' awareness that infants and their families are formed by their stories, (whether these are authentic or not entirely non-authentic).

- Offer an exploration about the meaning of the parents' views on conception/disclosure/non-disclosure. These will be stories that embrace the experiential, gendered, transgenerational, moral, ethical and cultural aspects unique to them and to their children.

Conclusion

Many parents believe children need to be shielded from their parents' past, even that which is directly intertwined with the child's history. Some people reassure themselves that there are "lots of individuals in life who are without full knowledge of their birth genesis". This may be so; however, it dodges the dilemma that we would do well to reconcile, and to find the compassion we need to be effective in allowing for the hidden implications of ART to emerge, with honesty and without shame.

Fonagy and Target (1997) and Slade (2005) suggest that what needs to be therapeutically supported are the parents' own feelings and preconceived notions, as this can lead to the parents' capacity to offer family narratives which reflect upon their child and his/her own unique identity needs. Applying this to ART conceptions means attending to any feelings around previous traumatic birth histories, tragic losses, and great disappointment and sorrow dashed on the rocks of huge efforts and finances. Whilst painful, parents may need help to tolerate thinking about the buried consequences of biological or social infertility. Not being able to explore this sufficiently risks the transgenerational transmission of feelings into the infant's sense of identity. It is important that the infant does not get lost in residual, unacknowledged feelings about the need for, and subsequent distresses often inherent in, participating in the ART process.

An infant-centred practitioner holds in mind the infant, and at the same time can help parents aim to make some peace with their personal and physical war wounds. However, babies have urgent needs, and sometimes parents cannot travel emotionally as far as the babies need them to travel. Cuthbert and Fronek (2014) raise concerns about how these infants, children and soon-to-be adults "will have questions to ask about their identities, the mothers who bore them, the women and men who donated ova and sperm to whom they are genetically linked" (p.64). They assign responsibilities to professionals who need to ask further questions about the policies and legislative regimes (or the absence of these) that allow births to take place without due regard to the inevitability of the future adults' questions regarding their identity, community and belonging. The way parents develop a meaningful story, we now know, does influence the relationship and thus the mental health of the baby.

Acknowledgements

I would like to sincerely thank Dr Wendy Bunston, Dr Paul Robertson, Ms Emma Toone, Dr Julie Stone and Ms Natalie Saunders, all of whom helped me bring to life the ideas held within this chapter.

References

Becker, G., Butler, A. & Nachtigall, R. (2005) 'Resemblance talk: A challenge for parents whose children were conceived with donor gametes in the US.' *Social Science and Medicine 61*, 6, 1300–1309.

Blyth, E. & Cameron C. (1998) 'The welfare of the child: An emerging issue in the regulation of assisted conception.' *Human Reproduction 9*, 13, 2339–2355.

Bowlby, J. (1980) *Attachment and Loss, Volume 1*. London: Penguin Books.

Culley, L., Hudson, N., Rapport, F., Blyth, E., Norton, W. & and Pacey, A. (2013) 'Crossing borders for fertility treatment: Motivations, destinations and outcomes of UK fertility travellers.' *Human Reproduction 26*, 9, 2373–2381.

Cuthbert, D. & Fronek, P. (2014) 'Perfecting adoption? Reflections on the Rise of Commercial Off-Shore Surrogacy and Family Formation in Australia.' In A. Hayes and D. Higgins (Eds) *Families, Policy and the Law: Selected Essays on Contemporary Issues for Australia*. Melbourne: Australian Institute of Family Studies.

Daniels, K.R. & Taylor, K. (1993) 'Secrecy and openness in donor insemination.' *Human Reproduction 12*, 2, 155–170.

de Lacey, S., Peterson K. & McMillan J. (2015) 'Child interests in assisted reproductive technology: How is the welfare principle applied in practice?' *Human Reproduction 3*, 30, 616–624.

Deonandan, R. (2015) 'Recent trends in reproductive tourism and international surrogacy: Ethical considerations and challenges for policy.' *Risk Management and Healthcare Policy 8*, 111.

Feast, J. (2003) 'Using and not losing the messages from the adoption experience for donor-assisted conception.' *Human Fertility 6*, 1, 41–45.

Fonagy, P., Luyten, P. & Strathearn, L. (2011) 'Borderline personality disorder, mentalization, and the neurobiology of attachment.' *Infant Mental Health Journal 32*, 1, 47–69.

Fonagy, P. & Target, M. (1997) 'Attachment and reflective function: Their role in self-organisation.' *Development and Psychopathology 9*, 679–700.

Galhardo, A., Pinto-Gouveia, J., Cunha, M. & Matos, M. (2011) 'The impact of shame and self-judgment on psychopathology in infertile patients.' *Human Reproduction 26*, 9, 2408–2414.

George, C. & Solomon, J. (1996) 'Representational models of relationships: Links between caregiving and attachment.' *Infant Mental Health Journal 17*, 3, 198–126.

Holmes, J. (1993) *John Bowlby and Attachment Theory*. London: Routledge.

Kirkman, M. (2003) 'Parents' contributions to the narrative identity of offspring of donor-assisted conception.' *Social Science and Medicine 57*, 11, 2229–2242.

Konrad, M. (2005) *Nameless Relations*. New York: Berghahn Books.

Landau, R. (1998) 'The management of genetic origins: Secrecy and openness in donor assisted conception in Israel and elsewhere.' *Human Reproduction 13*, 11, 3268–3273.

Lieberman, A.F., Padron, E., Van Horn, P. & Harris, W.W. (2005) 'Angels in the nursery: The intergenerational transmission of benevolent parental influences.' *Infant Mental Health Journal 26*, 6, 504–520.

Lycett, E., Daniels, R., Curson, S. and Golombok, S. (2004) 'Offspring created as a result of donor insemination: A study of family relationships, child adjustment, and disclosure.' *Fertility and Sterility 82*, 1, 172–179.

McGee, G., Brakman, S. & Gurmankin, A. (2001) 'Gamete donation and anonymity: Disclosure to children conceived with donor gametes should not be optional.' *Human Reproduction 16*, 10, 2033–2036.

Nordqvist, P. & Smart, C. (2014) *Relative Strangers: Relative Strangers, Family Life, Genes and Donor Conception*. London: Palgrave Macmillan.

Nygren, K., Adamson, D., Zegers-Hochschild, F. & de Mouzon, J. (2010) 'Cross-border fertility care – International Committee Monitoring Assisted Reproductive Technologies global survey: 2006 data and estimates.' *Fertility and Sterility 94*, 1, e4–e10.

Readings, J., Blake, L., Casey, P., Jadva, V. & Golombok, S. (2011) 'Secrecy, disclosure and everything in-between: Decisions of parents of children conceived by donor insemination, egg donation and surrogacy.' *Reproductive BioMedicine Online 22*, 5, 485–495.

Salter-Ainsworth, M.D. & Bowlby, J. (1991) 'An ethological approach to personality development.' *American Psychologist 46*, 4, 333–341.

Slade, A. (2005) 'Parental reflective functioning: An introduction.' *Attachment and Human Development 7*, 3, 269–281.

United Nations International Children's Emergency Fund (1989) *Convention on the Rights of the Child*. Globalization and the Workplace Portal – International Labor Standards: Child Labor. New York. Retrieved 20/4/2019 https://www.unicef.org.uk/wp-content/uploads/2010/05/UNCRC_united_nations_convention_on_the_rights_of_the_child.pdf

Victorian Assisted Reproductive Treatment Authority (2017) *Annual Report 2017*. Melbourne: VARTA.

Winnicott, D.W. (1960) 'The Theory of the Parent–Infant Relationship.' In *The Maturational Processes and the Facilitating Environment*. London: Hogarth Press (reprinted Karnac, 1990).

Zeanah, C.H., Benoit, D., Hirshberg, L., Barton, M. & Regan, C. (1994) 'Mothers' representations of their infants are concordant with infant attachment classifications.' *Developmental Issues in Psychiatry and Psychology 1*, 1–14.

About the Authors

Kerry Arabena is a Meriam woman, Consultant, Business Owner and former Chair for Indigenous Health, University of Melbourne, Australia. With a Social Work degree and a doctorate in Human Ecology, she leads research projects, owns several Indigenous business, and is a mentor and trainer. She is also the Director and Chair of Aboriginal community organisations.

Wendy Bunston (Editor), PhD, is a Senior Clinician, Trainer and Consultant who has worked with infants, children, young people and their families for the past 30 years in mental health and community health. She presents on her work internationally and has published multiple academic papers, chapters and books.

Louise Dockery is a Registered Nurse, Registered Midwife and Maternal and Child Health Nurse. She has worked as an Enhanced Maternal and Child Health Nurse (EMCHN) in Victoria, Australia, since 2006. EMCHNs clinically assess, monitor and refer children with complex needs to appropriate health and community support services.

Kathy Eyre is a Senior Infant Mental Health Clinician with a background in Occupational Therapy and Family Therapy. Kathy has worked in public Child and Adolescent Mental Health Services for over 25 years, and in recent years with many vulnerable and traumatised infants.

Ben Grey, PhD, is a Senior Lecturer in Attachment Studies at the University of Roehampton, England. Ben has worked in different roles carrying out assessments of children and families for the family courts, and local and health authorities in the UK. He developed and validated the Meaning of the Child Interview (MotC), an interview-based procedure for assessing parent–child relationships.

Jeremy Gunson is a Child and Adolescent Psychotherapist working in the NHS and in a social enterprise independent practice in Birmingham, England. He trained at the Tavistock Clinic in London, having previously qualified as a Social Worker in Liverpool. Jeremy is an Executive Member of the Association for Infant Mental Health (AIMH) and of the Training Council of the Association of Child Psychotherapists (ACP) in the UK.

Robyn Hemmens has worked in the children's sector in South Africa since the 1980s. After serving girl children living on the streets in Durban, she moved into preventative work to strengthen emotional connections between adults and children in high-risk communities. She holds relationship and service as a great privilege.

Christine Hill, PhD, is a Perinatal Psychotherapist, Midwife and Writer in Melbourne, Australia. In her work she makes frequent border-crossings between the arts and psychoanalysis to encourage linking and thinking about infants and their relationships. As a volunteer she facilitates baby playgroups for refugee and asylum-seeking families.

Angelique Jenney, PhD, is an Assistant Professor and the Wood's Homes Research Chair in Children's Mental Health in the Faculty of Social Work, University of Calgary, Canada. She has spent decades in the children's mental health sector, with her research and intervention focusing on the impact of violence in families.

Sarah J. Jones (Editor) is a Psychotherapist/Mental Health Social Worker in Melbourne, Victoria. Her clinical interests include working with infants/children, couples and individuals with both perinatal and infertility concerns. She is a Clinical Supervisor/Trainer to hospitals (both public and private), ranging from Maternal and Child Health to Palliative Care.

Maria McCarthy, PhD, is a Family Therapist in the Children's Cancer Centre at the Royal Children's Hospital (RCH) and a Senior Research Fellow with the Murdoch Children's Research Institute,

Melbourne, Australia. Her research interests include the psychosocial impacts of cancer and serious childhood illnesses on children and their families.

Jennifer McIntosh is a Clinical Psychologist, Professor of Attachment Studies at Deakin University and Director of the ATP-G3 Melbourne Attachment & Caregiving Lab. Her research focuses on early developmental trauma and translation of evidence into practice. Her family law-related interventions and resources are housed on the site www.ChildrenBeyondDispute.com.

Amity McSwan is an accredited Mental Health Social Worker and trained Family Therapist. She has worked in a number of Child and Adolescent Mental Health Services in Victoria, Australia and in private practice. She is currently Senior Clinician on the specialist child team at Eastern Health Child and Youth Mental Health Service (CYMHS).

Nicole Milburn, DClinPsych, is a Clinical Psychologist and Infant Mental Health Specialist who has been working in private and public practice for 20 years. She has expertise in the assessment of maltreated infants and their families and is passionate about ensuring infants and young children have their experiences recognised and respected.

Luella Monson-Wilbraham is Executive Officer for First 1000 Days Australia. Her career focus has combined social and emotional wellbeing, research, healing, therapy and technical writing with strategic programs and services targeting Australia's First Peoples. She is committed to working with Indigenous communities to build capacity and relationships and effective partnerships.

Paul Robertson, MBBS, is a Child and Adolescent Psychiatrist with a long interest in infant mental health in Melbourne, Victoria. He works in a range of settings including public Child and Adolescent Mental Health Services, medical education in the training of child and adolescent psychiatrists and other professionals, and educational and public health initiatives in the broader Asia-Pacific region.

Rachel Rozentals-Thresher, Dlalanathi's Director since 2007, trained in commerce and psychology. At that time, South Africa's inequalities and the ravages of the AIDS pandemic on families demanded action. Under her leadership, Dlalanathi develops sustainable ways to strengthen families and communities, emphasising strong relationships as the bedrock for healthy development.

Helen Shoemark, PhD, is an Associate Professor of Music Therapy at Temple University, Philadelphia, Pennsylvania. Her primary research focus has been on the pre-vocal expressive capability of hospitalised infants and the role of parental voice and meaningful auditory stimulation to support attachment. She previously worked as a Senior Clinician at the Royal Children's Hospital, Melbourne.

Julie Stone is an Infant, Child and Family Psychiatrist in Melbourne, Victoria, who has learnt so much from generous, creative colleagues around the world. As a clinician, Churchill, and Zero to Three Fellow, Julie's commitment now is to return that generosity, sharing what she has learned with others to support them in their work.

Lisa Thorpe is a proud Gunditjmara/Gunnai woman in Melbourne, Victoria, and current CEO of Bubup Wilam for Early Learning Aboriginal Child and Family Centre. She has a Masters in Public Health and has worked extensively in education and community services. She is committed to programmes and services that assist Aboriginal children and their families to achieve self-determination.

Fiona True, LCSW, is a Family Therapist who specialises in helping children and families overcome the effects of family violence. A Faculty Member of the Ackerman Institute in New York and Co-Director of its Center for Children and Relational Trauma, she has published and presented her work within the United States and internationally.

Jenifer Wakelyn is a Child Psychotherapist in a mental health service for children in care in London. She teaches at the Tavistock Centre and has presented research across the UK, Europe and the Ukraine. Her current work on a 'Watch Me Play!' manual is funded by the Tavistock Clinic Foundation.

Hisako Watanabe, MD, PhD is a graduate of Keio University, Tokyo, specialising in infant, child and adolescent psychiatry. She is an

Executive Board Member of the World Association for Infant Mental Health, President of the FOUR WINDS, a national forum for infant mental health in Japan, and works with traumatised communities.

Natasha Whitfield is a Clinical Psychologist who splits her time between a school board position and her private practice office. She received her PhD in Clinical Developmental Psychology from York University, Toronto, in 2015. She currently lives in Kingsville, Ontario.

Angie Zerella has 30 years of experience in Early Childhood Education and is the Education and Training Manager at Bubup Wilam for Early Aboriginal Child and Family Centre. She delivers a high-quality Aboriginal early years curriculum and supports the training and employment of Aboriginal and non-Aboriginal people within the organisation.

Subject Index

Author Index

Adamson, P. C. 247
Adelson, E. 50, 92, 114, 269
Ahlfs-Dunn, S. M. 126
AIHW 126, 135
Ainsworth, M. D. S. 202, 269
Aitken, K. 32, 167
Ake, J. 137
Alaggia, R. 91
Allen, N. E. 137
Alleva, E. 38
Alvarez, A. 77
American Academy of Pediatrics 83, 248
American Psychiatric Association 91
Anda, R. F. 75
Anderson, F. S. 247
Anthony, J. 162
Appleyard, K. 93
Armstrong, N. 179
Arnold, G. 137
Australian Border Force 229
Australian DIBP 231
Ayling, P. 77

Bakermans-Kranenburg, M. J. 86
Balaam, M. 235
Bancroft, L. 94
Baradon, T. 9
Barlow , M. R. 100
Barnard, K. 163
Barr, R. 80
Barton, L. R. 229
Bassuk, E. L. 126
Batchelder, S. 93
Battiste, M. 148
Baxt, C. 247, 248, 255, 256
Becker, G. 287
Beebe, B. 8, 202
Beeghly, M. 92, 201, 207
Beek, M. 81

Benoit, D. 272
Bergstraesse, E. 247
Bernier, A. 69
Berry, A. 38
Bick, E. 52, 78, 128, 233, 269
Bion, W.R. 10, 239
Bird, I. 173
Birk Irner, T. 75
Black, D. 110
Black, M. 176, 178
Blyth, E. 283
Bogat, G. A. 92
Bohr, Y. 191, 192
Bond, E. A. 255
Bond, M. J. 269
Booth, R. P. 75
Borelli, J. L. 109
Bouvette-Turcot, A.-A. 7
Bowlby, J. 32, 61, 110, 163, 201, 269, 284
Boyce, W. T. 248
Brakman, S. 289
Brandon, M. 75
Bratton, S. 77
Brawner, T. 109
Brazelton, T. B. 231
British Columbia Provincial
        Mental Health and Substance
        Use Planning Council 94
Britto, P. 178
Browning, A. S. 81
Bryant, W. 108
Buckley, H. 91
Buckner, J. C. 126, 127, 135
Bullows, M. 233
Bunston, W. 29, 36, 37, 38, 91, 94,
        111, 114, 120, 125, 126, 128,
        130, 131, 134, 135, 136, 138
Butler, A. 287